Resolving Disagreem
in Special Educationa

Local Education Authorities are now obliged to put in place arrange-ments to try to settle disputes over the assessment and provision for children with special educational needs. This practical book aims to help those charged with making these arrangements and those directly involved in the conciliation and mediation process.

While there is no 'right way' to resolve disputes of this kind, the ultimate goal must be to reach a positive conclusion as quickly as possible for the benefit of the child involved. In this book, the authors look at a range of approaches and issues to achieve this such as:

- How to plan disagreement resolutions
- Skills and techniques for mediation
- Tools for training and self-assessment
- The SEN tribunal
- Ethical and legal issues

The book includes contributions from leading practitioners in special educational needs, law, and mediation and conciliation. It is the ideal handbook for all those working in the area of special education needs, both in schools and for LEAs and other agencies.

Professor Irvine S. Gersch is Course Director for the MSc profes-sional training for educational psychologists at the University of East London. **Adam Gersch** is a Barrister and the Managing Director of Global Mediation Ltd.

Resolving Disagreement in Special Educational Needs

A practical guide to conciliation and mediation

Professor Irvine S. Gersch
and Adam Gersch

RoutledgeFalmer
Taylor & Francis Group

LONDON AND NEW YORK

First published 2003 by RoutledgeFalmer
11 New Fetter Lane, London EC4P 4EE

Simultaneously published in the USA and Canada
by RoutledgeFalmer
29 West 35th Street, New York, NY 10001

RoutledgeFalmer is an imprint of the Taylor & Francis Group

© 2003 Irvine S. Gersch and Adam Gersch

Typeset in 10/12pt Goudy by Graphicraft Limited, Hong Kong
Printed and bound in Great Britain by TJ International Ltd, Padstow, Cornwall

British Library Cataloguing in Publication Data
A catalogue record for this book is available from the British Library

Library of Congress Cataloging in Publication Data
A catalogue record has been requested

ISBN 0-415-26613-0

Contents

Contributors

Cathy Casale (now known as Cathy Pierce) is a Senior Educational Psychologist in the London Borough of Lambeth.

Hugh Clench is Regional facilitator for SEN, South Central region.

Sarah Gale is the Equalities and Partnership Development Manager in the London Borough of Tower Hamlets Education Directorate. Until last year she was the borough's Parent Partnership Officer and was responsible for setting up the Parents Advice Centre in Tower Hamlets. Sarah has worked as a teacher and in a range of Education roles in Inner London authorities since 1971.

Adam Gersch is a barrister in independent practice and Managing Director of Global Mediation Ltd. He was called to the Bar at Lincoln's Inn in 1993 and is a member of 8 King's Bench Walk (Chambers of Lord Gifford, QC).

Barbara Gersch is the Principal Officer for Special Educational Needs, for the London Borough of Tower Hamlets.

Professor Irvine S. Gersch is Course Director of the MSc Professional training for Educational Psychologists at the University of East London. Prior to 2000, he was Principal Educational Psychologist at the London Borough of Waltham Forest. He has been a part-time Open University tutor and counsellor for twenty-five years. His PhD was in the field of educational management and leadership. He is an Ofsted Team Inspector, a member of the DFEE advisory group on the future role and training of educational psychologists and a Fellow of the British Psychological Society.

Zanne Findlay has worked as a freelance mediator and trainer for the last seven years. She is co-author of the *Workplace Mediation Manual* and has worked with the DfES on the implementation of mediation within SEN. She is Programme Director of the Certificate in Applied Mediation (SEN), and has worked with a number of LEAs on the introduction of disagreement resolution. She was a lay member of the SEN tribunal and is a former Assistant Director of Social Services.

Jeff Frank was Head of Special Educational Needs in Hillingdon. It was here that he managed the West London Mediation pilot on which his chapter is based. In January 2002 Jeff took up the post of Head of Special Educational Services in Buckinghamshire.

Nick Knapman is Co-facilitator of SEN Regional Partnership (South West).

Mary Kuhn is Partnership Manager for London SEN Regional Partnerhip.

Tom Leimdorfer is Development Worker for Disagreement Resolution Service, SEN Regional Partnership (South West).

Mari-Cruz Taboada Lopez is a lawyer by training, who moved from Barcelona to London four years ago. Qualifying originally as a commercial mediator with the Centre for Dispute Resolution (CEDR), she trained as a community mediator joining Southwark Mediation Centre as a full-time mediator. In her current role as Development Officer, she is responsible for introducing peer mediation throughout Southwark.

Chris Luck was formerly the Assistant Education Officer, Special Services, in the London Borough of Waltham Forest and now works as a consultant in special education.

Moray McLaren is a trained mediator and has been a member of the SMC management committee since 1998.

Simon Oliver is a barrister, practising in family and education law from Guildford Chambers, where he is joint head. He has co-written *Enforcing Family Finance Orders* and is currently writing the second edition of *Special Educational Needs and the Law*. Both are published by Jordans. He has been a part-time chair of the Special Educational Needs Tribunal since 1994 and of the Probation Children Act Tribunal (now known as the Care Standards Tribunal) since 2000.

Lindsey Rousseau has since January 2000 been a manager of the South East SEN Regional Partnership. The SE region includes the

LEAs of Brighton and Hove, East Sussex, Kent, Medway, Surrey and West Sussex. Before this post she was Head of Physical and Sensory Services in Kent LEA and her professional background is as a teacher of the deaf and educational audiologist. She has worked in various aspects of SEN in mainstream and special schools in London boroughs, Berkshire and Kent since qualifying and working as a teacher in ILEA in 1973. She has been a trained counsellor since 1985 and has worked extensively with parent groups and voluntary organisations with regard to disability.

Janet Rowley is an educational psychologist with the London Borough of Barking and Dagenham.

Philippa Russell is Director of the Council for Disabled Children and Disability Rights Commission.

Philippa Stobbs is the Principal Development Officer for the Council for Disabled Children.

Acknowledgements

We would like to express our thanks to the following people and organisations for their help with this book and consent to reproduce material.

We are indebted to Taylor & Francis Ltd for their permission to reproduce the articles 'The Waltham Forest Conciliation Service' (Gersch *et al.*, 1998) from *Educational Psychology in Practice*, 14(1): 11–21, and Rowley and Gersch (2001) 'Referrals for Conciliation: Is There a Pattern to Referrals?' from *Educational Psychology in Practice*, 17(4). For the purpose of this book, the latter article has been abridged. The website for this journal is www.tandf.co.uk/journals.

Our thanks to A. Acland for his kind permission to reproduce extracts from his book *A Sudden Outbreak of Common Sense: Managing conflict through mediation*, published in 1990 by Hutchison Business Books.

We would also like to thank the DfES for their consent to reproduce Section 3 of the SEN Toolkit, Resolution of Disagreements, published 2001 and which is and remains Crown Copyright.

A large number of friends and family have provided support and practical help with this book. The meticulous proofing, assistant editing and advice given by Barbara Gersch throughout the book project has been invaluable. Kirstie Soar, a doctoral research student at UEL, has provided speedy, efficient and effective administrative back-up. We have benefited from the patience and wise advice of Alison Foyle, the editor.

We would like to thank SCRIP/SERSEN for permission to reproduce their tender, referral flow diagram and referral criteria, which have been developed by Hugh Clench and Lindsey Rousseau. We should also like to thank Global Mediation Ltd for their consent to reproduce their mediation agreement and statements and documentation.

We should like to acknowledge the help of Professor Sheila Wolfendale (UEL) for her advice in respect of further sources and reading, Christine Willett (Parent Partnership Officer, EduAction, London Borough of Waltham Forest) for her ideas and notes and to our friend Charles Stevens for his discussions and ideas on philosophical and spiritual issues, which contributed to and helped develop some underlying themes.

And finally, we pay tribute to all the children, parents, teachers and other professionals who have participated in disagreement resolution, and have acted as our teachers on this subject.

Much of the book was prepared and written in the village of Week St Mary, Cornwall, which provided an atmosphere of peace, quiet and reflection amongst friends who took a sincere and supportive interest in the project.

Disclaimer

Irvine S. Gersch and Adam Gersch

Preface and how to use this book

This book is intended to serve as a practical handbook for all those involved in dealing with SEN disagreement resolution. It is written for LEA officers, schools, parent partnership officers, other professionals involved in SEN, educational psychologists and medical and social service professionals, as well as for parents. It is, of course, intended for professional conciliators and mediators, a growing body of people in a field, as yet unregulated.

Our aims have been:

- to provide a practical handbook;
- to share ideas and projects without wishing to be prescriptive;
- to outline the 'state of the art' at this time in UK SEN history;
- to provide readers with quick and easy access to information they might need, in one place;
- where interesting projects are described, to include descriptions by the practitioners themselves, in their own words;
- to include contributions from people who are actually working as practitioners at the cutting edge of developments in this field.

The book is organised into eleven chapters, which can be dipped into as needed. The chapters are organised to enable easy access, and for the material to be used as a reference.

The first chapter outlines the legal and historical background, and explanation of the key concepts, which themselves often can lead to confusion. Chapter 2 reviews some considerations for LEA Officers when planning disagreement resolution arrangements, and concludes with a staged model. Chapters 3 and 4 describe projects in respect of *conciliation* and *mediation* respectively. Chapter 5 describes the work of the SEN tribunal. Chapter 6 examines the skills and techniques used by mediators and includes self-assessment activities and training tools. Chapter 7 explores some ethical issues, principles and dilemmas using casework vignettes. Chapter 8 focuses on training.

Chapter 9, the conclusion, looks forward to some emerging applications and future possibilities. In the final chapters, 10 and 11, we provide a source of further information, websites, references, extracts from the DfES toolkit and exemplar codes of conduct which we hope will be of practical help to those involved in this field.

A number of themes, which emerge through the book, are noteworthy:

1   The arrival of the book coincides historically with major legal developments in the UK, to use mediation rather than adversarial mechanisms to deal with disputes.

2   There is no single right way of resolving disagreements, rather these need to be managed at different levels, at different times and with different styles.

3   It is helpful to construct a *staged model* in respect of LEA SEN disagreement resolution arrangements.

4   There is a great joy in being of help to humans in conflict and perhaps helping them to resolve differences. Perhaps this is all the more potent when the dispute is about children with special educational needs, where the goal must be to reach a positive and speedy agreement in the best interests of the child.

5   Any mediator needs to be very much aware of their own wishes and feelings; the dispute does not belong to them and nor does the resolution. Not all disputes are ready for resolution, and thus a failure to end up with an agreement should not necessarily be regarded as a personal failure, tempting though it is to view it this way. All negotiators, conciliators and mediators need to be *reflective practitioners*, and indeed *self*-reflective practitioners. Perhaps every would-be 'disagreement resolver' should ask themselves, privately, but deeply, why they became involved in this field. The answers are likely to be very revealing.

6   We have observed a growing interest in spiritual issues, and open-mindedness about what is often termed alternative or complementary therapies. The term spiritual, in this context, means that there is more to people than their material or physical being; people act in ways according to deeper needs, their spirit or soul. There is much, as humans, we still have to learn about our experience and there is a growing openness and indeed interest in such issues.

At the very least, the editors have taken a humble view about what can and cannot work in disagreement resolution, allowing for the magic of personal relationships, understanding, trust and synchronicity.

7 Dealing with conflicts and human emotions as a mediator or conciliator is highly emotionally charged. Professionals working in this area will need to consider how they are to receive appropriate emotional support themselves, how they are to deal with ethical dilemmas as they might arise, and how they are to ensure their effective training and ongoing professional development.

8 The area is fast changing and developing, and this book aims to set out some of the most exciting and up-to-date initiatives.

The reader will need to keep a close eye on future developments and watch this space closely.

We wish you well in your endeavours.

Irvine S. Gersch and Adam Gersch

Chapter 1

Introduction

Adam Gersch

1.1 ALTERNATIVE DISPUTE RESOLUTION (ADR): A BRIEF HISTORY, CONCEPTS AND DEFINITIONS

Introduction

This section provides a brief history and overview of the key concepts and terminology commonly used in ADR – Alternative Dispute Resolution. The term ADR itself is one that has crossed the Atlantic from the USA to describe procedures other than litigation used to settle disagreement. As ADR has grown in popularity and communities begin to embrace the use of ADR, some commentators have suggested that the acronym should now stand for 'Appropriate Dispute Resolution'.

Whilst this book focuses on mediation and conciliation in the context of SEN, it is important to understand the context of these methods of ADR within the wider range of available models.

It is interesting to note that the DfES has discouraged the use of the word dispute by promoting 'disagreement resolution'. The term disagreement has a softer connotation – a disagreement may be small or large; dispute conveys a major, entrenched difference more closely associated with court proceedings.

Within a culture that should avoid confusing terms and acronyms like ADR and describe procedures in a clear and accessible way, the term disagreement resolution is preferred here to ADR and the thinking behind the use of this term is sound.

History

One of the earliest disagreements avoided by ADR (Alternative Dispute Resolution) is described in the Book of Genesis at chapter 18, when

Abraham learns that the cities of Sodom and Gomorrah are to be destroyed and engages the Almighty in a successful negotiation. Thousands of years later, a significant disagreement was resolved with the signing of the Magna Carta in 1215 and recognition that subjects had rights and royal government had limits. Even by that time, the aggrieved citizens were a long way from demanding a statement or assessment of SEN for their child or threatening to take a case to the SEN tribunal.

Whilst Article XIII of the Bill of Rights, 1689, provided that 'for the redress of grievances, Parliament ought to meet frequently', use of a mediation process for resolving disputes was merely a distant vision. History often comes full circle. The original official forms of dispute resolution would now in fact be described as 'alternative'. Trial by ordeal or trial by duel may be fondly remembered, but are certainly not now regarded as conventional.

In the Dark Ages there were local community assemblies or 'moots' to resolve disputes according to local custom. These assemblies came to be administered by the Crown and at the centre was the Curia Regis (King's Court).

In the sixteenth and seventeenth centuries, the functions and jurisdictions of different courts sometimes overlapped, and each had a different reputation and standing. The more notorious Court of Star Chamber was famous for its handling of political crimes, and was even more feared than the SEN tribunal until it was abolished in the 1640s.

Gradually justice became a royal function, with royal court supervising local courts and travelling judges administering justice through what became known as the 'assize system' and reporting the results to London.

In 1846 a system of local civil courts was established in the form of new statutory county courts, although some of the original successors of the old local assemblies survived, gradually declining until they were formally abolished in the 1970s.

Following the Judicature Acts 1873, our legal system has been highly formalised. The High Court and Court of Appeal were created to replace and streamline the number of old courts including the Queen's Bench, Common Pleas, and Exchequer.

In the 1800s, the only formal dispute resolution process as an alternative to litigation was arbitration. Whilst the arbitration process has now been modernised and may take a variety of forms, early arbitration was effectively a form of tribunal or private court.

Examples of tribunals can be found from very early times, particularly those dealing with tax and revenue matters, but one of the first major tribunals was the Railway and Canal Commission established in 1873 to settle disputes between companies and customers; it later became the Transport Tribunal.

The development of the welfare state led to an increase in the use of arbitration. Following the Workmen's Compensation Act 1897 disputes over compensation for industrial injuries were supposed to be settled by arbitration but most were taken to the county court.

The use of arbitration was also favoured for international dispute resolution and decisions became increasingly enforceable worldwide, particularly following the 1958 New York Convention.

By 1971, the tribunals and Inquiries Act was passed in England creating a formalised system of dispute resolution outside the courts. In due course, many tribunals became so formal that they are simply regarded today as another type of specialised court, and are no longer an 'alternative' to litigation but represent just another litigation forum.

During the 1970s, the term ADR was first coined in the USA where there was a real demand for practical and realistic problem-solving alternatives to litigation. The demand in the USA was particularly prompted by the problems of insurance-led litigation, contingency fees, unpredictable awards by civil juries and the fact that legal costs are not ordinarily recoverable as they are in other jurisdictions. A constant rise in litigation from an increasingly consumer-led society meant that alternatives were sought which would not bear the hallmarks of litigation – cost, delay, uncertainty, inequality and damaging to future relationships.

By the 1980s, the concept of ADR had spread to other countries. In the UK, the Centre for Dispute Resolution (CEDR) was formed in 1990 and championed the use of ADR as a philosophy.

By 1992 there were some 1,200 ADR programmes serving state and federal courts in the USA streamlined throughout the federal system by the US Civil Justice Reform Act 1990. The US ADR Act 1998 provides that every federal court must make available some form of ADR, and mediation has been widely embraced.

In 1996 judges of the Central London County Court established a pilot mediation scheme for civil disputes over £3,000. This pilot project has been continued and there are now several court mediation schemes currently being evaluated throughout the UK. In the same year, a new Arbitration Act codified and streamlined the arbitration process.

The whole civil justice system was overhauled by Lord Woolf with the introduction of the Civil Procedure Rules in 1999 that encourage settlement of disputes at the earliest possible stage through ADR and mediation rather than going to court.

Use of ADR falls within the primary objectives of the new Civil Procedure Rules including promotion of early settlement, saving costs, encouraging a cooperative approach, allowing the parties to keep control of the dispute and, therefore, control of the costs involved.

Litigation should now be the method of last resort and courts have a duty to encourage the use of ADR wherever appropriate. One year after these reforms were introduced the Lord Chancellor said, 'There is no doubt that mediation can provide quicker, cheaper and more satisfactory outcomes than traditional litigation in a wide range of disputes; and I certainly want to see mediation achieve its full potential.'

Mediation is now strongly encouraged as the favoured initial process of resolving disputes by courts and tribunals alike. Mediation is also widely used as a method of resolving disagreement in Australia, Bermuda, Canada, Hong Kong, the UK, the USA and Japan. In some jurisdictions, such as Florida, USA, a civil trial cannot be brought unless attempts have been made to try mediation.

With an increase in awareness of people's rights and higher number of cases where litigation is threatened, alternative forms of disagreement resolution are both necessary and advantageous to all involved.

1.2 ADR DEFINITIONS AND SOME COMMON MYTHS ABOUT MEDIATION

Negotiation

The most widely recognised and commonly used form of disagreement resolution is negotiation. Many of us take for granted the techniques associated with negotiation and some would argue that this is not a form of ADR at all. The various methods of negotiation are far from straightforward, however, and it is possible to train for many years to an advanced level through various schools such as the Harvard Business School, and still have much to learn.

The widely accepted models of negotiation are 'principled negotiation' described by Fisher and Ury in their famous text, *Getting to Yes* (1981), and the more commonly used 'positional negotiation'.

In positional negotiation models, parties go back and forth making offer and counter-offer, trading concessions until some middle ground is reached, depending on the bargaining powers of those involved. The model can be described figuratively as a dance, with each party knowing the unwritten rules of engagement, one often-cited rule being 'never accept the first offer'. Such a 'dance' may not be very useful where SEN issues are concerned – particularly where more (money, hours of support, etc.) may not necessarily be best for the child or young person.

In principled negotiations, the principles are considered as the basis for discussions and a problem-solving approach is encouraged. Negotiators separate 'the person from the problem', avoiding emotional game-playing. Objective standards are used to support decisions and the competitive 'dance' is avoided. The concepts of a BATNA (Best Alternative to a Negotiated Agreement) and WATNA (Worst Alternative to a Negotiated Agreement) are used by each party to measure the options for mutual gain against the alternative of reaching no agreement.

Negotiations can fail for a number of reasons including the ability and skill of the negotiators, lack of a realistic assessment of the options, lack of trust, emotional baggage, poor communication of respective needs and plain deadlock. These problems may be capable of resolution by the intervention of a third party.

Conciliation

The term conciliation has been used in a confusing variety of ways, and by some is used interchangeably with 'mediation'.

Conciliation in SEN has emerged as a more evaluative, and less independent form of mediation. A Parent Partnership Officer may offer to 'conciliate' a disagreement, and other LEA staff can meet with parents to see if a solution can be achieved (see the Waltham Forest project at pp. 45–65).

Whereas mediation involves a completely neutral facilitator who does not offer any view or evaluation, conciliation may involve an expert neutral who can explain and advise the parties to assist with the resolution of their disagreement. Conciliation is also taken to be the process of resolution by negotiation and meetings before a disagreement is referred to independent mediation.

In some models of healthcare or workplace mediation, the independent neutral is referred to as a conciliator, although they are completely independent. Sometimes conciliation implies a greater emphasis on counselling skills and dealing with emotions as a bar to the resolution of a disagreement.

Throughout this book, conciliation is taken to be the process of disagreement resolution that takes place 'in house' by the LEA and Parent Partnership Officer or other supporter, and mediation is an independent service provided by a neutral third party as one of the final phases in the disagreement resolution landscape.

Mediation

This is a voluntary, non-binding and confidential disagreement resolution process using an independent mediator to assist the parties to reach a negotiated settlement. In SEN mediation, the parties are usually contacted by an impartial mediator who explains the procedure and establishes a rapport with each party. A joint meeting is then arranged at a neutral venue and all parties are given an opportunity to be heard uninterrupted. The process continues with a mixture of joint and private sessions led by the mediator who manages the process, but does not impose a solution. The mediator acts as a facilitator, and discussions are confidential and non-binding until an agreement is signed. In SEN mediation, parents retain the right to continue with a tribunal case or legal action, although lawyers are specifically excluded from the process.

Expert Determination and Early Neutral Evaluation

Used where there is a specific technical matter of dispute, an Expert Determination is where a neutral expert is instructed to investigate and report to both parties who agree that the expert's decision shall be binding. Another version along the same lines is Early Neutral Evaluation where a neutral expert provides a report that is used to guide negotiations and assess the prospects of success on both sides, and may be binding if the parties agree this in advance.

Arbitration, tribunal, litigation

The aim of any arbitration, tribunal or court hearing is to impose a binding settlement on parties where they have not been able to reach one themselves. The hallmarks of this process are that it is formal, adversarial, can be time-consuming, governed by rigid rules of procedure, and usually based on law and precedent. Lawyers usually advise parties on the basis of their legal case based on the available evidence. The determination is usually final subject to any appeal on a matter of law. Parties are encouraged to put their best case forward, but the boundary of factual consideration may be limited. In SEN cases, the most common forum is the SEN tribunal (considered more fully at pp. 148–60) and litigation through the civil courts.

Baseball Arbitration and online dispute resolution

In Baseball Arbitration, the neutral receives offers of settlement in a sealed envelope from all parties to the disagreement, and selects the proposal for settlement which most closely fits with their assessment of the case. Such techniques are well suited to resolving small financial claims where there is a single financial issue, and have been used as 'online' models of dispute resolution via the internet, either by automated computer formula that calculates the award, or using neutrals who communicate with all parties through the medium of the internet.

Med-Arb and mediator evaluation

This technique is a combination of mediation and arbitration, used when a final binding solution is needed. Mediation techniques are used in the first instance, followed by arbitration if the mediation does not achieve a solution. In some models, the neutral starts as a mediator and then becomes arbitrator if necessary, which poses its own challenges on how mediator confidentiality is handled. In other models, a new neutral is brought in to impose a solution where one was not found by agreement. Med-Arb can also incorporate Baseball Arbitration where all parties seal their best proposal for settlement in an envelope before the start of the mediation and hand these to the neutral. In the event of no agreement, the neutral uses the Baseball Arbitration procedure to impose a settlement.

In a watered-down form of Med-Arb, the mediator provides a report to both parties on a possible framework for solution, and this is sometimes known as Mediator Evaluation.

Ombudsman

There are a variety of different schemes, largely covering complaints of maladministration or incompetence in decision-making rather than disagreement over the merits of particular decisions, although there may be some overlap. Most ombudsman schemes, such as the Local Government Ombudsman will base decisions upon written evidence and parties are expected to attempt resolution before a decision falls to be considered on the papers. The Ombudsman will normally determine the issues to be examined after considering all the written evidence and submissions, and may circulate written questions to be answered in writing before making a written finding.

Common myths about mediation

'Mediation will affect my legal rights'

The process is not a bar to taking a case to the tribunal and does not take away any other legal rights. In fact, mediation can be helpful even where no solution is reached, as very often the number of issues disputed can be reduced and there can then be greater focus on the more fundamental areas of disagreement. Parties need not be fearful about 'disclosing their hand' in mediation, as the parties remain in control throughout, and everything remains confidential. A court or tribunal will not take into account what was said in mediation, and any such statement would be regarded as a 'without prejudice' settlement discussion. If parties do not wish to be seen to make an offer or concession during the mediation, the suggestion could be presented as the idea of the mediator.

'Mediation is for people who have a weak case'

The potential for success is high and those who believe they have a strong case can use the process to convince others. It provides an opportunity for cases to be looked at in detail and considered with greater care than usual, and for misunderstandings to be resolved face to face that otherwise could take lengthy correspondence. Compromise is less important than creative and imaginative solutions that may not have been considered before, and the opportunity to rebuild trust and re-establish a working relationship.

'We use these techniques all the time, and there is no point in further discussions'

However skilled or able the party or however many techniques are employed, the key component – mediation with an independent third party has often not been tried. Even a genuine attempt to resolve disagreement may not be effective if the parties do not perceive that there is complete neutrality in the process. A neutral mediator is completely detached from the problem, the areas of disagreement, the emotions and the political pressures and can manage the process in a way that is perceived to be completely impartial and focused on mutual gain.

From experience, even the fact that mediation is proposed by one party can lead to suspicions on the part of another party that it is done for some ulterior motive. How much greater, therefore, is the suspicion attached to an offer or proposal made by one party directly to another where trust and confidence has broken down?

'Mediation is just about compromise and meeting half-way'

Most mediation settlements are not simply a splitting of differences, and many creative solutions are achieved. There are a variety of methods employed to break deadlock, and very often the outcome is a solution that neither party had considered prior to the mediation process. One of the strengths of mediation is that parties can examine the issues perceived to be important in detail and remain in total control of discussions which may cover past, present and future. There is no limit to what can be discussed, unlike in a more formal legal setting where feelings, emotions, trust and confidence, correcting miscommunications, and rebuilding relationships are usually of no significance.

'Mediation is a waste of time if parties are too entrenched'

Very often the parties have an opportunity to listen to each other and highlight their perspective in the presence of a neutral third party for the first time. What a party reveals in confidence to the mediator may be totally different from what they are prepared to reveal to their 'opponent'. Thus parties who appear to be unmoveable are simply putting their best case forward and refusing to compromise. These are precisely the kind of cases where negotiation cannot proceed further without the intervention of a mediation to break the deadlock.

Why mediation works

Mediation works for a variety of reasons – including the fact that it

- Allows communications to take place freely
- Overcomes deadlock

- Assists negotiations
- Focuses on important issues and needs
- Gets the right people and information together at the same time
- Makes everyone part of the solution
- Rebuilds trust
- Restores and safeguards relationships
- Explores options for mutual gain.

1.3 RECENT DEVELOPMENTS IN UK LAW

Irvine S. Gersch

Special educational needs has been high on the agenda of the Labour government since they came to power in 1997. Following a White Paper in education (1997) 'Excellence in Schools', and a Green Paper on SEN (1997) 'Excellence for all children – meeting special educational needs', an Action Programme 'Meeting Special Educational Needs – A Programme of Action' was issued in 1998, and subsequently a new SEN framework put in place.

The framework comprises three main pieces of legislation.

1 The 1996 Education Act and Regulations, and under its powers, the revised Code of Practice on Special Educational Needs (2001). This Code replaced the very first SEN Code of Practice (1994).

2 The SEN and Disability Act 2001 and Regulations, which similarly require codes of practice to be published. A draft has been issued (a) for schools and (b) for post-16 students. The final versions come into effect in September 2002.

3 The statutory guidance on 'Inclusive Schooling for children with SEN' which was issued in November 2001.

The SEN Code of Practice (2001) deals with general principles and policies, partnerships with parents and pupil participation. It details clearly the system for identifying, assessing and providing for the needs of children with SEN and for carrying out a statutory assessment. There are comprehensive sections on Statements, Annual Reviews, the role of the Special Educational Needs Coordinator (SENCO) and on working in partnership with other agencies.

The SEN and Disability Act and Regulations explain how to avoid discrimination against disabled people in education, and ensure that their treatment is no less favourable than for people without a disability.

This Act also revised the operation of the SEN tribunal, which will become the SEN and Disability tribunal (SENDIST) in 2002. (See Chapter 5 by Simon Oliver.)

In 1993 the general principle that children with SEN should normally be educated in mainstream schools, subject to parental wishes, was enshrined in law (Education Act 1993, consolidated into the Education Act 1996). This followed agreement by the UK government to the 'Salamanca Statement'. This Statement, agreed in Salamanca, Spain, in 1994, at a UNESCO world meeting, called upon all countries to include in their laws or policies the principle of 'inclusive education, enrolling all children in regular schools, unless there are compelling reasons for doing otherwise'.

Statutory guidance was provided for LEAs, schools, health and social services in England in November 2001, in a document entitled 'Inclusive Schooling' which aims to provide practical advice and must not be ignored.

Some of the key principles highlighted are that inclusion should be viewed as a *process*, encompassing virtually all children, if the right training, strategies and support are put in place. The interests of pupils must be safeguarded, schools and others should seek to remove barriers to participation and all children should have access to opportunities to achieve their potential. Finally, it is acknowledged that mainstream education will not always be right for every child at all times, but rather a child might be included appropriately at a later stage.

Most importantly, recent educational legislation has now included a requirement on LEAs to put in place arrangements for independent disagreement resolution or mediation.

The new Code of Practice for SEN has a particular section on resolving disputes, in chapter two on 'Working in Partnership with Parents'. Sections 2:22 to 2:31 (pp. 22–5) which gives guidance to LEAs, headteachers, school governors, early-education practitioners and other interested parties.

In addition the DfES have produced a useful and clear toolkit on the whole Code of Practice, of which section 3, entitled 'Resolution of Disagreements' is intended to be read alongside chapter 2 of the SEN Code of Practice. This section of the toolkit is reproduced, by kind permission, in Chapter 10.

The Code itself begins with the reminder that all LEAs are required to make arrangements, that include the appointment of independent persons, to help avoid or resolve disputes between LEAs and parents of children in their area. Further, LEAs are required to make their disagreement resolution services known to parents, headteachers, schools and others they think are appropriate.

In short, it is clear that conciliation, mediation and disagreement resolution and avoidance have come of statutory age!

It is probably fair to depict the stance of the DfES in this area as open to developments in practice, whilst setting a clear remit and brief.

It seems to be the case that this government is keen to set out key principles and to encourage good practice to develop, rather than being highly prescriptive, thus allowing local variation and determination. This will inevitably lead initially to some regional variation, but over time, given ongoing sharing of good practice, it is likely that clearer practice will emerge.

The SEN Code of Practice views Parent Partnership schemes as key in helping prevent disagreements in the first place, through early meeting of any difficulties, but notes that this service is essentially a voluntary one. Thus it is helpful to regard Parent Partnership services perhaps as the first step in the ladder.

The Code states too that parents should be able to access local disagreement resolution procedures at any time during the SEN process, including if disagreements arise between parents and the school over arrangements and provision.

A central point is that all LEAs must provide disagreement resolution services, and the Code sets out the minimum standards required of these services.

The Code indicates that such services should demonstrate independence, credibility and they should work towards informal and early resolution. Parents must be given good information about the services, and how they can access them. Parents must also be informed that their legal rights are in no way affected by their use of such services, and indeed the process runs alongside the appeals process.

Many LEAs have thus reviewed their existing mechanisms for dealing with complaints and disputes in SEN and some are developing a staged approach.

Such a staged approach might include

1   School and parent direct
2   LEA officer and parent direct
3   Parent Partnership services
4   Conciliation arrangements or service
5   Independent mediation.

An aim of resolution services is to reduce the number of appeals, which are placed before the SEN tribunal. In doing so, the Code stresses the importance of genuine neutrality and independence, with the service being able to offer 'practical educational solutions' to which all parties can agree, ensuring the minimum disruption to the child. This last point is worth stressing and highlights the importance of acting in the best interests of the child.

In section 2:28 the Code specifies that the facilitator, as it terms the neutral mediators, should have a range of experience, knowledge and qualifications. This should certainly include (a) training and experience in mediation (b) counselling and negotiation skills (c) effective communication skills and (d) knowledge of SEN legislation and framework and the Code of Practice.

The models of operation suggested include:

1   Using a panel of trained mediators, with the LEA buying in services as needed
2   Expanding existing services
3   Using regional panels such as the SEN Regional Partnerships to provide a pool of facilitators.
4   LEAs working in partnership with other existing services which provide mediation.

In a helpful section (2:27) depicting the actual mediation process, the SEN Code of Practice goes on to envisage the facilitator bringing the various parties together in a non-threatening way, using discussion and negotiation to resolve the dispute. The facilitator is not seen as an arbitrator or someone who will determine the solution, but rather as someone who encourages the key parties to discuss all the issues and explore options, hopefully coming to an agreement.

On the basis that many disputes are the result of misunderstanding and not seeing the other person's point of view, such a process could prove to be extremely helpful in enabling a meeting of minds and creating a climate for understanding and compromise.

The Code does not envisage that parents will require legal representation, since that might not reflect the correct spirit of disagreement resolution. However, the Code does stress that all parties – and the child is included in the list, which is of note – need to feel confident that their point of view will be respected.

It is perhaps worth underlining the issue of child involvement. This Code of Practice dedicates a chapter to *pupil participation* and strongly encourages pupils to be as actively involved as possible in all aspects of their education. There is certainly a role for the child to play in attending part of the mediation process, at least, subject to age and circumstances.

Two annexes to the toolkit are provided. Annexe A outlines one suggested model, notably that which appears in the manual of mediation (UK) and Annexe B presents a case example.

The status of the toolkit is to explain the legal requirements and to provide detailed guidance. It reflects current research and models, and previously reviewed examples of good practice.

This research is based on the survey carried out by Jane Hall, whose findings are published in a booklet entitled *Resolving Disagreements between Parents, Schools and LEAs: Some Examples of Best Practice* (1999). This can be obtained from the DfES free of charge.

References

Department for Education DfEE (1994) *Code of Practice on the Identification and Assessment of Special Educational Needs*. London: HMSO.

Department for Education and Employment (DfEE) (1997) *Excellence for All Children – Meeting Special Educational Needs*. London: DfEE Publications.

Department for Education and Employment (DfEE) (1998) *Meeting Special Educational Needs – A Programme of Action*. London: DfEE Publications.

Department for Education and Skills (DfES) (2001) *Inclusive Schooling: Children with Special Educational Needs*. London: DfES Publications.

Department for Education and Skills (DfES) (2001) SEN Toolkit. London: DfES Publications.

Department for Education and Skills (DfES) (2001) *Special Educational Needs: Code of Practice*. London: DfES Publications.

Hall, J. (1999) *Resolving Disputes between Parents, Schools and LEAs: Some Examples of Best Practice*. Special Educational Needs Division, DfEE.

Special Children (2002) *Practice Makes Perfect: The Revised SEN Code of Practice: Special Children*, January 2002, pp. 20–5.

Stobbs, P. (2001) The SEN and Disability Act 2001. National Children's Bureau Highlight no. 186, July, National Children's Bureau.

Stobbs, P. (2001) The SEN and Disability Act 2001. Schools' Duties in the Disability Discrimination Act 1995. National Children's Bureau Highlight no. 187, October, National Children's Bureau.

The Disability Rights Commission (2000) Draft Code of Practice (Schools); Draft Code of Practice (Post-16). Consultation documents.

The Education Act (1996) London: Stationary Office.

The Salamanca Statement on Inclusive Education (1994) Salamanca, Spain, UNESCO.

The SEN and Disability Act, chapter 10. London: Stationary Office.

1.4   MEDIATION IN ACTION – MESSAGES FROM THE USA

Philippa Russell

There has been a general welcome for the proposals to introduce a new duty on LEAs to establish dispute resolution services within the SEN and Disability Rights Act 2001. As the number of appeals registered with the SEN tribunal has continued to rise, so has the proportion of those appeals, which are withdrawn prior to the hearing. It is clear that in many cases, disputes can be resolved if parents, the LEA and any other relevant professionals have the opportunity (and time) for an open and honest exchange of information, aspirations and concerns. Late withdrawals of appeals are stressful and expensive – for parents, LEAs and schools. The introduction of mediation arrangements in the SEN and Disability Act 2001 should help all parties to get together earlier to resolve differences.

In thinking about best options for mediation or dispute resolution in the United Kingdom, we can learn from the USA. When IDEA (Individuals with Disabilities Education Act) was amended in 1997, the USA was facing many of the dilemmas that are confronting us today. Parents were bringing more appeals through the 'due process' procedures. Litigation was very stressful for families – a research study showed how many parents wished that their dispute could have been resolved earlier, even if they had 'won' – and it was expensive. Schools were spending money on financial compensation after court cases, which could have been better spent on making schools more accessible and inclusive. Some schools were literally 'paying off' disabled children whom they did not wish to accommodate, regarding the financial compensation as a legitimate price to pay for not – as they saw it – changing the nature of the school.

In the USA, Minnesota and a handful of other States had already introduced mediation in the 1980s. Mediation was optional, was always carried out by a trained mediator and was independent of education services. Ongoing evaluation suggested that parents using mediation very often resolved their difficulties without needing any formal legal proceedings. Messages from parents using mediation were positive:

> Mediation is much quicker than the Courts. The service can set up a meeting in up to 20 days. And we felt in control of the process.

The process really allowed us to clear the air and to resolve issues which had been problematic for several months. We and the school really understood each other for the first time. We stopped being angry and irritated with each other.

(Minnesota Special Education Mediation Service)

Because of parental support for mediation in those States which had introduced schemes early, the USA federal government formally introduced mediation with a range of other amendments to IDEA in 1997. Section 615 (e) of the Act now requires all Education Departments to offer a mediation session to all parents who are seeking a due process hearing (roughly the equivalent of going to the SEN and Disability Tribunal).

Mediation in Minnesota (which has one of the longest running schemes) is seen as a *process* of dispute resolution. To be effective, it requires:

- *Orientation* – clear ground rules, clarity about the information required
- *Information and advice*, including support from a relevant parent organisation
- *Sharing of different perspectives, issues and options* – emphasis upon honest and open sharing of concerns
- *Caucus* – both sides can have separate meetings with the mediator
- *Discussion of options for resolution and possible solutions* – parents and schools need to understand how different options might be implemented; what are the barriers to implementation and what additional resources might be required
- *Agreement* – conclusions are written as formal documents. The conclusions may be incorporated within the child's IEP and form part of regular reviews of the USA equivalent of the Statement. In the USA, the IEP can include both SEN and any disability specific issues. If a child is disabled, the IEP will include a special 'impact statement' on any implications – i.e. transport, special equipment, which will impact upon, but may be separate to, any special educational needs.

An important issue for success is the *status* of mediation services. In most states, the mediator is not only trained but is part of the equivalent of a local authority's mediation/conciliation services. The service is not provided through the education department. There have been discussions about possibly running services through independent contractors or the voluntary sectors. But the functions of a mediation service are seen as quasi-judicial and not appropriate for independent providers. Conciliation services are also available, but are seen as a distinct, more formal and discrete phase in dispute resolution.

In the USA, as in the United Kingdom, parent support groups and voluntary organisations are seen as having key roles in reducing disagreements and misunderstandings. The USA voluntary sector and parent training and information centres have in general seen themselves as providers of information and advice to parents rather than as providers of mediation. They often offer an 'independent friend' (or independent parental supporter) role during dispute resolution and frequently also provide more formal advocacy and representation at any formal hearing.

Under IDEA, as amended in 1997, all USA states are now required as a minimum to:

- Maintain a list of 'individuals who are qualified mediators and knowledgeable in laws and regulations relating to the provision of special education and related services'.
- Ensure that any meetings relating to mediation are held in convenient and accessible locations and in a timely way.
- Regard discussions which take place in mediation sessions as confidential. They may not be used in evidence in due process or in civil proceedings. Participants may be required to sign a confidentiality pledge at the start of any proceedings.
- Agreements reached by mediation are set out in formal mediation agreements.

Although the parents are only required to participate in mediation on a voluntary basis, the State is required to make every effort to encourage them to do so. Education Departments or the State may establish procedures (often on a contract basis) with parent training and information centres or community parent resource centres (roughly the equivalent of parent partnership services) to meet with parents to discuss their complaint or dissatisfaction at a time and place to suit them. Parents may also be referred to another form of dispute resolution if this seems more acceptable.

Considerable emphasis is placed upon all parents having appropriate information. If parents register a complaint, they must be given copies of a Procedural Safeguards Notice (section 1415), which must contain:

- A full explanation of the procedural safeguards, written in the native language of the parents wherever possible and written in an accessible and understandable manner.
- Information on how parents may access educational records, and independent educational evaluation.
- The child's placement during the resolution of the dispute, if relevant.
- The arrangements for mediation.
- Information on the appeal process from registering complaints, to mediation, due process hearings and state-level appeals.
- Information in a format or language appropriate to the family's needs.

The effectiveness of any dispute resolution arrangements will depend upon the clarity of procedures around the assessment of special educational needs and any special educational provision specified to meet such needs. In effect, it is purposeless to try to introduce a less adversarial approach to resolving disputes, unless there is shared understanding about the basis for decision-making and the provision of accessible and comprehensive information 'on the table' for all parties to review and reach a shared conclusion about. Therefore, the introduction of a formal requirement to provide mediation arrangements under IDEA was accompanied by a review of (and amendments to) the wider framework for the assessment of special educational needs.

As Turnbull and Rainbolt (1998) noted:

> IDEA is targeted at retaining and enhancing the rights that students and parents have, while *increasing* the effectiveness of schools to implement those rights and to ensure that students' proposed outcomes are met . . . it identifies barriers to effective special education and proposes solutions based on research and experience, namely:
>
> - High expectations
> - Strengthening of parents' roles (in terms of rights and responsibilities)
> - Coordinated service delivery
> - Clarity about resources
> - Redefinition of special education as a service not a place and
> - Improved assessment with clear outcomes and evaluation arrangements in place.

The USA, like the UK, has seen a growing debate about increased bureaucracy in education and an emphasis upon the need for more streamlined assessment arrangements. Evaluation (assessment) is seen as a team affair, with the team containing the students' parents, at least one regular (mainstream) teacher if the child is or may be attending a mainstream school and at least one special education teacher or provider. The team will also include a representative of the local education department who is qualified to provide or supervise 'specially designed instruction to meet the unique needs of students with disabilities and who is knowledgeable about general curriculum and the availability of local agency resources', together with an individual who can interpret the 'instructional implications of evaluation results' (who may already be a member of the team) and any other individuals who have relevant knowledge. Parents may propose these additional team members if they so wish. Students also have the right to participate as team members, subject to agreement about the appropriateness of so doing.

IDEA introduces 'more enriched, more extensive evaluation [assessment]' (Guidance Notes, IDEA, 1997), which incorporates new safeguards for parents), namely that:

- The evaluation (assessment) team must include the parent of the pupil being assessed, in addition to any other parent representatives. Parents therefore must be part of all the assessment proceedings.
- Parents may submit and require the evaluation team to consider any assessments or reports, which they initiate.
- Parents, as in the UK, receive copies of all relevant reports.

But – and it is an important new qualification – assessment teams must now

- Consider using (and justifying) a variety of assessment tools and techniques
- Consider reviewing existing data on the student, including current class-based assessments and observations, together with the views of teachers and any other relevant service provider
- Clarify what, if any, additions or modifications to the students' special educational provision might be required in order to meet the measurable goals set in the IEP and to ensure participation in the general curriculum as appropriate.

These changes in effect provide the context for effective mediation by substantially increasing parents' rights to information and participation in assessment. They presume that effective assessment will be a team process, with a collective responsibility for agreed outcomes and they clearly link assessment to the IEP and associated programmes of work. They are also seen as taking forward the State programme on school improvement by requiring the assessment team to use *tools and strategies* that indicate whether the school is actually meeting the student's educational needs and thereby adding yet another *accountability provision* which can be tested out and explored when there is disagreement with parents about the provision being made.

IEPs are themselves redefined, to include new requirements relating to inclusion, namely:

- *Performance and inclusion*: this involves a statement on the student's current performance together with the impact of the student's disability on his/her involvement and performance in the general curriculum.
- *Annual goals and inclusion*: they must set bench-marks (short-term annual objectives) relating to the involvement and progress of the student in the *general* curriculum.
- *Measuring progress: information for parents*: the IEP must state how the student's progress towards annual goals will be measured and how parents will be informed about that progress. Parents of children with special educational needs or disabilities must receive information *at least as often as parents of students without special educational needs or a disability* would be informed of their children's progress. Many parents of children with special needs had complained that they received much less information on progress than was the case for parents of children without such needs.
- *'Impact statements'* with targets relating to the child's disability: the reprovisioning of IDEA recognises that children's ability to learn may not only depend on the appropriateness of their special educational provision but also upon practical provision such as the child needing to sit at the front of the class; requiring a special chair or piece of equipment; needing assistance in mobility training or personal care or in participating more fully in the social or sporting life of the school. Importantly, targets relating to disability may include requirements on non-educational agencies to provide and monitor a service (such as speech and language or physiotherapy or to provide support for a healthcare need). The 'disability impact

statement' is of particular relevance to the implementation of the SEN and Disability Act 2001 and to the extended role of the renamed SEN and Disability Tribunal. Mediation processes may relate to the specific *disability*-related targets or provisions made for the child as well as to special educational needs.

The greater specificity about *what* must be included within a pupil's IEP, combined with targets which must be regularly reviewed, makes any mediation scheme more practical, with the disputes in question covering a wide range of issues ranging from provision of equipment to the differentiation offered in the child's access to the curriculum.

The development of mediation in the USA must also be put in the wider experience of the use of a variety of dispute resolution approaches in industry and also, most significantly, in family law. There are various legal definitions of mediation, the State of Louisiana Mediation Act defining the mediation process as:

> . . . a procedure in which a mediator facilitates communication between the parties concerning the matters in dispute and explores the possible solutions to promote reconciliation, understanding and settlement.

The State of Louisiana, like Minnesota and others which have well-established mediation programmes for use in education, sees mediation as a *process* – a voluntary and non-adversarial process involving a trained third party and which will only be effective if the process is based upon:

- Clear understandings of roles and responsibilities, with careful consultation and training prior to the service commencing work
- Clarity about the independence and neutrality of the service offered. In the majority of USA services, mediation is provided as part of an existing 'arms'-length' mediation service (e.g. a wider local authority service for dispute resolution).
- A recognition of the time entailed in successful mediation (including the need for preparation of relevant information or reports).
- Proper support for parents and other family members, who may feel angry and disempowered and see mediation as a diversion from a settlement of their difficulties.

Perhaps less importantly for the United Kingdom, lawyers have become involved in mediation in some States. A USA family lawyer (personal communication) commented that:

> Lawyers do not usually attend mediation sessions. We aim to make those sessions as neutral and conducive to cooperative thinking as possible. However, we have found that some families insist on their lawyer playing a role. In the USA, families may not feel safe without their legal adviser present, even if the procedures are confidential and evidence from mediation procedures cannot be subsequently used in the courts. If this is the case, we would emphasise that the lawyer's role (and sometimes this is still an important one) is to advise his or her clients throughout the mediation process on their legal rights and also on their obligations. In the rare case where the lawyer is a mediator (some of our lawyers are trained to be, and may act as, mediators in family courts), then the lawyer specifically does not give legal advice to either party. Instead he/ she is a personal adviser and interpreter. We find it essential to spell out to parents what mediation means – it is not an extension of a court, it is not a legal battleground and it is not adversarial. Nobody will win or lose because the desired outcome is a mutually agreed settlement.

A parent (personal communication) similarly noted the importance of understanding roles and responsibilities. She saw her mediation sessions as leading to:

> . . . less 'posturing' on both sides – the problem is that you only get to mediation, when there has been a serious breach of trust on both sides. The real role of the mediator is to initiate and keep the conversation going without anyone rushing out of the room! Mediation offers you space to think.

The same parent cited the importance of independent parental support and advice, referring to the role of PACER (the Parent Advocacy Coalition for Educational Rights) and the value of good-quality written information on special educational needs and provision. She observed that:

> When parents have concerns about their children's special educational needs, they are worried, often disappointed and angry. They

may have missed opportunities to contribute to their child's IEP or to query proposed provision at the right time. In some cases, they themselves feel inadequate and afraid to challenge an education system which seems intimidating and bureaucratic. Very few parents understand disability rights in education – and they may have no idea of the range of options that might meet their child's needs without support. Education Departments may feel that supporting independent parental support is expensive and unnecessary – I would argue that if you want to reduce disputes, then you have to invest in good parent support services.

Mediation has a potentially crucial role in helping parents to understand the full range of possible options. Norman Pickell (2000) comments that mediation means neither 'giving in' nor 'giving up', but presuming that it will be possible to find practical solutions in a positive environment. Key issues in such practical solutions are:

• Communication (both parties frequently failing to understand each other).
• Exchanging positions (probing the underlying and often unspoken issues).
• Exploring interests and needs.
• Generating options – mediators may be able to suggest options which neither party has considered.
• Assessment of merit of different options, with accessible information, and negotiating their acceptance.
• Recognising that sometimes mediation can result in more creative solutions than are possible through the courts – but that time and energy may be needed to work through hostility and low expectations. The voluntary sector and parent groups have an important role in providing informal support and, if requested, providing 'best friends' to accompany families to mediation sessions.
• Accepting the growing challenge of involving children and young people in decision-making, particularly when parents' views differ or where there is confidential information (e.g. on degenerative medical conditions) which professionals are reluctant to share with the young person.

The new provisions in IDEA have only just been implemented but there is already enthusiasm for mediation. Parents feel that their views are taken seriously. Children and young people are beginning to be included within mediation sessions. Cases are being withdrawn before due process hearings because everybody has agreed a way of working together. But the final message is that dispute resolution is not a single activity. Mediation is most effective when parents have good information, feel respected and valued and have the confidence to negotiate. It also has the capacity to engage schools and a wider range of services in thinking through their policies and practices in a non-adversarial way.

As one parent commented (Minnesota Special Education Service):

> Mediation is not a soft option. You need to be very clear about what you want and understand what the barriers are. The trouble is, your child only has one life and sometimes you feel so worried and angry, you don't know how to work with other people. But when you go somewhere neutral, with a mediator who really listens, somehow you begin to see the school differently. You start working together again, which is what it is all about. If you can work with your school and your education department, then the outcomes are good not just for your own child. Our mediation sessions helped 'John's' school not only to understand our concerns and respond to them, but also to think strategically about developing an action plan to make the school more inclusive and accessible over time. Suddenly we moved from crisis intervention to shared planning, with parents as partners and not the enemy!

In the United Kingdom, the SEN and Disability Act will raise new challenges not only around the requirement to provide a mediation service, but also in requiring schools and LEAs to think strategically about improving access and inclusion for disabled pupils. Because the Act covers the whole life of the school and because the tribunal will be able to hear disability specific cases, mediation services will need the capacity to handle a wide range of different referrals and to have the capacity to create positive dialogues about creating more accessible school environments. There are also likely to be new and extended roles for parent partnership services, whose potential role has been strengthened by the new legislation and the revised SEN Code of Practice. The USA equivalents of our parent partnership services have had an important role in informing and supporting parents in mediation, in conciliation and in 'due process' legal hearings. The role of the independent parental supporter can be essential in providing the independent and facilitative support, which many parents will need in order to enter into a mediation.

The American experience tells us that mediation can work – and work well – but a final message is that its success will depend upon careful investment in setting up mediation schemes and attention to the quality of training and the expectations of those using and providing it. As one education administrator commented at a meeting of the President's Committee on Mental Retardation (2000 – personal communication),

> ... the new rights-based approach to meeting special educational needs means that we have to be prepared to be clear about the rationale for making (or withholding) any special educational provision. Education departments, schools and parents must understand their mutual roles and responsibilities. Allocation of resources must be transparent – and we must involve all players in strategic action planning to improve capacity in schools and the wider range of services. Our former litigation-based approaches meant that some families used the courts to get good services. But there was no incentive to invest in the wider infrastructure of services for pupils with disabilities or SEN. Mediation requires honest and open discussion – sometimes disclosure – of difficult and often painful issues and information. But it has opened up a new honesty in decision-making for SEN.

References

Individuals with Disabilities Education Act, 20 USC, chapter 33 as amended by IDEA Amendments 1997, Public Law 105–17 (June 1997).

Landau, B. (1997) *Family Mediation Handbook*, second edition, Canada, Butterworths.

Minnesota Office of Dispute Resolution, MINSEMS (Minnesota Special Education Mediation Service) and related publications for parents, schools and education departments.

National Information Center for Children and Youth with Disabilities (August 1997), The IDEA Amendments of 1997, National Information Centre, Washington DC.

Noble, C. (1999) *Family Mediation: A Guide for Lawyers*, Canada Law Books.

PACER (Parent Advocacy Coalition for Educational Rights), Parents' Summary of IDEA '97, PACER, Minneapolis, USA.

Pickell, N. (2000) *In Family Law, How Is Mediation Different from a Settlement Meeting?*, Mediation Services, Mediation Books, USA.

SEN tribunal (2000) Annual Report of the SEN tribunal

Turnbull, R. and Rainbolt, K. (1997) *Individuals with Disabilities Education Act: Digest and Significance of 1997 Amendments*, Beach Center on Families and Disability, University of Kansas, USA.

Chapter 2

Setting up local disagreement resolution, conciliation and mediation arrangements

Irvine S. Gersch

2.1 ISSUES FOR LEA ADMINISTRATORS

In order to comply with the law, LEAs are required to set up local independent mediation and disagreement resolution arrangements. Many will already have informal and perhaps formal systems in operation, which will require review. It is fair to say that LEAs are likely to be at different stages of development in respect of such schemes.

Some have experience of using external and independent agencies for disagreement resolution, others will have used their own agencies, such as the Educational Psychology Service (EPS) or Parent Partnership Officers. Others may have joined a syndicate of LEAs to consider working together and still others may have used a partnership model whereby LEAs use colleagues in a neighbouring LEA to mediate cases, on a reciprocal basis.

For the purpose of this chapter the following areas will be considered.

1 Where the LEA is now: a disagreement resolution audit
2 Which cases might qualify
3 Level of demand and funding
4 In-house versus independent of the LEA
5 Format
   - Procedures and operational issues
   - Venues
   - Trust and confidence
   - Quality standards
   - Monitoring and evaluation
   - Time-scales
   - Literature and publicity
   - Confidentiality

6   Equal opportunities
7   Other issues to consider.

The disagreement resolution continuum

Before analysing the above issues it is worth outlining a concept which may be found useful in conceptualising arrangements which LEAs might set up for disagreement resolution and mediation in SEN, namely, that of the *disagreement resolution continuum*.

This concept suggests that arrangements in reality fall along a continuum from (a) informal to formal and from (b) non-independent to independent.

LEAs may be placed on different stages of the continuum for either of the dimensions. Further, there may not be a direct correlation between the place on the continuum and outcomes for disputes. For example, in some LEAs with very few cases ending up in a SEN tribunal they may adopt informal and in-house methods only. Little research is available to indicate the relationship between these parameters and success or otherwise in respect of dispute resolution.

In recent years, there has been increasing concern and indeed suspicion about bodies which investigate themselves when complaints are made about them. This has extended to bodies where attempts have been made to use their own sub-systems to undertake the investigation. Some agencies, for example the Police Force, have used other forces within the Police Service but from a completely different region or locality to investigate complaints but this has led to public disquiet about independence, fairness and bias.

The idea of 'the Police investigating themselves' has been criticised as inconsistent with natural justice and fairness, whatever the result of the particular inquiry. The issue of independence is not only about justice but rather relates to 'justice being seen to be done'.

Before the advent of the SEN tribunal, parental disputes in respect of their children with SEN were dealt with by local appeal panels convened by the local council, and often chaired by elected council members, in council offices. The move towards regional independent SEN tribunals removed a potential criticism about such hearings, namely that they were inherently biased in favour of the LEA from the outset.

To some extent, the outcome or procedures for such in-house processes did not matter in relation to the criticism; justice required that the procedures be regarded as even for all players. It now seems fair to say that there has been a move in the public mood towards disputes being resolved by neutral people in a context, which starts from a self-evidently independent stance.

There are, however, some disadvantages in such an independent system.

First, they are more costly than in-house systems. Second, it could be argued that the further one removes the resolution from the actual dispute (either locationally or in respect of involving other previously uninvolved agencies) the larger the dispute becomes, and the harder it may be to resolve. Third, one could argue that those who know the context best are likely to be those who are working in the specialist area, and thus LEAs with local knowledge and expertise are well equipped to investigate and resolve local complaints. Officers from their own LEAs, may come up with their own creative solutions, and have the power to implement them through their knowledge, status and relationships with key players (e.g. headteachers, health authority and social services professionals) within the locality. Outsiders are unlikely to have such a level of local knowledge, power or relationships to effect such creative changes. Finally, one could argue that officers are frequently able to operate with an open mind and to show fairness, compassion and justice in their dealings. Many LEA officers will have selected this type of work fuelled by a sense of fairness, parental rights, equal opportunities and to improve the lot of children. Accepting that LEAs Officers have a duty to be prudent with public funds, and there is undoubtedly a significant concern to avoid unnecessary over-expenditure of budgets, it would be erroneous to tar all officers with the brush of wanting to offer parents and children with SEN a poor deal.

There is a good case for an LEA exhausting its own in-house disagreement resolution arrangements before resorting to neutral mediation.

Future Planning

Where the LEA is now: a disagreement resolution audit

When considering what sort of disagreement resolution services would be desirable for an LEA, a starting point might be to determine where the LEA is currently positioned, not only in respect of the continuum regarding formal/informal and independence/in-house, but in respect too of the number of tribunal cases currently taking place, the patterns of disputes and how these are being dealt with.

It is likely that, whether *ad hoc* or not, there are a number of practices in the LEA which are both effective and desirable to emphasise.
Perhaps the first step therefore in the exercise should be a comprehensive audit of *all* the procedures, agencies and personnel who are con-
tributing, directly and indirectly, to the effective resolution of disputes
in SEN.

One could argue that schools themselves should be included in
this auditing process since early resolution of difficulties, and potential
major disputes, is by and far the best policy. Consequently, a rapid,
effective response in the early stages of a parental concern may well
save a much more serious dispute from arising or developing.

At this stage it is also useful to audit the nature and types of appeals
that are leading to appeals to the SEN tribunal, and to review whether
there are any discernible patterns. In the author's experience, such an
exercise can be most interesting and challenge what is taken to be
preconceived patterns of disputes.

A 2001 study by Rowley and Gersch (described in Chapter 3) found
that the most common disputes dealt with by a disagreement resolution
service in one urban LEA, over a three-year period tended to be in
respect of boys, aged between ten and twelve years and who had physical
difficulties. This challenged the preconception that the major difficulties
were in relation to dyslexic-type cases.

In order to audit the current situation it is worth going beneath
the surface of the LEA SEN climate through identifying those factors
which are having an impact upon the disagreement resolution climate
overall.

Such factors will serve to increase or decrease the volume of disputes
going on, and their chances of successful resolution. This will also
assist the development of a staged model of disagreement resolution,
which we shall suggest and develop at the end of this analysis.

Some of the factors worthy of consideration at this point are:

* The role of the SEN panel
* Parent Partnership scheme
* The role of the LEA's named officer
* The role of the school
* The role of allied professionals (health authority, social services)
* Local context and policies
* Local community
* LEA agencies and providers of SEN support services
* Voluntary agencies

The role of the SEN panel

In considering disagreement resolution arrangements it is important to establish which person or persons or panel makes decisions for individual children in respect of the draft statement of SEN, on behalf of the LEA. In some LEAs an SEN panel will consider all the advices and compile a draft statement, some LEAs will delegate the task to others, for example educational psychologists, whilst some LEAs may now have most draft statements prepared by individual officers.

Whatever the local system, which for the purposes of this section we shall regard as the SEN panel, it would be relevant to establish whether

- the panel takes a flexible line,
- is open to changing its mind in the light of new evidence,
- has any 'blind spots' or hobby horses such as specific issues of belief and viewpoint which it regards as unchangeable irrespective of the individual case.

In summary, it may be possible to characterise the attitude of the SEN panel through asking the following questions:

Is the SEN panel

- Parent-friendly within LEA policy parameters?
- Flexible?
- Rigid/inflexible?

The parent partnership scheme

Beyond the SEN panel, LEAs now have some form of parent partnership officer, service or scheme that has been set up to support and help parents of children with SEN deal with the process of statutory assessment and arranging support for their child. Clearly, the operation of such a service will have an impact upon the disagreement resolution environment in an LEA.

In auditing this environment it would be important to know whether the scheme has been in operation for some time, whether it is effective and accessible to parents, and what its role in dispute resolution is. It is also pertinent to ask whether there is any specific pattern of referral to this service, since this could be a signal that some more general LEA response might be required rather than a focus upon the individual case and similar dispute repeated over and over again.

It would be important to question whether the parent partnership scheme is effective in resolving parental disputes with the LEA or schools.

LEA named officer

The LEA named officer is 'the person from the LEA who liaises with parents over all the arrangements relating to statutory assessment and the making of a statement. LEAs must inform parents of the identity of the Named Officer when they issue a notice of a proposal to make a statutory assessment of a child' (DfES, 2001, SEN Code of Practice, p. 204).

This person represents the LEA and is the official LEA contact. In the author's experience named officers can view themselves as primarily LEA officers, others as supporters of parents and others as mediators on behalf of the child. Mostly, it is a combination of all three roles and almost all named officers would be involved in informal disagreement resolution.

In auditing the LEA disagreement resolution current scene, it is important to discover how effective such officers are in respect of disagreement resolution. This should not of course be judged simply by the number of cases resolved in favour of those parents who make the most fuss, nor, conversely, in favour of overpowering parents who might have a justifiable complaint. What we do need to know, however, is whether disputes are resolved generally to the satisfaction of all parties, and in the interests of the child, and whether after the involvement of the named officer there are a large number of appeals lodged with the SEN tribunal. If so, again an analysis of patterns of referrals would be helpful. Key questions would ask whether the named officer is

- A creative problem solver
- Parent-friendly within LEA parameters
- Approachable.

The role of the school

Schools in the LEA will make an enormous impact upon the SEN disagreement resolution climate: their attitudes are critical in the determination of how many disputes occur, how many of these are resolved and how many prolonged.

In particular, the attitude and beliefs of the headteacher and SENCO and indeed the governing body are vital. Is the school a friend or foe of the LEA, does it help or hinder the case under dispute?

Schools are in a special position in relation to both parents and the LEA. There are situations in which they can make things work well for the child through making in-school provision quickly, and of course, conversely, by not doing so. They could inform the parents that they need more resources and thereby encourage parents to be the agent of resource collection for the school. The parental dispute with the LEA over their individual child with SEN thus becomes a vehicle for resolving a resource dispute between the LEA and the school.

Schools could well argue that they are empowering parents to fight for their rights, and indeed are encouraging the dispute between parent and LEA as a matter of principle. Indeed, they may have justice on their side. In any event it is the parents who now become caught up in the crossfire. And, it is fair to note, such disputes will not cease through them being dealt with on a case-by-case basis. Indeed, each case may be used to reopen a more underlying battle. What is needed here perhaps is an agreed policy between LEA and schools to which all parties adhere.

SEN audit systems have been used to deal with such issues with funding being allocated to schools in a fair and transparent way. Case disputes over statements can allow funding to be adjusted at the margins.

There are many examples of schools actually averting disputes through their ongoing contact with parents and the trust and confidence that has developed. Indeed these factors would appear to be fundamental to the avoidance of disputes.

In some LEAs, the idea of an attached LEA SEN officer to a group of schools has been found to be very successful in developing ongoing relationships, trust and resolving difficulties early. This emanates from the SEN section, which administers the SEN assessment process, being organised in such a way that individual casework officers have regular responsibility for all the cases in a set list of schools. This makes contact between school and LEA easy and reliable and can avoid misunderstandings arising.

Bearing in mind the importance of school as a factor, three separate barometers have been suggested to audit their impact on the disagreement resolution environment in an LEA. In particular are they

- SEN-friendly?
- Parent-friendly?
- LEA-friendly?

Role of allied professionals

It has been a major plank of the Labour government's educational policy to promote and develop collaborative and multi-professional work in the area of SEN. In the formulation of Statements of SEN, a number of parties contribute Advices, any one of which could become an issue in a dispute.

Medical colleagues may have different views about inclusion, provision or even diagnosis from those of educational professionals; social workers may hold different values about schools than others, and thus there is potential for significant inter-professional misunderstanding and disagreement.

Similarly, the health authority, social services and education departments have typically managed and are held accountable for their own distinct budgets. Consequently, disputes have arisen about which department should pay for certain items.

Fortunately, there are moves for pooled budgets and shared decision-making which are very helpful.

However, in auditing an LEA's disagreement resolution climate it is useful to assess how far such agencies are working together, share values and priorities.

It is also useful to note whether parents may be in receipt of contradictory advice from different professionals, whether some exceed their remit through perhaps encouraging parents to a particular view (for example in seeking transfer to certain schools) and how far some are working harmoniously with the LEA.

Examples do arise occasionally whereby an individual professional feels very strongly about a particular provision. In one case, for example, a specialist teacher accompanied a parent to visit a special school, prior to any LEA decision, thus building up expectations and a head of steam. This laid the foundation for a dispute, which might have been averted. Clearly all parties do need to agree to and adhere to rules of protocol and act in harmony in following agreed procedures. Although, that said, there must be scope in any system for disagreements between professionals to be aired properly and hopefully be resolved. It might be useful to question whether other agencies are

- highly collaborative with the LEA and supportive of parents
- supportive of parents only
- working unilaterally.

The local context and policies

Every LEA will have developed policies in respect of SEN, inclusion, behaviour support, children in public care, the standards of services, educational development of schools, strategic plans, and plans for working with children and adolescents with mental health problems. Other action and strategic plans perhaps in response to LEA Ofsted reports might also exist. Few could complain that LEAs are under-planned at this time in their history.

Indeed, many feel that there is such an intensity of planning activity and large number of plans that it is difficult for all intended actions to be implemented! It is also fair to comment that there is sometimes a difference between actual practice and what is sometimes called 'espoused theory'. In short, a discrepancy between plans and actions in the real world.

In auditing the SEN disagreement resolution climate, it is important to be clear about what plans are in play, both theoretical and actual and which superordinate principles might be influencing decisions made for individual children. An obvious example is the strength of an LEA's inclusion policy and practice which will certainly impact directly upon decisions made in respect of individual children with SEN. This might conflict with the LEA's policy of listening to parents and customer orientation. In any event, in order to plan for disagreement resolution arrangements, it is essential for such policies, practices and values to be considered.

The barometer for such policies might be determined by the following question: are the LEA policies understood, appreciated and welcomed by parents and schools, or indeed not understood or resented by schools and parents?

The local community

A further set of factors which determine the disagreement resolution landscape are the nature and make-up of the local community. Training exercises have revealed different issues and causes of disputes in different areas. In some, the trend is towards a large number of parents seeking costly residential education for their children; in others, parents in dispute seemed more concerned to raise levels of resources for children with reading difficulties in school.

This is also affected by the LEA's own policies and indeed by the provision they are currently offering to all children. Were all dyslexic children catered for to their parents satisfaction, one would envision that it would be less likely for there to be disputes in that area.

What is required is a careful analysis of the local communities, their needs and perspectives and the issues currently which are subject to dispute at all levels. There are likely to be less disputes where LEAs are responsive to and meet the needs of its local community, and involves them in the disagreement resolution arrangements.

LEA agencies and SEN support providers

Any comprehensive audit of the disagreement resolution landscape requires taking account of all the players in the game. Several key players include those who are providing assessment of and/or support to children with SEN in the locality.

Although there will doubtless be regional organisation and management variations, and different names used, such players are likely to include the Educational Psychology Service, Learning Support Teaching Service, learning support assistants, special schools, outreach teachers, specialist teachers (for example who support children with hearing or visual or behavioural difficulties), education welfare officers and others.

Some of these agencies might be funded by the LEA directly and thus held centrally, others might be delegated, meaning that they have to be purchased direct by schools themselves, for their continued existence. These funding arrangements will have direct impact upon the nature of the service, in that a service reliant upon schools for their existence will not wish to fall out with what is their valued customer. The customer relationship inevitably affects priorities.

The relevance of this point to disagreement resolution and disputes is that situations do arise whereby such agents are asked to support schools and parents in disputes with the LEA, on occasion for additional resources. These agencies then become involved in a dispute, albeit indirectly.

Obviously, there may be times when such professionals also feel that they need to advocate a case in support of parents, or indeed in the interests of the child. In any event, an audit of the LEA scene does need to make some assessment of the power and influence of such agencies.

The barometer questions in this category would pertain to whether the agencies are:

- highly acquiescent or combative with the LEA
- sympathetic to the LEA perspective
- supportive of parents
- hold the child's needs as paramount.

Voluntary agencies

There are a number of voluntary agencies which support parents with children with special needs, typically relating to types of disability. Some of the most well known include SCOPE, MENCAP, the British Dyslexia Association, The Autistic Society and others.

Parents frequently derive considerable support, information, and advice from such voluntary associations and agencies. LEAs sometimes can experience them as pressure groups, advocating provision for children in their area of focus and pressing for improvements. The LEA perspective will reflect their responsibility for all children in their care, and thus tensions and different viewpoints can arise, leading to disputes.

In auditing the disagreement resolution landscape, it is useful to know which voluntary agencies are dominant in the area, how they are operating, and the power and influence they wield. Which, if any, are adopting a primarily adversarial approach and which might be willing to engage in, or already engage in, collaborative creative problem-solving with the LEA?

Which cases might qualify

An LEA will need to take a view about which cases are referred to its formal disagreement resolution service, whether in-house or independent.

Some of the choices include:

- All those that are accepted by the SEN tribunal for a hearing
- All those referred to the SEN tribunal
- All those where parents have lodged a dispute with the SEN panel or LEA formally

- All those whereby parents make a direct referral to the disagreement resolution service
- Referrals by schools and other agencies, such as the EPS.

In the last section of this chapter, a *comprehensive staged model* will be advocated for all LEA dispute resolutions, which further develops this point. Nonetheless, there remains a case for having a somewhat flexible system, since time can be of the essence in resolving some cases.

Level of demand and funding

This will obviously depend upon the decision reached for referrals, above.

One starting point is to assess the number of cases currently being lodged with the SEN tribunal, and then add a percentage. A mediation case may cost around £800 to £1,000 at 2002 prices.

In-house or independent

At the beginning of this chapter we discussed the independent continuum in detail and thus the points will not be re-visited here. Suffice to say that the LEA does have some choices to make, along the lines of the continuum.

The world is changing, however, and one can readily predict a future when some parents might regard the move towards external bodies more favourably. Some LEAs might also feel that moves toward delegation militate towards the use of external bodies, who require less initial investment and long-term financial commitment. One can appreciate the fear, however, that external bodies might prove to be an expensive challenge to the LEA in their decision-making.

Format

LEAs setting up disagreement resolution arrangements will need to consider the following elements:

Procedures and operational issues

A detailed specification about how the disagreement resolution will operate will need to be agreed. There are several models which are utilised, each of which will require somewhat different methodologies.

A typical mediation, undertaken for example in two half days, will involve the mediator hearing all sides, reviewing files and then exploring common ground as a basis for resolution.

For example, Jane Hall (1998) in her account of best practice, identifies at least six stages in the mediation process. These are:

1   Establishing contact with both parties
2   Preparation
3   Hearing the issues
4   Exploring the issues
5   Building agreements
6   Closing and following up.

Venues

These will need to be selected and be such as to be conducive, providing confidentiality and the possibility of formal meeting with all parties, and at other times, private meetings between the mediator and one party. Coffee and tea will need to be provided.

Trust and confidence

Trust and confidence is critical to the whole process and outcome, and will be enhanced through a transparently impartial role being adopted by the mediator and very clear information being provided about the procedure and ground rules.

Quality standards

The LEA will need to set operational standards for the service, as with all other services now undertaken by the LEA or its agencies. Such parameters as response time and telephone contact will all need to be specified.

Monitoring and evaluation

The whole mediation arrangement will need to be monitored and, at the end of a set period, say twelve months, be carefully evaluated. Agreements about what aspects should be evaluated need careful thought. Such factors include the number of disputes which have been resolved (quantity) or clarified (if not resolved) and those which have led to a satisfactory outcome from the point of view of, for example, parents, schools, the LEA.

Time-scales

Agreements will be needed on times allocated for an average disagreement resolution and of course responses within deadlines perhaps set by SEN tribunal appeal hearing dates.

Literature and publicity

It is important that procedures are transparent and accessible for all parents, and to this end any literature needs to be clear and straightforward for parents and users of the service. Points of contact need to be quickly identifiable and costs included, or information about these, if they are free of charge to parents but funded by the LEA. Parents will also wish to know about their legal rights in respect of their SEN tribunal appeal. They may also need to know to whom they may turn if they wish to make a complaint about the service.

Confidentiality

Confidentiality is critical to the process and should not be breached, save for cases of child protection. Information gleaned during mediation should not be released to any parties, and indeed any written records should be destroyed within agreed time lines. Information which has been agreed by all the parties involved in the mediation may be released to other parties.

General data held for monitoring and evaluation purposes would need to be retained, albeit anonymously, and should be kept for this purpose; this being explained to the parties concerned.

Equal opportunities

Access to the service needs to be fairly open to all and thus it is important that any literature is available in community languages and Braille, and is provided on tape where needed. The service needs to take care not to discriminate against people with disability from minority groups and diverse backgrounds. Interpreters and others to support and represent the family may be needed.

Other issues to consider

Some cases are not appropriately handled through disagreement resolution. For example, parents may feel they wish to have their case heard by the SEN tribunal. In such cases, this choice should be respected.

2.2   ISSUES FOR PROFESSIONALS

In setting up successful local disagreement resolution arrangements it is important to consider the role of professionals who typically contribute to statutory assessments and who will be quite directly affected by the scheme.

Such professionals include educational psychologists, speech therapists, occupational therapists, medical officers, social workers, school staff, SENCOs, specialist teachers, education welfare officers and others.

Obviously it would be helpful for professionals to be consulted about the scheme during the course of its development, and thereafter to be fully aware of its nature and operational details. Indeed, their input will be needed, in several ways.

First, such professionals may need to draw parental attention to the scheme in some instances and also to alert the LEA as early as possible to potential difficulties and disagreements.

Second, they may need to provide updated information and advice to the LEAs to help resolve specific issues. For example, disputes can arise in respect of the number of hours required for speech therapy or the type of treatment needed. Should this be called into question, either a second opinion or more detailed updated information might prove to be a critical way of agreeing a way forward, satisfactorily to all parties. Thus, such professionals do need to be willing to provide such additional information quickly and effectively.

Third, it is important that professionals adhere to working within agreed boundaries. SEN panels can experience their decision-making scope fettered by an individual professional who goes beyond his or her remit, and for example, recommends specific schools before a full picture has been provided. This can create the context for disputes and is best avoided.

Fourth, professionals who provide for SEN may be required to offer rather more flexible support than sometimes obtains. There are examples of support set up with very tight criteria. For example providing certain sorts of therapies only for primary children, in our experience, has caused major problems and set the background for disputes. They are also quite questionable, and indefensible for particular children, but have often been set up to ensure that the service can cope with the demand. Consequently, where such instances have been identified, a greater degree of flexibility may be required by professionals for the future.

Finally, some disputes might be averted by professionals adopting a very listening third ear; and being very ready and open to encourage parents to express their views and feelings in what is, after all, an emotional and difficult experience for many. Meeting professionals about one's child with SEN can be, of course, an emotionally challenging, anxiety-provoking and distressing experience for parents, and indeed the whole process of statutory assessment is often experienced by parents as fraught.

In our experience, professionals who gain the confidence and trust of parents, who give them time, and listen carefully to their views have less disputes than those who are perhaps less flexible, less patient, and more 'bureaucratic' in their approach. One could argue that relationships, reliability, clarity and openness are the keys to dispute avoidance and resolution.

2.3   A STAGED MODEL FOR DISAGREEMENT RESOLUTION

Reference has been made earlier to a possible staged model in respect of disagreement resolution, and to what has been termed a disagreement resolution climate. It is perhaps useful to consider disagreement resolution within an LEA as a comprehensive set of activities, rather than focus too much on the final perhaps formal episode.

Consequently, dispute and potential disagreements are best dealt with in a staged way: first, directly in the context when they arise and then going up a line if a resolution cannot be achieved.

Such a model could include the following stages, although variations would be needed to the early stages depending upon the nature of the case.

1   Negotiation
2   Conciliation
3   Mediation
4   Tribunal

The first and second stages could be dealt with by

- school staff: SENCO and headteacher and perhaps a school governor
- the LEA officer concerned with the case
- a specific professional relevant to the nature of the dispute
- a second LEA officer or chair of the SEN panel or their representative within the LEA
- a parent partnership officer

The second stage might be carried out through a developed and semi-formal service.

The third stage will clearly require the employment of an independent and neutral qualified mediator.

The fourth stage, as a last resort, would involve an SEN tribunal hearing.

Consequently, where a disagreement arises about, for example, provision, the first point of call would be the school, with the parent and school staff attempting to resolve the disagreement, but adopting a disagreement resolution approach. That is, the aim would be to listen carefully to all sides and, through collaborative, creative and effective problem-solving work, to resolve the dispute.

Within school, key staff might include the teachers, SENCO, headteacher and perhaps school governor, if it was felt that their contribution might assist and this was welcomed. Some governors do hold a specific brief for special needs and, in certain circumstances, could play a useful role.

It would be important for one person to steer a parent through these stages and monitor progress, and the best placed most appropriate person would appear to be the LEA's named officer, who would act as the initial point of contact.

It should also be stressed that such stages should be used as a guide rather than bureaucratic hurdles, and that they should be used flexibly, in accordance with the needs of the particular case. However, as a guide and checklist, they could serve the purpose of ensuring that all options are included.

Most importantly, these stages serve to reflect *the principles* that all disputes are dealt with

- as quickly as possible
- as near to the context of disagreement as possible

- by those who know the situation well
- with the lightest touch as possible
- with the least adversarial process as possible
- with the involvement of those who have the power to make decisions
- with regard to school staff, including those who might be able to offer personal flexibility and changes in respect of their own scope of work.

Checklist of considerations

To sum up the LEA's guide for setting up local arrangements:

1 Audit present disagreement resolution climate
2 Review operations of local landscape
3 Review the position on the formality and independence continuum
4 Decide where there are any gaps
5 Decide where one wants to be
6 Review the operational aspects one wishes
7 Set up a steering group
8 Set up monitoring and evaluation procedures
9 Implement the scheme
10 Review in a year and fine-tune in the light of the review.

Chapter 3

SEN conciliation

3.1 THE WALTHAM FOREST CONCILIATION SERVICE

Irvine S. Gersch, Cathy Casale and *Chris Luck*

Introduction

In this chapter we aim to outline the background to the Waltham Forest Conciliation Service, conciliation and mediation, describe the key stages and details of the service, report on an evaluation study of the conciliation service and discuss some possible future implications for local education authorities (LEAs), educational psychology services (EPSs), schools and parents.

Within the first 6 months of the implementation of the 1993 Education Act, i.e. by 31 March 1995, the LEA had experienced three tribunal hearings. Early experience had shown that the tribunal process can be extremely time-consuming, anxiety-provoking and, by dint of its adversarial nature, can serve to harden attitudes. There may also be delays in resolving conflicts which may not be in the best interests of the child. Further, in some cases, the LEA was not aware of the concern of a parent or carer until the receipt of a letter from the special educational needs (SEN) tribunal, despite the fact that each parent or carer had been offered (and in most cases took up) an interview with a senior officer in the SEN section of the LEA. A further filter was therefore needed to avert the overall stress of the tribunal whilst at the same time ensuring a rapid response to the child's difficulties and the concerns of the parent or carer.

This article was first published in *Educational Psychology in Practice* (1998) **14.1**, pp. 11–21. It is reproduced with the kind permission of Taylor & Francis Ltd. Some changes have been made to the original.

The conciliation service began after the principal educational psychologist (PEP) had attended a particular tribunal hearing in 1995. During the hearing it became apparent that it should be possible to organise a local problem-solving mechanism that might be acceptable to both parents and the LEA. The PEP traditionally had a problem-solving role where conflicts had arisen. It was decided that this process could be formalised and developed as a local conciliation service to enhance its effectiveness.

Accordingly, the conciliation service was established in order to provide a rapid response to conflict resolution.

Referrals to the conciliation service are made formally by the LEA once an appeal to the tribunal has been lodged. The service provides an independent review of the particular case, usually involving the PEP, often working with a colleague.

Background

Literature review

This section provides a brief overview of the relevant literature on legislation concerning appeals and conciliation and on conflict resolution.

There has been an increase in the past few years in the use of litigation by parents to obtain what they consider to be their rights for their children with SEN. This is reflected in the increase in the numbers of parents taking cases to the Ombudsman, to appeal and to judicial review.

The right to appeal was introduced within the 1981 Education Act. This system of appeal was criticised for being inconsistent, slow and unfair because the local appeals committee lacked independence. The formality of the system was a daunting prospect for many families and the process of appealing was described as extremely difficult. Pressure to reform the system led to a new system of appeal (SEN tribunals) introduced by the 1993 Education Act. It replaced the 'flawed' system of local authority appeals committees with a new independent system to deal with appeals against LEA decisions about statements of special educational needs.

The new system of appeal, through the SEN tribunal, came into existence in September 1994; based on industrial tribunal procedures it aims to be informal, flexible and able to reach decisions quickly. It is independent of central and local government. Tribunals have been set up in regions throughout England and Wales; each is chaired by a legally qualified person and has two lay members with knowledge and experience of SEN and/or local government. Hearings usually take place in private unless a public hearing is requested and agreed by the LEA and the parent.

The tribunal is able to consider appeals against:

- LEA refusal to carry out an assessment
- LEA refusal to carry out a further assessment
- LEA refusal to issue a statement after assessment
- the content of the statement, insofar as it relates to the child's needs and the provision to be made to meet those needs, including the school named in the statement or the failure to name a school
- LEA refusal to agree a subsequent change of school
- LEA decision to cease to maintain a statement (DfE, 1994).

Reports on the first year of the SEN tribunal

The Independent Panel for Special Educational Advice (IPSEA) produced a report regarding the first year of tribunals for the House of Commons Education Committee (IPSEA, 1996). The report concluded that, in general, children with SEN and their parents have been well served by the tribunal in the first year of its operation. However, IPSEA identified several areas of concern which they believed should be addressed by the President of the tribunal, the Department for Education and Employment (DfEE) or Parliament, as appropriate. One of these concerns is of particular relevance for this chapter: IPSEA identified the need for a mechanism or power, within the remit of either the tribunal or the DfEE, to prevent unnecessary appeals, i.e. a tribunal hearing in cases where an LEA has clearly acted in breach of its legal duties when compiling the statement (IPSEA, 1996).

A report submitted by the Association of Educational Psychologists (AEP) indicated that members generally regarded the SEN tribunal system as an improvement over the previous arrangements (AEP, 1996). It highlighted the perceived greater independence of the tribunal and the improvement in time taken for appeals to be dealt with. There were a number of concerns expressed including: a lack of balance in the composition of the tribunal members, lack of any screening process for appeals, the large number of appeals being lodged, the cost to LEAs and educational psychologists (EPs), and the inflexibility of the tribunal in relation to adjournments. More specifically the AEP report argued that there was a lack of any screening process, and that if a parent appeals, this automatically proceeds. The AEP suggested that the SEN tribunal should register the appeal and advise both parties to arrange a meeting or process whereby they can exchange their major concerns and to let the tribunal know the outcome of this by a certain date. The report went on to suggest that any unresolved situations should automatically be referred to the tribunal, provided there was a *prima facie* case.

Given the large number of appeals being lodged by parents, the AEP believed that LEAs might be encouraged to set up conciliation mechanisms. Additionally, the AEP expressed concern regarding the inflexibility of the tribunal in relation to adjournments and thought that there could be more scope for more informal 'out-of-court' settlements' (AEP, 1996).

According to the DfEE *Newsletter* of July 1996 (SENCL 2/96), some LEAs have indicated that they currently have, or would like to have, mechanisms in place to mediate formally with parents about their children's special educational needs. Such mediation could take place either before or during parents' appeals to the SEN tribunal. Apparently, there has been some concern expressed by LEAs that any such mechanism could conflict with the remit of the SEN tribunal and might, therefore, be seen as undesirable or, possibly, unlawful. In fact, the DfEE states that they very much welcomed continuing dialogue between LEAs and parents (DfEE, 1996). They did not think there was any legal impediment to LEAs establishing such systems (DfEE, 1996).

However, LEAs were advised to ensure that any system for local mediation is not presented to parents as an alternative to an appeal to the SEN tribunal, and LEAs should continue to make clear to parents their rights to appeal to the tribunal and the timetable for doing so, and LEAs should themselves operate within time-scales to ensure that parents are able to appeal to the SEN tribunal within two months of the LEA's decision.

The present government has indicated its commitment to reviewing the provision and arrangements for children with SEN in their 1997 White and Green Papers (DfEE, 1997a, 1997b). There is an intention to build upon the SEN Code of Practice to reduce bureaucratic procedures and to look urgently at the scope for improved mediation, in order to reduce the need for disputes to reach the SEN tribunal.

Conflict resolution

Often, when faced with a problem or disagreement, people start from the assumption that most conflict is destructive and the only outcomes possible are 'win' or 'lose'. Most of the ways parties try to deal with conflict are themselves based on conflict and confrontation and are premised upon an adversarial approach. A more productive way of approaching conflict is suggested by Acland (1990) who states that conflict can be viewed as:

- a problem to be solved
- a mutual predicament to be escaped, and
- a situation which is uncomfortable, stressful, risky and expensive for all involved.

(Acland, 1990, p. 8)

This approach focuses on the problem or situation as the reason for the dispute, rather than the people involved. The main methods which are commonly used when trying to settle disputes are coercion (forcible compulsion), the law (decision made by court or use of justice system), arbitration (dispute settled by independent body appointed by the two parties), negotiation (process of conferring to bring about agreement), mediation or conciliation (assisted negotiation using a third party). (Definitions provided by *The Pocket Oxford Dictionary*, 1957).

For the purposes of this chapter the focus is upon negotiation and mediation. According to Acland (1990) negotiation uses a problem-solving approach and is a realistic and effective means of resolving disputes. However, negotiation can, at times, focus again on the outcome being a matter of winning or losing. He argues that there are a number of problems with negotiation:

- Negotiations can turn into power struggles.
- Strong emotions can prevent effective communication and make direct negotiation unrealistic and the conflict worse.
- Fear of 'losing face' can prevent either side admitting the fault or making the offer which unlocks the situation.
- Negotiation usually involves people taking and then giving up a series of positions which can cause problems with relationships.
- People can dig themselves into entrenched positions and refuse to move.
- Problem-solving negotiation has to be a creative process, but people in conflict often feel too insecure and too concerned with keeping up their guard to be creative.
- The outcome depends heavily on the skills of those involved.

(Acland, 1990, p. 11)

Mediation is an alternative method increasingly being used, for example, in cases of divorce. In this article the terms mediation and conciliation are used interchangeably. According to Acland (1990):

> mediation is assisted negotiation with the mediator holding separate and joint meetings with those in conflict in order to:
> - reduce hostility and establish effective communication
> - assist people to understand each other's needs and concerns
> - ask questions which reveal the real interests of each side
> - raise and clarify issues overlooked or inadequately covered
> - assist people to develop and communicate new ideas
> - help reframe proposals in more palatable terms
> - moderate unrealistic demands
> - test receptiveness to new proposals
> - help draft agreements which solve current problems, safeguard relationships and anticipate future needs.
>
> (Acland, 1990, p. 18)

The mediator requires certain skills and qualities in order for the process to be successful, including the ability to defuse tension and aggression, listen actively and empathise, enable others to define and clarify, work to build trust and respond professionally.

Techniques

Some interesting negotiation techniques which have been found to be particularly useful to the Waltham Forest Conciliation Service are 'win–win negotiation' and 'negotiation jujitsu'.

Win–win negotiation

Win–win negotiating is a framework explained by Jandt (1985) and is described as negotiation within a conciliatory context. The framework contains specific defusing techniques designed to address needs before positions polarise which should improve the chances for an agreement that provides something for everyone (Jandt, 1985).

Negotiation jujitsu

Fisher and Ury (1981) outline an interesting strategy called 'negotiation jujitsu'. The strategy suggests that the negotiator does not react but side-steps any attack and deflects it against the problem. Rather than resisting force, energy should be channelled into exploring interests, inventing new options for mutual gain and searching for independent ideas (Fisher and Ury, 1981).

Description of the conciliation service in the London Borough of Waltham Forest

Aims of the conciliation service

The aims of the conciliation service are to listen carefully to every person's point of view, to collect additional data as required, to go beyond the written evidence and to produce a recommendation for the SEN panel for a mutually acceptable and amicable agreement. Underpinning such agreements, however, is the fundamental principle that the child's needs and interests are always paramount.

The types of cases referred to the conciliation service have so far included appeals against the LEA deciding to issue a note-in-lieu instead of a statement, the degree of resourcing allocated, choice of school, type of school, speech therapy, diagnoses of autism, clarity of terms and provision, guarantee of arrangements, lack of trust and amount of integration experience in mainstream school.

The key principles of the conciliation service

The key principles of the conciliation service are as follows:

- reconciliation of differences, if possible
- listening to all sides (the latent as well as the manifest issues)
- impartiality
- fairness
- transparency
- clarity
- honesty
- integrity
- confidentiality
- collection of new data where needed
- negotiation based on win–win model where possible
- innovative ideas where needed, i.e. negotiating jujitsu.

Key stages of the conciliation service

The conciliation service is designed specifically to address individual cases. Following a review of all the papers, a decision is made about the most appropriate way forward. Typically this will involve meetings, collection of evidence, further psychological assessment, collection of reports, observing the child in school and meetings with individuals and all parties. Whilst the PEP is always involved in every case, it has been found to be useful to involve other colleagues, e.g. the EP for the school, a trainee EP or the SEN adviser. It is important to stress that each case is viewed individually and each process is tailor-made, hence the judgement made at the 'setting-up' stage is a critical feature of the final outcome.

There are six key stages of the conciliation service: referral; introducing the service to parents and carers; identification of issues; negotiation phase; recommendation to SEN panel; and reporting back. These key stages are discussed below.

Referral

Any appeal made to the SEN tribunal is automatically referred to the PEP in writing by the LEA, usually the chair of the SEN panel. The PEP takes the responsibility for contacting the parents and informing them of the operation of the conciliation service.

Introducing the service to parents and carers

The PEP contacts the parents or carers and explains the role of the conciliation service. During the introduction to the service the following points are clarified as detailed below.

EXPLANATION OF SERVICE

The process of conciliation and procedures of the conciliation service itself are explained and the aims of the service outlined. The voluntary nature of the service is emphasised but the potential benefits are also discussed.

EXPLANATION OF ROLE

The role of the PEP in respect of the conciliation service is explained, including the fact that, in this situation, he is impartial and not representing the LEA. In order to maintain neutrality, it is pointed out that, although the PEP is normally a member of the SEN panel, he will not vote on this particular case and thus the final decision is made by the other panel members. This gives the conciliator greater freedom than if he were acting as an SEN panel member. Interestingly, this has not proven to be a problem: no parent has refused conciliation on the basis of perceived conflict of interest and the LEA has respected the independence of the mediator at all times.

LEGAL STATUS

The legal status of the conciliation service is clarified: namely that involvement with the service does not in any way affect the legal rights of the parents or carers and that if they are not satisfied with any agreement or recommendation made they are still free to continue with their appeal, but that any mutually acceptable agreement reached will be referred to the SEN panel for decision. Indeed it is only the parents or carers who can withdraw the SEN tribunal appeal.

ACKNOWLEDGEMENT OF PARENTAL OR CARERS' CONCERNS

The concerns of parents or carers are acknowledged in the context that they clearly want to do the best and to secure the appropriate provision for their child. It is stressed that their understanding of the child, as parents or carers, will be valued.

Identification of issues

The direct issues for all parties involved are identified as clearly as possible. The latent issues are also seen as very important, i.e. what do parties really want. It has been felt to be very important to 'go below the surface' and to probe sensitively those issues that are really worrying parents or carers. On many occasions we have found that the deep, latent and troubling issue has been very different from the presenting one and that only by addressing this latent concern has a valid resolution been agreed. For example, in one case the parents requested additional resources whereas, in reality, they wanted a guarantee that sufficient resources would be provided by the school.

Negotiation phase

MEETINGS AND/OR VISITS

Meetings and/or visits are arranged for parents or carers and schools to meet the conciliator(s). Initial meetings, organised in order to establish all the facts and issues from all parties, are held separately to ensure that everyone has a chance to speak openly and honestly.

DATA COLLECTION

At this stage in the conciliation process, data are collected using the EPS files, school files and/or records, reports from EPs, social workers, doctors or other professionals involved with the child.

FURTHER ASSESSMENT

If necessary, further assessments of the child are carried out in order to provide up-to-date information to help inform the negotiation and decision-making process.

SELECTED ACTIONS DEPENDING UPON CIRCUMSTANCES

Further data will be collected as required.

Recommendation to SEN panel

WRITTEN REPORT

A written report is submitted to the panel including a summary of the issues, data, options discussed with all parties and recommendations agreed upon.

ATTENDANCE AT PANEL

The PEP attends the panel session where the case is discussed and the recommendations considered. However, the PEP does not take part in the final decision.

DECISION

A decision is made by the members of the SEN panel based on the information provided.

Reporting back

DISCUSSION AS NEEDED

The panel decision is reported back to all parties and this is discussed where necessary. On some occasions further negotiation is needed.

INFORMATION TO PARENTS, SCHOOL AND EP

Information is given to all parties involved and the implications of the decision explained. Where necessary, statements are redrafted and recirculated.

LIFE-LINE FOR THE FUTURE

A line of contact is established in certain cases, with involvement of the PEP where necessary, in order to enable regular reviews of the effectiveness of the negotiated agreement.

An evaluation study of the Waltham Forest conciliation service

Introduction

The evaluation study of the conciliation service was carried out in July 1996 by the second author as a research dissertation of the MSc educational psychology course. The aim of the investigation was to discover the views of consumers concerning the conciliation service as well as the perceived effectiveness of the service and the satisfaction consumers have with it.

The sample

The evaluation of the conciliation service involved surveying the views and perceptions of the service from the following groups:

- fourteen parents and carers who had been involved with the conciliation service
- three headteachers and/or special educational needs coordinators (SENCOs) in schools that had been closely involved with the conciliation service
- the Assistant Education Officer (reflecting views from the Special Needs Department and the LEA)
- the PEP.

Fourteen cases were investigated, being the total sample referred to the conciliation service during the period September 1995 to June 1996.

Method

Data for this evaluation study were collected in different ways:

1   postal questionnaires
2   telephone interviews
3   face-to-face interviews
4   number of tribunal appeals lodged
5   number of tribunal appeals withdrawn.

Postal questionnaires

A postal questionnaire was compiled which addressed the key questions central to this evaluation study. These were:

1   reasons for the appeal to the SEN tribunal
2   referral to the conciliation service
3   attitude about participating in the conciliation service
4   experiences of the conciliation service
5   degree of satisfaction with the decisions and outcomes of the conciliation service regarding the final statement of SEN.

The questionnaire was accompanied by a covering letter which outlined the aim of the study, conveyed to its respondents its importance, assured them of confidentiality and encouraged their replies. Seven parents completed the postal questionnaires (50 per cent). Of the seven parents who did not return the questionnaire, four explained that they were still actively involved with the conciliation service and therefore did not feel able to complete the questionnaire at that time.

Telephone interviews

To complement the data collected by the postal questionnaires, tele-phone interviews were conducted in order to explore parents' feelings and perceptions in more depth, and in order to include the rich elements of personal opinion and experience. A random sample of four parents was selected from the total sample for the telephone interviews. During the interviews the same questions were used for each parent.

Face-to-face interviews

The following people were interviewed in order to obtain a sample of opinions and perceptions from different perspectives:

- school staff (n = 3)
- the Assistant Education Officer
- the PEP.

Results

Key findings

Of the fourteen cases investigated all were successfully resolved and appeals to the SEN tribunal withdrawn. The majority of the referrals were boys (which is consistent with the high number of boys in any SEN sample). The majority were children in mainstream infant and junior schools with a small minority from either secondary or special school settings. The four main areas of contention were:

1   school placement
2   level of resourcing
3   opposition to note-in-lieu
4   disagreement with LEA's refusal to assess.

Most of the children concerned presented learning difficulties, with about half of these presenting specific learning difficulties or dyslexia.

Of the seven cases who responded to the postal questionnaire, two (29 per cent) were very satisfied with the outcome, three (43 per cent) were satisfied and two (29 per cent) did not know; there were no negative responses.

Also of these seven cases, four (57 per cent) said it was clearly explained, all indicated they had sufficient time to talk and their views and concerns were listened to, six (89 per cent) said their views were valued, five (71 per cent) thought that they had some control regarding decisions made, and all seven (100 per cent) still retained some choices of action.

The results of the questionnaires and interviews resulted in several common themes which identified the strengths and weaknesses of the conciliation service. The results are presented as emerging themes with quotations from the questionnaires and interviews to illustrate and expand upon the themes or views.

Perceived strengths of the conciliation service

The following were strengths of the conciliation service as identified by the parents, headteachers and/or SENCOs.

Interpersonal skills

All staff interviewed mentioned that they believed the effectiveness of the conciliation service often depended on the negotiator's skills as a negotiator and communicator. In addition staff identified other important skills: the ability to manage and direct meetings; and the ability to remain calm and patient throughout the process.

The conciliation service reduces hostility

During the interviews this was an area which was discussed at length and thought to be one of the most important features of the conciliation service. It was thought that involvement of the conciliation service helped to calm down the situation and allowed the opportunity for more rational thought.

> The conciliation service takes the heat out of a situation.
>
> (Parent)

> The situation was almost in a deadlock and relationships had become very strained before the conciliation service became involved.
>
> (Headteacher)

> It is helpful to have someone to manage the meeting, especially when everyone is angry or frustrated.
>
> (SENCO)

[It was possible] to mollify the situation by dealing with any bluntness and rudeness expressed due to frustrations and dissipate the bad feelings. The problems seemed to be reframed and put in a more positive way.

(Headteacher)

The conciliation service brings people together

It is a good chance for everyone to get together and talk.

(Parent)

It is a time of bringing together opposites and finding common or middle ground on which to build an agreement.

(SENCO)

It provides an opportunity to discuss the problems in a different forum.

(Headteacher)

The conciliation service listens to all sides and values opinions

Arranging both separate and joint meetings was seen as a beneficial characteristic of the conciliation service as it was thought that this presented the opportunity to talk freely and frankly about concerns and difficulties. The fact that everyone was asked their opinion and feelings at every stage and not judged caused all parties to feel involved and valued.

Everyone was given a chance to have their say and say exactly how they felt but the negotiator managed to keep everyone on track and stopped people from moving away from the focus of the meeting.

(Parent)

The conciliator was able to appear to empathise with all sides which made you feel as though he understood.

(Headteacher)

I certainly felt like everyone's views and concerns were taken into consideration.

(SENCO)

The conciliation service is supportive

> The staff certainly felt supported throughout and I know M's mother did as well.
>
> (Headteacher)

> The conciliation service was felt to be very supportive and it was a relief to be listened to.
>
> (Parent)

The conciliation service is methodical and thorough

> We had to go through the statement line by line to tease out where the problem went. It was tedious but I suppose it ensured that all the concerns had been brought up for discussion.
>
> (SENCO)

> [The process] was very thorough and this must stop any extra worries appearing afterwards.
>
> (Parent)

The conciliation service adopts a positive approach

Staff reported it was refreshing to approach a problem with the attitude and belief that there was a solution.

> The problems were approached with the attitude that there was a solution.
>
> (SENCO)

Perceived weaknesses of the conciliation service

The conciliation service is time-consuming

> The whole process is extremely time-consuming. It seems so unfair that you spent so much time devoted to one child when there are all the others to think about.
>
> (SENCO)

It worries me slightly that it all takes so much time. Each meeting there were about eight salaried people talking for an hour and a half about one child. This happened at least four times.

(Headteacher)

But

The input of time is necessary and I don't really see a way around it.

(Headteacher)

There is a lack of information about the conciliation service

There is no information about the conciliation service and therefore I am unclear about the role of the service to the school.

(SENCO)

The conciliation service does not offer continued support

Some of the members of staff interviewed expressed concerns in terms of a lack of support following the resolution of the disagreement and thought that it could be necessary to follow up the case to ensure that there were no continuing problems.

The conciliation service becomes involved at a late stage

It would be good if the conciliation service could become involved before things reach crisis point.

(SENCO)

By the time the conciliation service becomes involved relationships between different people have become very strained and tense.

(Headteacher)

We feel that this service was very helpful as it resolved our child's SEN statement. However, parents should be made more aware of this service at a much earlier stage of the statement process.

(Parent)

Progress of the conciliation service 1996/97

The conciliation service has continued; some ten cases (up to November 1997) have been referred and all but one have been resolved. Some cases have been revisited but with different queries from the parents. The number of referrals has reduced to approximately one per month. The conciliation service has been undertaken by senior educational psychologists in the EPS during the absence of the PEP.

Conclusions

In response to a series of cases being referred to the SEN tribunal it was decided to explore a more creative, alternative way of resolving disputes. The aim was to arrive at a response which was quicker and more economic and which satisfied the needs of all parties at a local level. What has emerged is a formal SEN conciliation service headed by the PEP but involving other colleagues. This conciliation service has evolved gradually, building on previous experience and has become a formalised part of the SEN provision in the borough. An evaluation carried out in 1996 gave further impetus to the development of the service; the study found that all the cases referred to the tribunal had been resolved by conciliation, there was a high degree of parental satisfaction and various recommendations were made for further improvement.

Although it is acknowledged that the conciliation service work is time-consuming, such time has to be compared with that required for an actual tribunal appearance. The local procedure is quicker, less adversarial and has led to a speedier outcome for children.

Before considering the next section of implications for LEAs, EPs, schools and parents, we will highlight some aspects of our experience which appear to us to be important.

First, as mentioned earlier, we have been struck by the disparity between the ostensible complaint and that which parents are really worried about; what some psychologists refer to as the manifest versus latent content. The benefit of a mediator being able to explore deeper concerns has proved to be important. It is thought that EPs are particularly well equipped to undertake this sort of work either directly or through training others, although it is acknowledged that some other professionals may have skills in this area and be able to undertake mediation.

At first there was some anxiety as to whether the PEP could be seen as independent by parents and whether parents would want to take up the offer of conciliation. No parents have declined the conciliation service and this has not proved to be an issue. However great care has been taken to provide a transparent, fair and honest approach.

In evaluating some of the effects of the conciliation service, one colleague (Beaver) has commented that the existence of the conciliation service could have influenced the ethos of the borough and encouraged the further development of a negotiating ethos. We have no evidence about this but it is an area for further research.

Finally the evaluation study shows clearly that any mediator/conciliator would need considerable training and support in developing appropriate skills.

Implications for further development

It has generally been agreed locally that the conciliation service should remain on a permanent and formal basis within the LEA.

The conciliation service methods could be developed as a training pack; invitations have been received from different services and LEAs to share information about the Waltham Forest Conciliation Service. It is clearly a Service of interest to other LEAs who have reported that too much time is being spent on tribunal work, not always with a successful outcome for either party.

Implications for educational psychology services

The psychological skills of a PEP may be of particular value and have proven to be locally. However, the service can be very time-consuming for an EPS and thus it is necessary to consider some time allocation issues. We have found it to be important to involve the EP for the case as much as possible.

An interesting role has developed with the use of trainee EPs on placement with the PEP. It has become evident that they can take a more active role – e.g. providing new assessment information, collating existing information – provided that adequate supervision and support are made available. They too have commented on the value of this experience for their training.

Implications for LEAs

From the perspective of an LEA, any conciliation service developed needs to be credible to both the LEA and parents, flexible in respect of its ability to be commissioned rapidly for a particular case, and locally aware of political and educational dynamics.

It is clear that a conciliation service can be an extremely useful tool in the LEA's stock of SEN provision, being both cost-effective and parent- or carer-friendly.

It is also clear that SEN tribunal preparation is costly in terms of staff time and attendance is even more so. It follows that the development of a service such as a conciliation service can give much needed release from such pressures.

Implications for schools

A conciliation service which is able to work consistently with schools, identifying blocks and providing solutions, is clearly of immense value. Such work might also provide valuable training opportunities for schools.

Implications for parents and carers

Perhaps the greatest benefits are in this area. For all but the most articulate parent or carer, the whole business of identification of SEN and consequent provision can be a daunting one. Hence, the opportunity for local discussion with a sympathetic audience when serious problems have arisen has proven to be invaluable.

The additional opportunity to penetrate to the root of a dispute in a relatively informal setting is available through the conciliation service to all parents and carers. It is difficult to overstate the value of this, as parents and carers are naturally keen to achieve the best for their child and may see the LEA as 'an enemy' in the quest for provision. A successful conciliation service may facilitate resolution of even the most difficult cases with dignity and honour on both 'sides'. After all, it is likely that the LEA will, for most children, continue to be the same throughout their schooling and a trusting and supportive relationship with LEA representatives is likely to be of lasting benefit to the child concerned. One can only agree with Acland (1990) who states that, ideally, people should emerge from the process feeling satisfied that all their needs and interests have been taken into account, that they have achieved the best possible outcome, and that they are ready to re-enter the process the next time a problem comes up.

Acknowledgements

We would like to acknowledge the help and support of all our colleagues who undertook work in relation to the conciliation service, as well as Natasha de Lantivy (trainee EP) who assisted in further data analysis. We would also like to acknowledge the help and participation of the parents, school staff and colleagues who participated in the research.

References

Acland, A. (1990) A Sudden Outbreak of Common Sense. Managing Conflict through Mediation. London: Hutchinson Business Books Limited.

Association of Educational Psychologists (1996) Special Educational Needs: The Working Code of Practice and the Tribunal Report together with the Proceedings of the Committee, Minutes of Evidence and Appendices. Memorandum submitted by AEP in Education Committee (1996). Ordered by the House of Commons to be printed on 21 February 1996. London: HMSO.

Department of Education and Science (1981) Education Act 1981. London: HMSO.

Department of Education and Science (1993) Education Act 1993. London: HMSO.

Department for Education (1994) The Code of Practice on the Identification and Assessment of Special Educational Needs. London: HMSO.

Department for Education and Employment (1996) Newsletter (SENCL 2/96), July 1996. London: HMSO.

Department for Education and Employment (1997a) Excellence in Schools. CM3681. White Paper. London: The Stationery Office Ltd.

Department for Education and Employment (1997b) Excellence for all Children. CM3 785. Green Paper. London: The Stationery Office Ltd.

Fisher, R. and Ury, W. (1981) Getting to Yes. Negotiating Agreement without Giving in. London: Hutchinson Business Books.

House of Commons Education Committee (1996) Special Educational Needs: The Working of the Code of Practice and the Tribunal Report together with the Proceedings of the Committee, Minutes of Evidence and Appendices. Ordered by the House of Commons to be printed on 21 February 1996. London: HMSO.

Independent Panel for Special Education Advice (1996), Memorandum submitted by IPSEA in Education Committee (1996): Special Educational Needs: The Working of the Code of Practice and the Tribunal Report together with the Proceedings of the Committee, Minutes of Evidence and Appendices. Ordered by the House of Commons to be printed on 21 February 1996. London: HMSO.

Jandt, E.E. (1985) Win–Win Negotiating. Turning Conflict into Agreement. New York: John Wiley.

3.2   THE ROLE OF PARENT PARTNERSHIP IN DISAGREEMENT RESOLUTION

Sarah Gale

What is a parent partnership service? Different models of parent partnership

Parent partnership services have their origins in the 1993 Education Act and the accompanying SEN Code of Practice (1994). Funding was first made available through the then DfE Grant for Education Support and Training (GEST) grants for 1994–95 and LEAs were invited to submit bids to set up parent partnership schemes to 'encourage parental partnership, to reduce conflict and to minimise the number of statutory appeals over the LEA processes of identifying, assessing and making statements for pupils with SEN' (DfE, 1993).

At the heart of this new area of LEA activity was the development of information and advisory services for parents of children with SEN. LEAs could, if they wished, bid as consortia and were encouraged to be imaginative in devising their own schemes. The main elements of expenditure, however, were expected to be the salary of a parent partnership officer, the training and expenses of volunteers (to be known as 'Named Persons') and the production of printed materials.

Over the three years for which DfEE funding was available (1994–97), a range of schemes emerged, varying from the creation of an LEA officer post (full or part time), often based at the LEA offices in the town or county hall, to the funding of an established, local voluntary organisation, which could build on existing networks of support for parents and operate independently of the LEA. The London Borough of Newham adopted the latter approach, since it was fortunate to have a well-used, independent parents' centre, which provided a ready-made base from which the parent partnership team could offer advice and support to parents. Inevitably, the parent partnership schemes between these two ends of the continuum differed, not only in their degree of independence from the LEA, but also in the levels of funding they could access. Since GEST funding provided by the government had to be matched by the LEA and parent partnership schemes were not a statutory requirement, some LEAs provided a minimal service or had no scheme at all.

It was hardly surprising, therefore, that when the three years of GEST funding ended in 1997, some of the smaller schemes disappeared, only to reappear in the late nineties, when Standards Fund (another

form of central government grant) money was again specifically allocated to provide parent partnership 'services' (as opposed to 'schemes').
The emphasis was still very much on giving parents information, advice and support, in partnership with voluntary sector organisations,
and on offering access to an objective source of help in the form of a
trained volunteer, known as an Independent Parental Supporter, the
successor of the Named Person. The original aim of reducing conflict
and minimising the number of statutory appeals was less prominent.
The role of a parent partnership service is perhaps best summed up by
the latest DfES guide for parents and carers on Special Educational
Needs:

> Parent partnership services provide support and advice to parents
> whose children have SEN. They provide accurate and neutral
> information on the full range of options available to parents. They
> do not 'take sides'. They help parents to make informed decisions
> about their children's education. Where parents want an inde-
> pendent parental supporter, the service should provide one.
>
> (DfES, 2001)

From 1 April 2002 all LEAs are required to provide a parent partnership service, funded from the core Education Budget rather than through
a Standards Fund Grant.

The creation of a parent partnership service in Tower Hamlets

The Tower Hamlets response to the DfEE initiative to establish parent
partnership schemes was to set up a Parents' Advice Centre (PAC),
located on the same site as the borough's SEN centre, alongside centrally funded SEN support teams. A feasibility study had already been
undertaken to explore ways of improving information to parents, following a key recommendation from an earlier review of SEN services
that the LEA should establish an advisory and advocacy service for
parents. The aim was to ensure that parents had the knowledge and
support necessary to play an active part in decision-making about their
children's education (Galloway, 1990) and, in particular, had access
to bilingual staff. In an inner-city, multicultural area such as Tower
Hamlets, where over 70 per cent of children speak English as an additional language, many parents struggle to understand the complexities
of the education system and the school curriculum. For parents of

children with special educational needs, even when no language barrier exists, the processes involved in identifying and assessing their needs can appear bewildering.

The initial proposal aimed to encourage partnership with parents by providing a designated centre, with office accommodation for advice workers, but, more importantly, space for parent groups to meet, crèche facilities for young children and interview and training rooms for workshops and short courses. One full-time and two part-time advice workers were appointed in April 1994. All were bilingual in Bengali/Sylheti and English (56 per cent of children in Tower Hamlets schools are from families of Bangladeshi origin) and had a wealth of previous experience in working with parents/carers of children with special educational needs. Over time the team has grown and now includes a total of six advice workers (two full-time and four part-time). Three are still bilingual, one now being a Somali speaker. Although all team members work generically, two specialise in offering support to families of children who have been excluded from school (either on a fixed-term or temporary basis).

The advice workers visit parents in their homes, their child's school or accompany them on visits, for example to look at alternative provision for their children. As well as interpreting at meetings, translating reports, letters and statements, they also help parents to contribute their views as part of the statutory assessment process and prepare for Annual Review meetings, making sure that they feel able to ask questions on all the issues about which they have concerns. To a great extent, the advice workers fulfil the role envisaged for the Named Person (Independent Parental Supporter), but because they are paid and not volunteers, they can provide a more reliable and consistent service. As LEA employees they are recognised and valued by schools, but they are completely independent of the statutory assessment process and of SEN provision (schools and support services), so are seen as being to a large extent neutral by parents.

In many cases, it is the advice workers who are the first point of contact when a parent feels unhappy about some aspect of either the assessment process or the provision being made for their child. Whether there has been a simple misunderstanding or a deeper-seated problem has arisen, the intervention of a third party can be invaluable. In some cases the advice worker may set up a meeting, usually with the school and the parent/s, and often acts as a go-between, helping to keep the channels of communication open. Occasionally the problem relates to a disagreement with the LEA. This may be resolved quickly by an explanation about procedures or it may require some informal telephone calls or possibly a meeting with the Named Officer, who is always willing to talk with parents.

The Parent Partnership Officer/Parents Advice Centre Manager post is part time, as all the feedback suggests that it is more important to concentrate resources in providing front-line advice workers who can empower parents. By offering advice by telephone and an effective outreach service, parents who lack confidence in expressing their views to professionals and who are unlikely to seek out the support of voluntary organisations, can be given a voice.

The role of the Parent Partnership Officer is to provide professional support and supervision to the team members, to develop greater awareness in schools of ways of engaging parents in active partnerships and provide training for volunteers. These may be members of parent support groups or community organisations, who are keen to offer up to date information to parents on special educational needs (whether or not they wish to be cast in the role of Independent Parental Supporters). The Parent Partnership Officer may be involved in individual casework, but not usually at the first point of referral. In complex cases, particularly when the referral has come through the LEA, as may occur with complaints, she will become involved in negotiating between the parent and the school to resolve the disagreement between them. However, in most cases, easy access to an advice worker gives parents a ready source of advice and a sympathetic listening ear, which helps to defuse tension and prevent the disagreement reaching the more formal complaint or appeal stage. It also provides the LEA with an early warning system.

An example of early intervention from a parent advice worker

June 1999: Sue Jackson – all names have been changed – first contacted the Parents' Advice Centre. She wanted advice about her son, Jason, who was currently attending a local nursery school and was due to transfer to primary school shortly.

Jason was small for his age, had some developmental problems and displayed inappropriate and violent behaviour. In addition to coping with a very demanding four-year-old, Mrs Jackson suffered from poor health and lived in cramped and poor housing conditions with her other two children. As is often the case, what started as an educational concern soon developed into a lengthy and elaborate search to assist the family with a range of difficulties which were impacting on Jason's life. The PAC advice worker also played a key part in negotiating first with the nursery and then the primary school, whose staff felt severely challenged by Jason's behaviour.

July 1999: the nursery staff state that they cannot request additional support for Jason until they receive an outstanding report from the Health Authority's Child Development Team. Mrs Jackson voices her frustration and concerns about Jason's education and the advice worker helps her to write a letter to the LEA formally requesting an assessment of Jason's special educational needs. She also helps Mrs Jackson to fill out a form applying for Disability Living Allowance and she contacts Social Services on her behalf.

August 1999: the report from the Child Development Team arrives. The primary school's educational psychologist, the PAC advice worker and Mrs Jackson meet at the school before the term starts to plan a programme of support for Jason. The LEA has agreed to fund support from a learning support assistant while the assessment is carried out.

September 1999: The 'first letter' arrives informing Mrs Jackson that the LEA has agreed to carry out a statutory assessment of Jason's needs and the PAC advice worker helps Mrs Jackson to draft her views as her contribution to the assessment. Jason, meanwhile, has started school and says that he likes it, but Mrs Jackson is called to school and asked to take him home on several occasions. The classteacher is off sick and the learning support assistant has resigned. Jason's behaviour deteriorates and the school is not sure that they can cope. Sue is despairing, a situation not helped by a violent death in the family. The PAC advice worker, following a discussion with the LEA's SEN section and the school's educational psychologist, arranges to take Mrs Jackson to a local school for primary-aged pupils with emotional and behavioural difficulties so that she is aware of other options.

October 1999: Mrs Jackson has been called into school three times in one week. She has to attend a funeral and does not know what to do if the school should call while she is unavailable. Social Services have agreed to collect Jason from school, but will not be on call during the day. The advice worker persuades Social Services to provide the name of a worker who will come to the school for Jason in the case of an emergency. The school submits a request to the LEA for additional support for Jason.

November 1999: a consultant has recommended Ritalin for Jason. Mrs Jackson doesn't know what to do. The advice worker gathers information about Ritalin for her to read and puts her in touch with a parent support group, whose members have children with similar difficulties. This helps her to come to a decision. The LEA's SEN panel approves twenty hours interim support from a learning support assistant while the statutory assessment is being carried out.

January 2000: Jason is now taking Ritalin. He is getting on well with his new teacher and learning support assistant.

March 2000: Mrs Jackson receives a copy of Jason's draft statement. She is distressed to see that only fifteen hours of support from a learning support assistant is proposed. She also has some other concerns about words and phrases used in the reports. She immediately phones the PAC advice worker, who reassures her that this is still only a draft. She helps Mrs Jackson to make a written response. A meeting is held in the school and the SENCO agrees to provide the LEA's SEN section with more detailed evidence of the support the school is providing. The wording of the final statement offers a compromise. The twenty hours' support is to be reviewed in six months' time with a view to it being reduced to fifteen hours.

September 2000: Mrs Jackson has a major operation and the PAC advice worker is instrumental in making sure that respite care is organised. Mrs Jackson makes a good recovery and is in better health. A review meeting is held in school. There has been considerable improvement in Jason's behaviour both at home and at school, so there is a consensus that the amount of support should be reduced.

A few months later the family is at last rehoused. The accommodation has more space and is in much better condition. Jason continues to make good progress at school and although Mrs Jackson makes occasional contact with the PAC advice worker, her calls are mainly social. She is delighted to report that it is now very rare for her to be called to the school.

As well as demonstrating the complexity of many of the referrals received by the Parents' Advice Centre, this case study highlights the important role played by a parent partnership service in early intervention at a stage before a parental concern has become a disagreement with either the school or the LEA. By ensuring that effective links are made between the various agencies involved in supporting the family, as well as guiding the parent through the maze of procedures, including those involved in the assessment process, the PAC advice worker makes sure that agreement is reached about Jason's future support. Mrs Jackson is helped to make informed decisions (about Jason's proposed medication and alternative provision at a special school, for example) and the school is encouraged to adapt its approaches to meet Jason's needs.

Because the advice worker, as an LEA employee, can communicate quickly and frequently with the Named Officer and the school's educational psychologist, the LEA is able to respond sensitively and flexibly to the unfolding needs of this very young child. Confrontation is therefore avoided and at no point does the school or the parent adopt an entrenched position, leading to a dispute which might be hard to resolve.

Skills needed by parent partnership service staff

Possibly the most important skill for a parent partnership worker (in a paid or volunteer capacity) is a clear understanding of the roles played by the various partners involved in any situation where conflict may arise. The advice worker, as is evident in the case study, was aware of the limitations of her role and the invisible boundaries that exist between her and other professionals. As a facilitator, she made links between these professionals and brought them together with the parent, when appropriate. However, she did not offer educational or medical advice, for example, but made sure that the parent had enough information on which to base her decision. If the disagreement about the level of provision outlined in the draft statement had not been resolved, she would, under the new regulations, have ensured that the parent was aware of the disagreement resolution service and how to access it.

The existence of disagreement resolution services should strengthen the role of parent partnership services, by clarifying the point at which the parent partnership worker must refer the parent to an independent mediator and withdraw into the background. It is a particularly helpful development in LEAs such as Tower Hamlets, where the parent partnership service benefits from being located within the LEA, but has had to respond to concerns about its independence from both parents and voluntary organisations.

References

Department for Education and Skills (2001) *Special Educational Needs (SEN): A Guide for Parents and Carers*. London: DfES.

Department for Education (1993) *Guidelines for Grants for Education Support and Training*. London: DfE.

Department for Education (1994) *The Code of Practice on the Identification and Assessment of Special Educational Needs*. London: DfE.

Galloway, D. (1990) *Support for Learning in Tower Hamlets: Report of the Consultant in Special Educational Needs to the Chief Education Officer*. Lancaster: University of Lancaster.

3.3 BEFORE MEDIATION – A VIEW FROM AN LEA SEN OFFICER

Barbara Gersch

This chapter has been written from the perspective of a Principal SEN Officer in an Inner London LEA, where I manage a team of eight staff. We are responsible for the administration of the statutory assessment procedure for children and young people with SEN. A large part of my time is spent in the role of 'Named Officer'. This role is statutory and each LEA must have a named officer who is available to meet with parents to discuss their concerns, seek their views and aim to resolve any disagreements or disputes.

In the LEA we have a very successful parent partnership scheme, which is part of a purpose built parents advice centre. I often meet parents together with a parent partnership officer who attends to support the parents. This is particularly helpful in the case of bi-lingual families as the LEA has a large population of families for whom English is their second language.

We have found that having a bi-lingual interpreter is invaluable and therefore one of my staff is a bi-lingual caseworker. Apart from the issue of language difficulties, it is particularly helpful for putting families at ease.

In the LEA we have only had two appeals to the SEN tribunal since the tribunal started in 1994. There are many possible explanations for this. It could be said that the particular population in the authority may feel daunted at the idea of tribunal proceedings; it is also true that the Parents' Advice Centre and Educational Psychology Service play a very valuable part in supporting parents through the process. I would, of course, prefer to believe that it is because we have a very strong ethos in the borough of 'listening' and of parental involvement. Our core values in the SEN team are about acknowledging and appreciating parents' thoughts, concerns and views and extending utmost respect at all times. Although the statutory assessment procedure is, as laid down in the Education Act and Code of Practice, lengthy, bureaucratic and somewhat cumbersome, we aim at all times to remember that the child and family are at the centre of the whole process. It is so important to remember that this is not a paper exercise for the families.

Ten years ago, when I started working in the LEA, I heard a parent of a child with SEN give an account about her feelings when her daughter was going through the statutory assessment process. I was new to the post, having come from the cut-throat, commercial world of advertising. I was keen, naïve, and idealistic about the wonderful work that I was going to do! I was horrified, therefore, to hear her describe the whole process as a 'nightmare'. She talked about the lack of communication with the LEA, the constant need to badger officers to find out what was happening, the endless appointments with professionals, in addition to her usual round of appointments with doctors, physiotherapists, etc. She also talked with great emotion about how the whole procedure had imbued her with a huge sense of guilt about the difficulties that her child had and the shock of seeing her child's statement with her difficulties and weaknesses so vividly described.

The lessons I learned from hearing the experience of this parent have stayed with me ever since and the issues that she raised are explored when I train and induct new staff. I ask my team to put themselves in the shoes of the parents. It is not always easy when parents can display a variety of emotional responses, sometimes even abuse. However, each parent has his or her story to tell and it is very often our job to listen to that story.

At every point of communication in the assessment process, parents are invited to contact me if they would like to discuss any concerns or would like me to help them to represent their views to the LEA.

Parents often telephone, sometimes in desperation, because they are having difficulties with their child's school. Mostly, they talk about not being heard about their child's difficulties – being 'fobbed off' and told that there is nothing to worry about. Other concerns relate to bullying and other school-based issues. In these instances parents are advised to get in touch with a parent partnership officer who can facilitate a meeting for the parents with the school.

Most parents meet with me at the point when a proposed statement is issued to them. Their concerns can range from details of information which are incorrect in the statement or in the accompanying advices, to more serious and fundamental disagreement with the provision being recommended in the statement.

All these concerns, even the seemingly trivial, such as a misspelt name must be taken seriously. Occasionally parents have waited what seems to them to be a very long time for their child's statement to be completed; they have received it, studied it, waited for an appointment to see the named officer and made arrangements to travel to the office, sometimes with several other children. Once there, they might explain that they are upset because, for example, the number of children in their family has been noted incorrectly on the statement.

It would be all too easy to dismiss this as a ridiculous concern but it is fair to say that spelling mistakes or erroneous details on a statement can lead to a more generalised breakdown of confidence and trust in the LEA. It is just as important to show equal respect for this parent's concerns, even though they are easily put right, as a parent who arrives with a thoroughly researched and well-evidenced argument against the LEA's proposals.

By far the most common parental disagreement is about the level of resources proposed by the LEA. Although schools have come a long way in being able to meet the needs of children with SEN, there is still a culture in some schools that once a child has been identified as having significant special educational needs, they relinquish responsibility for supporting that child to the LEA. This message is very often passed to parents, who are fearful that without considerable extra funding from the LEA, their child will not cope in a mainstream setting.

In these instances, careful listening is vital; honesty and trust are essential. Mostly I have found that parents of children with special educational needs, even with all their anxieties and concerns, are realistic and reasonable. In many instances parents have had to wage war, probably since their child was born, against a range of different agencies in order to secure the provision that their child needs. They may have built up an expectation of an adversarial stance to fight for the rights of their child. They are also often exhausted from having to deal with a multitude of agencies.

In my experience, when parents are given the time and space to discuss their views, fears and wishes, very few make extravagant demands. The important question to ask of them is, 'What is it that you really want for your child?' How can this best be achieved?

It is interesting that very often the answer to that key question is not the one you might have expected.

Sometimes parents are anxious that once the 'spotlight' of the statutory assessment has gone off their child, that they will be forgotten. In those instances I have often suggested an interim review of the statement after six months, perhaps with the LEA Statement Monitoring Officer present. This suggestion has often been sufficient to allay these fears. I have found that reviewing a child's progress is extremely reassuring for parents, and if the LEA can be involved in some way, it is even more effective. Some parents feel more secure if they feel that schools can be 'called to account' by the LEA.

Another frequent concern of parents is that the school will ignore the objectives in the statement and that the resources allocated to their child in their statement will be used in a general way in the school. I have found that the best way to deal with this issue is to have a three way meeting with the parent and the SENCO of the school. I have also found it effective to hold such meetings in the Education Offices. Parents seem to be reassured by the relative formality of this setting. Once the SENCO has explained the plans for their child in the presence of the LEA Officer, parents feel that they are more likely to happen.

Invariably, parents come to see me if the LEA has issued a Note in Lieu of a statement for their child. A Note in Lieu is issued if the LEA feel, having completed a statutory assessment, that provision for the child's needs could be met from within the school's own resources without additional funding from the LEA.

Recently, an enraged parent came to see me and requested information about how to appeal to the SEN tribunal. Her son had undergone a statutory assessment and the LEA had issued a Note in Lieu. Although it was clear that this child had special educational needs, it was felt that his difficulties were not so significant that he would require a statement. His mother would not accept this. Although she was extremely angry and upset, I attempted to untangle what it was that she really wanted. It finally emerged that she was most concerned about her son's concentration and his handwriting and spelling.

Once I had clarified her main concerns I was able to arrange for the LEA Information and Communication Technology specialist teacher to assess the child and report back to me with a recommendation. The outcome was that we were able to purchase a portable word-processor for this child, which had a very positive effect on his concentration and helped him with his spelling. The parent was delighted and felt that there was no need to appeal to the tribunal.

Not all issues can be resolved in a single meeting with the named officer. Sometimes it is important to allow parents time to collect further information, or seek advice from others, without pressurising them with bureaucratic and possibly insensitive time-scales.

It is also true to say that sometimes the LEA 'gets it wrong'. In those cases, it is very important to be honest and acknowledge that the LEA should re-examine the child's papers and reconsider their decision. Humility, and even apology when appropriate, is a very powerful method of returning to an even keel when negotiating with parents.

For the future, I have an idealistic wish list. I acknowledge and welcome the fact that there will always be the need for informal conciliation. The use of creative problem-solving skills and in-depth knowledge of local possibilities and arrangements is very effective for the resolution of the majority of most disputes. However, I can also see the benefit of more formal, independent mediation services for those cases that have become firmly 'stuck'. Most of all though, I do hope that the 'nightmare' experience of statutory assessment so vividly and memorably described to me some ten years ago will eventually become a dim and distant memory.

Statutory assessment of a child will always be a stressful experience for their parents, but I firmly believe that close, equal and meaningful partnership of parents with schools, the LEA, and other professionals will go a long way to making assessment the cooperative venture that it really should be.

3.4 PATTERNS OF DISAGREEMENTS IN SEN

Janet Rowley and *Irvine S. Gersch*

Introduction

The article, which follows by Janet Rowley and Irvine Gersch, originally published in 2001 under the title 'SEN Conciliation – Is There a Pattern to Referrals?' represents a study of thirty-one cases which were referred to a LEA conciliation service over a three- to four-year period of operation of a conciliation service. It is of interest to those who are in the mediation business and disagreement resolution business.

By way of introducing this article, it is helpful to bring the findings up-to-date, in the light of the author's further experience and to add a number of comments.

As a starting point, it is useful to note from the SEN tribunal booklet, 'How to Appeal' (September 2001), pp. 3 and 4, that there are nine main issues upon which parents can appeal against an LEA decision. It should be noted that there is a two-month time-limit within which appeals must be sent in, and further, even when appeals have been lodged and tribunal dates agreed, parties are still encouraged to try to resolve their differences. Indeed, in my own experience, some disputes have been resolved just a few hours before the actual hearing date.

First, it is useful to list the precise issues, which can lead to appeals to the SEN tribunal. Appeals can be lodged if the LEA:

- refuses to carry out a formal assessment
- refuses to issue a statement of SEN
- issues a statement but there is a disagreement over the nature of the special educational needs stated or the help being proposed, or the name of the school.

- refuses to change the school named in the Statement, if the statement is at least a year old.
- refuses to reassess the child if the LEA has not made a new assessment for at least 6 months
- decides not to maintain the statement (that is, to cancel it)
- decides not to alter the statement after a reassessment.

In my experience most disagreements have tended to come under the following headings:

- refusal to assess
- refusal to issue a statement
- issues of detail within the statement (being the largest grouping).

In exploring the nature of disputes, the majority in my experience, having conciliated in excess of sixty cases in more than six years, have been about:

- funding levels and degree of help provided or suggested, such as the hours of special needs assistance required or specialist tuition
- specificity of provision
- factual description of the child's needs
- speech therapy
- specialist therapy such as music therapy
- transport
- residential placement being requested by parents whilst the LEA wished the child to receive help in a local school
- choice of actual school
- teacher qualifications to teach the child, particularly with dyslexic children
- parental difference of opinion about the school placement
- trust between parents, schools and LEAs about whether any offer will actually be guaranteed to happen and be maintained, particularly with transfer of children from primary to secondary school
- lack of confidence in the professional advice and wish for second opinions
- administrative delays and errors.

In providing training on SEN Conciliation to different LEAs it has become evident that there are differences between areas and LEAs in the nature of disagreements. This may well depend upon

- local polices and provision
- local attitudes
- the stance taken by key LEA officers and the decision-making panels.

It has been my very strong impression that where there is good communication, trust and open-minded attitude by LEA officers with parents, then disputes are resolved readily. Where there is an attitude of mistrust or a lack of communication, whatever the nature or patterns of the dispute, resolutions are more difficult.

Finally, it is worth adding that the Code of Practice 2001 does suggest that mediations are monitored and reviewed and the information fed back to LEAs in order for them to identify whether there are distinct patterns of common disputes. Should such patterns become evident, it is clear that the LEAs might decide that, rather than deal with cases, one at a time, it would be better to see whether it would be possible to get to the root of the problem and perhaps consider changing a general policy or provision.

An obvious example might be, if there are a significant number of disputes over a lack of provision (e.g. occupational therapy) this could be taken as a signal to review access to this provision more widely, through collaborative agreements with colleagues in other departments, such as health or social services.

The article which follows examines some patterns in one LEA.

Rationale for the study

The study carried out by Rowley (1999) involved a small-scale evaluative and exploratory study of one outer London LEA's conciliation service, established by the Educational Psychology Service (EPS). A previous evaluation (Gersch et al., 1998) indicated a very positive response to the conciliation service from a sample of parents and schools that had had involvement, and identified strengths and weaknesses of the service. The focus of Rowley's study was to explore key features of conciliation within the field of special educational needs. Questions addressed included:

- Can patterns be identified among the cases that become involved in disputes or among the issues that lead to conflict in this particular LEA?
- Can suggestions for prevention of disputes be identified?

- What are the key features of the conciliation process?
- To what extent is the conciliation process a matter of 'giving the parents what they want' or does the final outcome present a more creative response?

It should be pointed out that, for the purpose of this paper and the research project described, the second author directly managed the conciliation service. Consequently, it was the first author who carried out the evaluation research and analysed the data. The conciliation team included the principal educational psychologist (PEP), the SEN advisor, and, on an *ad hoc* basis, EP colleagues and EPs in training.

Some of the data collected and reported in this paper, therefore, about the principles and techniques used were taken from interviews at the time with the second author and are reported in that context.

Methodology

The study reported here was carried out between January and April 1999. Both quantitative and qualitative methods were used.

Research materials

The following research materials were used:

- three semi-structured interview schedules eliciting qualitative data;
- a recording sheet for file data.

A pilot study was carried out of the questionnaire and interview schedule with one parent.

The sample

Information was obtained from the following sources:

- parents who had been involved with the conciliation service;
- EPs who had been involved with the conciliation service;
- The PEP who ran the conciliation service;
- The EPS files of conciliation cases.

The questionnaire was sent to all twenty-four parents who had had involvement with the conciliation service since the previous evaluation.

A total of eleven questionnaires were returned. Semi-structured interviews were carried out with six parents from the sample of twenty-four. One of the interviews was carried out face to face. The other five interviews were carried out on the telephone. Face-to-face semi-structured interviews were carried out with the PEP and with four EPs who had been involved with the conciliation service. Thirty-one conciliation case files were analysed for information using a recording sheet, which was refined as the research progressed. A thematic analysis was carried out on the qualitative data using the outline given in Smith (1995). The aim of this analysis was to detect key themes and views that emerged from the data collection, with a view to determining patterns of responses.

Key findings and commentary

Key findings are related to the following areas: characteristics of conciliation cases; suggestions for prevention of disputes; key features of the process of conciliation; and the outcome of the conciliation process.

Characteristics of conciliation cases

From the file data, it emerges that access to the conciliation service is not restricted to those parents who have lodged an appeal with the SEN tribunal. For twelve out of the thirty-one cases (39 per cent), the conciliation service provided a 'troubleshooting' or preventative function (see Table 1).

Table 2 shows the findings concerning the issues involved in conciliation cases. Some cases were found to involve more than one issue. Placement is the largest single issue for conciliation. Most of the cases with placement as an issue involved parents requesting either special provision or more appropriate special provision.

It emerged that a relatively large percentage of cases (29 per cent) involved children aged eleven. This suggests that secondary transfer

Table 1 Reasons for involvement

	Number	%
Appeal to tribunal made	19	61
Mention of possible litigation	5	16
Concerns expressed	7	23
Total:	31	100

Table 2 Issues for conciliation

Issue	Number
School placement	12
Resource level	9
	(including 3 against note-in-lieu)
Inadequate assessment	6
Statement wording	6
Provision	
Speech and language therapy	4
Home tuition	1
Some access to mainstream	1
Wanted statutory assessment stopped	1
Decision not to assess	1

Table 3 Nature of child's special educational needs

SEN	Number	%
Physical difficulties	8	26
Specific learning difficulties	6	19
Autism/Asberger's	5	16
General learning difficulties	4	13
Severe learning difficulties	2	6
Emotional and behavioural difficulties	2	6
Speech and language difficulties	1	3
Down's syndrome	1	3
William's syndrome	1	3
Hearing impairment	1	3

may be a key point at which anxieties and conflicts emerge. This finding may reflect the theory of 'Chronic Sorrow' described by Hornby (1995), which stresses the importance of transition points for triggering strong emotions and reactions on the part of parents.

Findings relating to the nature of the child's special educational needs (Table 3) indicate a high proportion of cases involving children with physical difficulties (26 per cent). This might suggest that there are issues relating to assessment and provision for this sub-group within this particular LEA context. The relatively high percentages of children with specific learning difficulties (19 per cent) and autism/ Asperger's (16 per cent) reflect national tribunal figures.

Table 4 shows that the largest percentage of conciliation cases occurred during statutory assessment (58 per cent). A reasonably high

Table 4 Stage of statutory assessment process

Stage	Number	%
Statutory	18	58
Annual review	11	35
Statutory reassessment	1	3
Unclear	1	3

percentage occurred following the child's annual review (35 per cent). This latter finding may indicate the need for greater partnership with parents at this stage.

Suggestions for preventative work

Suggestions for preventative measures emerged from the questionnaires and the interviews with parents and EPs. Parents' responses stressed the need for improved communication with the LEA. Overall, the need for improved partnership with parents was expressed, including listening more to parents, taking their views on board, providing more information to parents, and greater transparency and parental involvement in decision-making.

According to file data, the response of the conciliation service in 63 per cent of cases appears to have been very quick and efficient, reflecting a strength of the mediation process expressed by Acland (1990). Twenty-six per cent of cases did not involve a face-to-face meeting, and 37 per cent of cases involved only one meeting. The speed with which some cases appear to be conciliated may indicate the ease with which they could, perhaps, have been prevented. An analysis of the issues involved in conciliation cases revealed that there were some, such as statement wording and inadequate assessment, that might have been resolved at an earlier stage of the process.

EPs felt that the conciliation service becomes involved at too late a stage, which was an issue identified in Gersch et al. (1998). EPs suggested that more opportunities for face-to-face communication and support are needed from the LEA. EPs also suggested that more detailed scrutiny by the SEN panel of the evidence received would help to improve the quality of decision-making. Adverse comments were made by some EPs and parents about the clarity of statements and about the administrative process.

Table 5 Response by conciliation service

Response	Number	%
One meeting with parents	11	37
Contact with parents but no formal meeting	8	26
Two meetings with parents	4	13
Meetings with parents plus meeting at school	3	10
Three meetings with parents	1	3
One meeting with parents and other professionals	1	3
Meeting with parents and other professionals plus meeting at school	1	3
Two meetings with parents and other professionals	1	3
Two meetings with parents and two meetings with school	1	3

Table 6 Involvement of other professionals

Other professional	Number
Speech and language therapists	5
Mainstream support service	4
Occupational therapist	3
Child and family consultation	2
Physiotherapist	1
Orthoptist	1

Features of the process of conciliation

Data on key features of the process of conciliation emerged from the file data, the questionnaires and the interviews with parents, EPs and the PEP. Table 5 presents information from file data on the nature of the conciliation service's response to cases.

The findings in Table 5 suggest that, for the majority of cases (63 per cent), the process of conciliation is relatively simple, involving only one meeting with the parents or no meeting at all. Other professionals were involved in providing reports and advice to assist in the process of conciliation for ten cases. These included doctors, teachers, speech and language therapists, and occupational therapists. Some cases involved obtaining advice from more than one other professional, with one particular case requiring new or updated reports from five other professionals (see Table 6).

In some cases, this may raise questions about whether the initial multidisciplinary assessment could have been wider ranging. Findings from the postal questionnaires and the interviews indicate that the parents' level of satisfaction with both the process and outcome of conciliation is high. This corresponds with the findings from Casale's evaluation in 1996, reported in Gersch et al. (1998). Nine out of the eleven parents (82 per cent) who responded to the questionnaires were satisfied with both the process and outcome of the conciliation service. Of the sample of parents who were interviewed, five out of six parents reported that they were satisfied.

Questionnaire data showed that all the parents in the sample felt that their views and concerns had been listened to. Ten out of eleven felt that they had had enough time to talk, and that their views and concerns were valued. Nine out of eleven felt that they still had some control. Fewer parents, however, felt that they still had some choices (seven out of eleven). On the question of impartiality, seven out of eleven felt that the conciliation service was impartial and independent.

The efficiency and responsiveness of the conciliation service were appreciated by four of the parents interviewed. The fact that the conciliation service provided a very speedy resolution of difficulties was noted by three parents. Another parent commented:

> We got appointments whenever we wanted them, and they were kept. Our phone calls were always returned.

The conciliatory rather than adversarial approach provided by the conciliation service was appreciated. One parent stated:

> The meetings were very pleasant. Even though I walked in with all guns firing, there was no need to.

The ability of the conciliation service to focus on interests rather than on positions was suggested in one parent's response:

> Originally we wanted her to go to special school . . . When we sat down and talked about it, we realised that H would be better off in mainstream school. I suppose it reassured us, really.

Five of the six interviewees appreciated the listening skills and communication skills of the conciliator. One parent commented:

> We felt that this was the first time that we were listened to.

The specialist SEN knowledge and the status of the conciliator were felt to be important. One parent said:

> It is handy that the PEP also sits on the panel. It needs to be someone in his position and with his experience. He understands the ins and outs of issues.

Ambivalence regarding the impartiality of the conciliation service is noted in some of the parents' responses. One parent said:

> At the first meeting I couldn't work out: are they doing things for us or doing things for them? After a while I realised that, although you had guidelines to follow, you were working with us as well.

Another parent made the comment:

> When you first go there, you don't automatically accept that it will be independent . . . It's part of the borough and you are meeting with someone connected with the borough. So you don't go into it thinking that it's independent. In the end, we had no reason to think that it wasn't.

Two parents, who had not been satisfied with the outcome of the conciliation service, felt that independence and impartiality were lacking. One wrote:

> The object of the exercise [conciliation] seemed to be to bring you round to the borough's way of thinking – by making concessions . . . It was as though the 'conciliation service' was just the last stage in a very longwinded process.

Thus data from the questionnaires and interviews indicate aspects of the process of conciliation that are valued by the sample of parents. These include the efficiency and responsiveness of the conciliation service as well as its accessibility. Many parents contrasted these aspects with their experiences of trying to communicate with the LEA. The interpersonal skills of the conciliator were valued, as well as his knowledge, status and experience. The feeling of being listened to emerged as important in a number of parents' responses, reflecting the emphasis placed on this skill in the literature.

Personal qualities that the PEP felt were important were being honest, fair and calm, listening, being non-judgemental, having a 'helicopter mind' (i.e. being able to take an overview of the essential issues), being non-emotional, clear and transparent.

In addition to psychological knowledge and skills in the areas of negotiation and conferencing, key areas of knowledge that the PEP felt contributed were knowledge of the panel, and knowledge of the borough and of special needs. He noted that conciliation in this context would be very difficult for an outsider.

The question of impartiality and independence of the conciliation service revealed ambivalence in the parents' responses. Data from the questionnaires revealed that most parents in the sample felt that it was independent and impartial. Those who were not satisfied with the outcome felt that the service was not independent. Interview data revealed that some parents initially felt suspicious and uncertain about the independence of the conciliation service, in the context of their lack of trust in the LEA. By the end of the process, the view of many parents was that they 'had no reason to think that it was not independent'.

The EPs felt that the question of independence and impartiality was problematic. The fact that the PEP was an influential member of the SEN panel was felt to be a key issue. However, three EPs stressed the importance for the conciliation service of the PEP's inside knowledge of the SEN system and of what the panel would agree to. Further assessments, when needed, were also undertaken by professionals not involved in the conciliation.

The outcome of the conciliation process

Twenty-five of the thirty-one cases involved the conciliation service making recommendations to the SEN panel, which were all agreed. (Table 7 shows the range of recommendations made.)

The largest percentage of recommendations involved an increase in resource level (29 per cent). Other recommendations may also have resource implications. The fact that recommendations for four cases merely involved changing statement wording, without provision or resource implications, again suggests possibilities for preventative work.

Three of the EPs expressed the reservation that the conciliation service could be perceived as conceding to parental demands. The PEP, on the contrary, stressed the importance of creativity in the conciliation process, stating:

Table 7 Recommendations to SEN panel

Recommendation	Number	%
Increase in resource level	9	29
Amendments to statement writing	4	13
Reassessment	3	10
Provision: speech and language therapy	3	10
Placement (special school)	2	6
Provision: support	1	3
Provision: home tuition	1	3
Maintain resource level	1	3
Cease statutory assessment	1	3

> Creativity is 100 per cent important . . . The tribunal can only find for or against. The conciliation service is more creative.

In short, conciliation can involve not just finding a middle ground between the two positions, but sometimes suggesting a totally new idea. For example, in a dispute over the number of special needs assistant hours, rather than agree a number of hours as a compromise, instead the support of specialist technicians were proposed to help a child with specific subjects (e.g. cookery, science). In these lessons, technicians were already employed but agreed to increase their hours worked to undertake specific tasks for a child in a wheelchair. This idea was accepted by all the parties involved as a better solution than simply increasing the hours of a special needs assistant generally.

The file data were analysed to see to what extent the final agreements reached between parents and the LEA matched the initial parental request or whether they involved more creative problem-solving. The issue of whether the agreements entailed a resource implication was also examined. For three of the thirty-one cases analysed, the precise outcome was unclear from the file data. Table 8 shows the results for the remaining twenty-eight cases.

From an analysis of file data, it emerged that for twenty-one (75 per cent) conciliation cases, the outcome involved agreement to the original parental request. Some cases were conciliated very easily, and a number involved changing statement wording without having resource implications. However, for fourteen cases (50 per cent), the outcome involved agreement to the original parental request, which involved an increase in resources or had a resource implication for the LEA. In seven

Table 8 The nature of the agreements reached with parents

Type of agreement	Number	%
Agreement to parental request, with resource implication	14	50
Agreement to parental request, with no resource implication	7	25
Creative response, using existing provision	3	11
Partial agreement to parental request, with no resource implication	2	7
Creative response, with additional provision	2	7

(25 per cent) conciliation cases, the final outcome was different from the parents' initial position, involving more creative problem-solving.

Summary and implications

From this study, it would appear that there are some key themes running throughout the data collected. It should be stressed, of course, that the sample is both small, localised and probably very community-specific. Hence, the results should best be regarded as preliminary and tentative, and suggestive of the need for further research in other areas and with other samples. Some key implications of this study are as follows.

1   It would appear that the most common time for referral to concili-ation for a dispute is at age eleven years, the time of transition from primary to secondary school.

2   The most common categories of special needs that are related to disputes would seem to be physical difficulties, followed by specific learning difficulties, autism, and general learning difficulties. Argu-ably, this might also reflect local considerations and the incidence of SEN generally.

3   Most resolutions were settled in favour of the parents, and not all involved additional resources. The suggestion was made that very close involvement of parents throughout the process, right from the beginning, might avert conflicts, and indeed prevent some unnecessary concerns and misunderstandings.

4   Clearly, where LEA SEN sections operate efficiently and effect-ively, and have good communication with parents from the onset, disputes can be reduced. A further strand in resolving disputes

within a LEA would seem to be the operation of an effective Parent Partnership Scheme. Both mechanisms would serve to reduce the number of referrals made for conciliation and tribunal.

5   Perhaps one way of viewing the conciliation service is as part of a continuum of stages that aim to resolve disputes. The stages could include:

(i)   resolution with the relevant SEN Officer;

(ii)   resolution utilising a Parent Partnership Officer;

(iii) conciliation;

(iv)   tribunal hearing;

(v)   other legal proceedings.

6   A conciliation service can be helpful for some cases, but it would appear that conciliators require special training, support, and preparation. The conciliator's personal qualities and skills are important. EPs are suitably skilled for the role, either carrying out conciliation directly or training others.

7   However, issues of independence do arise, and it may be that cross-boundary agreements are needed that enable LEA employees from one area to carry out conciliation for other LEAs on a reciprocal basis. Some LEAs may wish to arrange and instruct totally independent mediation and conciliation services.

8   This research indicated that some disputes occurred at the Annual Review stage; this is an area worthy of consideration in LEA and EPS planning.

Finally, as emphasised earlier, the results from this study pertain to a limited sample and should thus be regarded with caution. Further studies are needed regarding models of effective conciliation in SEN and on the patterns of disputes leading to conflict in other localities and communities. However, what does emerge clearly is that conciliation does provide an effective and positive alternative to lengthy and adversarial disputes being referred for more formal litigation and to the SEN tribunal.

Acknowledgements

The authors would like to express their appreciation to all the parents, professional staff and colleagues who took part in this study. The views expressed in this article are those of the authors alone, and do not necessarily reflect those of the LEA in which the study took place, or of their employing LEAs or institutions.

References

Acland, A.F. (1990) *A Sudden Outbreak of Common Sense: Managing Conflict through Mediation*. London: Hutchinson.

Gersch, I., Casale, C. and Luck, C. (1998) 'The Waltham Forest SEN Conciliation Service: One Approach to Reducing Tribunal Appeals', *Educational Psychology in Practice*, 14(1), 11–21.

Hornby, G. (1995) *Working with Parents of Children with Special Educational Needs*. London: Cassell.

Rowley, J. (1999) 'Conciliation in Special Educational Needs: An Evaluative and Exploratory Study of One LEA Model', unpublished MSc dissertation, Institute of Education, University of London.

Smith, J.A. (1995) 'Semi-Structured Interviewing and Qualitative Analysis', in J.A. Smith, R. Harre and L. Van Langenhove (eds), *Rethinking Methods in Psychology*. London: Sage Publications, pp. 9–25.

Chapter 4

SEN mediation

4.1 DEVELOPING AN APPROACH TO CONFLICT RESOLUTION: THE CONTRIBUTION OF PARENT PARTNERSHIP SERVICES

Philippa Stobbs

In the summer of 2001 the government announced £1.5 million to develop a regional approach to the resolution of disputes between parents and local education authorities (LEAs) and parents and schools about the special educational provision being made for their child. Prior to the injection of this regional funding, the imminence of a statutory requirement on LEAs to provide conciliation services meant that each LEA was starting to look at what arrangements they might need to put in place.

This chapter draws together information about approaches being adopted across the country prior to the development of the regional approach. It is based substantially on information held by the Council for Disabled Children, which provides support to a national network for all the parent partnership services, the National Parent Partnership Network (NPPN). As part of its support, the Council publishes a range of information including occasional papers bringing together information on particular aspects of parent partnership work. One such paper looked at the development of conflict resolution arrangements and was based on responses to a survey of parent partnership services in autumn 2000. The illustrative quotations throughout this chapter are from this survey.

Linkage between parent partnership and conflict resolution

Central government pronouncements on conciliation have often linked together the provision of parent partnership services and the provision of conciliation arrangements, not least through illustrative examples of parent partnership services providing mediation (DfEE, 1997). Setting aside a confusion of terms – conciliation, mediation, conflict resolution – an issue to which I return later, such services and parent partnership services were linked together and the government clearly saw them both as holding the potential to reduce, or halt the increase in, the numbers of appeals being made to the SEN tribunal.

There are other ways in which parent partnership and conflict resolution are linked. Since the earliest days of parent partnership services there has always been discussion amongst LEAs and parent partnership coordinators about the role of mediation and conflict resolution in relation to their services. To most people parent partnership work is about trying to resolve difficulties, to improve partnerships between parents and the LEA, or between parents and the school. There are natural, common-sense links in people's minds between parent partnership and conflict resolution. Thus, when the government put forward its proposals for legislation that would require local education authorities to provide conciliation services (the term used at the time), there was much to suggest that these services, as a natural extension of the parent partnership role, could and should be located with the parent partnership service.

This view was very much in evidence in the response to the survey of parent partnership services in the autumn of 2000. The survey asked about the arrangements for dispute resolution that LEAs were starting to put in place by this time. Seventy-nine services responded to the survey, a response rate of just over 50 per cent. Of these all but three responses made specific reference to some form of conflict resolution being available locally, though the majority of these were informal arrangements.

Many of the services indicated that it was the parent partnership service that provided any mediation/conciliation that was available:

> The parent partnership officer mediates between parents and head teachers in school when there is a breakdown in communication.

> There is an informal mediation/conciliation service: the Parent Partnership Service facilitates meetings between LEA/parents/parents/schools.

> At present the LEA and some schools rely on the parent partnership service for mediation/conciliation.

> The LEA has no mediation/conciliation services, only the input from my service, where I try and offer conciliation if required.

At least initially, many LEAs were assuming that it would be the parent partnership service that would provide any mediation that was needed. In addition some assumed that mediation was a natural part of that service and that there would be no additional resource or staffing implications arising from the establishment of these arrangements. However, this approach presented some problems:

Firstly, there was the question of supply and demand. To meet any demand for mediation in these LEAs, there was an expectation that parent partnership services would train volunteers to mediate, or that parent partnership coordinators themselves would take on the role of mediator. There was a concern that, if volunteers were sought to train as mediators, this would have an adverse impact on the recruitment of volunteer parent supporters (Independent Parental Supporters or IPSs) where there were already difficulties in recruiting in sufficient numbers. Equally, if the parent partnership coordinator took on the role of mediator, the additional demand on their time would impact on their ability to run existing services: the very services that can reduce levels of conflict in the system, and thereby hold the potential to reduce the need to go to mediation in the first place.

Secondly, whilst there are natural links between parent partnership and mediation, in broad terms, there has always been a view that has held that it was not appropriate to ask the parent partnership service to mediate. This view starts from the assumption that parent partnership services are there for the parents: to be alongside them, inform, support and advise them. If the services are for the parents, and are identified so completely with support for them, then they cannot, by definition, take on responsibility for mediating between the parents and the LEA or the parents and the school. Some LEAs had clearly taken this view in the early days of their parent partnership service and long before there were any proposals to establish separate conciliation services.

Advice on providing mediation

There were more LEAs who, whilst not necessarily looking to their parent partnership service to provide mediation, were looking to them to advise them on how the LEA might develop their approach:

> The LEA does see a role for the parent partnership service and will look to the service for advice on how conciliation services may be set up.

The development of mediation/conciliation service is the responsibility of the Parent Partnership Service i.e. down to me. I haven't decided how it will be developed yet.

If LEAs were looking to their parent partnership services for advice, the parent partnership services themselves were looking for help in thinking through how the new arrangements might sit alongside their own existing service.

Training for mediation

The NPPN consultation identified a significant training need. Some parent partnership coordinators were already trained mediators, but there was a need for a much wider understanding of what mediation entailed. This was not necessarily in order to train more skilled mediators, but rather to develop a greater understanding of the nature and function of a mediation service, in particular:

• the implications of different models of conflict resolution;
• what might need to be done to set up a service;
• what might need to be done to support a service once it was up and running;
• who might be the appropriate agencies to act as mediators.

During 2000 there was an impressive national learning curve on conflict resolution: there was training in every corner of the country, and there was a heavy demand for skilled and qualified mediation trainers.

Defining the terms

One of the first things to emerge from all the training was a better understanding of the different models of conflict resolution, particularly the difference between mediation and conciliation. Parent partnership services increasingly adopted the definitions that they were offered through training opportunities:

• *mediation*: a process which brings people together in the presence of an impartial third party, who then guides/facilitates those in dispute to come to an agreement. The disputants, not the mediator, decide on the terms of agreement. The mediator does not offer advice or recommend solutions but remains neutral and manages the process;

- *conciliation*, on the other hand, involves a third party to help people negotiate with each other. Conciliators will offer people advice and possible solutions to their problems and play a more active role within the process.

The effects of adopting these working definitions helped significantly in understanding what might be the role of a parent partnership service in this area. Whilst the parent partnership service might not be able to provide that independent mediator role, there were common threads between parent partnership work and more informal conciliation arrangements.

Training in the nature of the task

Training not only helped people to understand the difference between different approaches, but helped everyone to an appreciation of what the distinctive contribution of parent partnership services might be. There was an increasing recognition that training was needed simply in order to understand what the process was. Parent partnership co-ordinators, who were being expected by their LEA to provide mediation as part of their service, were keen that LEA staff received training in order to better understand the nature of mediation and perhaps in order to assist the LEA in understanding why the parent partnership service was not necessarily best placed to provide the service. In some LEAs this need for training for understanding was recognised. Certainly in the NPPN survey there were references to training for this purpose:

> The LEA sees no role for the parent partnership service, although I think training will be offered to me as PPO. Not particularly to undertake mediation/conciliation, but to be aware of the service.

> The manager has given us a quote for a full or half day training session to enable colleagues to understand the process.

It also became clear from the training that there were significant other systems that would need to be in place to enable mediation to happen – referral systems would have to be agreed; information would need to be developed; neutral locations would have to be identified for meetings; SEN staff would need training in understanding what the process has to offer; senior SEN staff would have to be available to go to mediation on the day, in order to have someone present with the 'power to settle'; and perhaps most importantly of all, systems would need to be put in place to ensure that there were mechanisms for feeding back to the LEA how conflict arises and how it could be avoided in future – whether by provision of better information; by improved management of the procedures; by the changed organisation of provision; or by any other changes. Without this element there would be no potential for learning from experience and reducing conflict in the future.

All of this constitutes a significant infrastructure to enable mediation to work. There was an appreciation of this in some of the responses to the NPPN survey:

> Not clear yet, but I would envisage Parent Partnership would have a role to play, possibly in alerting parents to the fact that they can participate in mediation.

> The Parent Partnership Service has been instrumental in setting up the pilot and organising in-service training for LEA and PPS staff. We will be completing the analysis of the pilot study. The Parent Partnership Service will liaise with parents when mediation is offered to ensure that they are aware of what to expect from the process.

A variety of arrangements

Gradually emerging from the national debate was a better understanding of how parent partnership services and other arrangements for resolving conflict might sit alongside each other. However, at the time of the survey of autumn 2000, there were several different approaches emerging, some of which have endured, others of which, have not.

It was evident, from the survey, that in some LEAs it was officers of the LEA who were seen as providing conflict resolution:

> At present the student Assessment Officer tries to settle disputes as part of the statutory process.

> Presently, parents who are not satisfied have the opportunity to meet with Statutory Assessment Managers in the LEA with the aim of resolving problems before application is made to the SEN tribunal.

There may be some confusion here with the meeting that parents can request with an officer of the LEA as part of the statutory procedures and the separate arrangements that were being proposed by the government – and it is important to remember that the responses to the survey were descriptive, not necessarily aspirational. However, assuming for a moment that what was being described was proposed as a possible model for conflict resolution, there are some difficulties with this approach:

- such a meeting has to be offered anyway as part of the statutory procedures, so does not offer an additional means of resolving conflict;
- such arrangements do not offer a mechanism for resolving conflict between parents and schools, an increasing issue in some areas;
- there was concern amongst parent partnership services that parents would be too readily persuaded of the LEA's point of view on any issue where there was disagreement;
- how could the LEA conciliate between parents and itself: the parallel argument to the one that was used in some areas to point to the inappropriateness of parent partnership services providing independent mediation arrangements;
- the manpower argument: if SEN staff took on the role, how would this impact on the workload of SEN sections, and possibly render them less efficient in meeting the statutory demands on them?

With time it became clear that, to enable parents to have confidence in the system, conflict resolution arrangements needed to be located somewhere away from the LEA, or at least away from the SEN department. With time the DfEE increasingly emphasised the need for independence from the LEA. This aspect of the arrangements was gradually strengthened, so that when the legislation was passed it said:

> The arrangements must provide for the appointment of independent persons with the function of facilitating the avoidance or resolution of such disagreements.
>
> (Section 332B, Education Act 1996)

However, this is to jump ahead by a year. Other approaches were emerging during the year 2000.

One LEA had appointed its own conciliation officer, the person who had previously worked as their parent partnership coordinator. Another LEA had a long-established conciliation service, provided by the local educational psychology service (described elsewhere in this book). Some LEAs were working with local or national voluntary organisations to provide a conciliation service locally.

At least two pairs of LEAs were developing 'swapping' arrangements. This involved the parent partnership coordinator of one LEA mediating in disputes in the partner LEA, and vice versa. An important consideration in setting up these arrangements was how well matched the LEAs were in terms of likely demand, that is: levels of appeals to the tribunal, size of the LEA and so forth. Another consideration was the ability of the two parent partnership coordinators to feed back to each other (on the generalities of what might be learnt from a number of cases, not the specifics of individual cases). There were not many areas where such matching was possible.

Some LEAs were looking to local mediation services that already existed and provided mediation in a range of other contexts – for example, housing. These LEAs were considering how, with training in the SEN legislation, these services might be able to meet any demand for mediation in the SEN context. In effect they were seeking out the mediation expertise and topping it up with an understanding of SEN, rather than plugging in the SEN expertise and topping it up with mediation skills.

The seeds of the regional approach

At the time of the survey the vast majority of services referred to informal arrangements for conflict resolution. Only eleven of the seventy-nine respondents stated that their LEA already had formal arrangements for conflict resolution to which parents of children with SEN had access. A further nine respondents said that their LEA was either piloting or about to pilot some form of service over the coming months. This was a comparatively small number, twenty, who either had in place or were proposing specific arrangements. Amongst these were two important groupings of LEAs in West London and in the West Midlands who were seeking to establish a regional approach to the provision of mediation.

In the end it was this approach that attracted DfEE funding, through the regional groupings of LEAs (the SEN Regional Partnerships). The regional approach is discussed in more detail in a separate chapter. However, this is not the end of the story.

The future of conflict resolution and parent partnership services

In the Eastern Region the funding arrived too late to be used for the development of services. These were already established. The regional funding is therefore being used to evaluate a number of different approaches which have now been adopted by member LEAs. This will be an important evaluation in identifying key elements of the most successful approaches and informing national developments in conflict resolution.

The role of parent partnership services has become more clear. Apart from having played an important role in supporting and informing the development of local, now regional arrangements, it is apparent that many LEAs are now thinking in terms of a two-stage process. The first part draws significantly on the parent partnership service in trying to resolve difficulties and improve joint working at earlier stages. In other words continuing to invest in and develop parent partnership arrangements is an important part of avoiding and resolving conflict. The second stage is when all else has failed and parents have lodged an appeal with the SEN tribunal. At this stage many LEAs now recognise the need for a more formal mediation process to be provided.

The development of a regional approach to the more formal stages still has implications for what goes before: the quality of the SEN procedures, the quality of the SEN provision, the relationships between parents and schools and parents and LEAs, the quality of parent partnership services themselves will all clearly have an impact on the extent to which LEAs will need to avail themselves of services at the more formal stages. If these services are being provided regionally, will LEAs start to examine each other's use of these services and start to challenge those who are making the most use of them? Comparative information used in a professional dialogue at a regional level could help LEAs to identify ways of making provision, ways of establishing a more constructive dialogue with parents that hold the potential to reduce conflict in the future.

In the mean time other features of the surrounding landscape are changing: new disability discrimination duties on schools are accompanied by a conciliation service provided by the Disability Rights Commission; the 2001 SEN Code of Practice places a new emphasis on the voice of the child in SEN decision-making; increased delegation of funding to schools holds the potential for greater conflict between parents and schools about how funding is deployed to meet children's special educational needs. In seeking to develop a constructive partnership with parents, services whose purpose is to resolve conflict will encounter a range of new partners with whom they will need to work in an educational context which does not yet offer a universal welcome for children with special educational needs.

References

Department for Education and Employment (1997) *Excellence for All Children: Meeting Special Educational Needs*. London: The Stationery Office.

National Parent Partnership Network (2000) *Arrangements for Avoiding and Resolving Disagreements*, Information Exchange, 11, December 2000, Council for Disabled Children.

4.2 DEVELOPING REGIONAL ARRANGEMENTS FOR DISAGREEMENT RESOLUTION

Nick Knapman and *Tom Leimdorfer*

The purpose of this chapter is to describe the role of the SEN Regional Partnerships in developing regional arrangements for disagreement resolution under the SEN and Disability Act 2001.

It is now accepted that parents have a vital role in the education of their children. The importance of partnership with parents, particularly when their children have special educational needs, should not be underestimated. The government's Green Paper *Excellence for All Children – Meeting Special Educational Needs* (DfEE, 1997) stressed the value of empowering parents to work with schools and local services to ensure that children's needs are properly identified and met. Since the introduction of the first SEN Code of Practice (DfE, 1994) Parent Partnership Services had begun to play an increasingly important role as a source of information, advice and support for parents (Wolfendale, in press). This led to a commitment in the government's subsequent Programme of Action (DfEE, 1998) that all Local Education Authorities (LEAs) would be expected to provide a parent partnership service and significant additional funding was made available through the SEN Standards Fund to promote the development of these services.

Recent legislation has reinforced the importance of effective partnership with parents. Under the SEN and Disability Act 2001(HMSO,

2001) all LEAs now have a duty to arrange for the parent of any child with special educational needs to be provided with relevant advice and information and extensive guidance is provided in the revised SEN Code of Practice (DfES, 2001).

However, all partnerships can come under strain. It was recognised in the Green Paper that, even with the involvement of parent partnership services, circumstances may arise where disagreement between parents, schools and LEAs might cause delay in making effective provision. It is to be expected that parents will seek the best possible educational arrangements for their child, while LEAs have to ensure that the support available is adequate to meet the child's needs. LEAs are not under a duty to provide 'the best' and have to consider the equitable use of limited resources. Disagreements can also result from a conflict of values; the debate about inclusion and separate, specialist provision frequently illustrates this. Furthermore parents, schools and LEAs may place different value on what the child needs in a particular case or on considerations of safety, academic progress and social inclusion.

Since its introduction in September 1994 the SEN tribunal has seen a steady increase in the number of appeals registered. These have risen from 1,161 in 1994/1995 to almost 2,500 in 1999/2000 (DfEE, 2000). However as many as 44 per cent of appeals are subsequently withdrawn (Hall, 1999).

In some areas parents began to explore the scope for mediation (Leimdorfer, 1998) and the steady increase in the number of appeals led to a minority of LEAs experimenting with conciliation and disagreement resolution. The DfEE commissioned research into best practice in resolving disputes between parents, schools and LEAs, and a report describing the models of mediation being trialled was published in 1999 (Hall, 1999). As a result of this work the DfEE's Programme of Action included a commitment that every LEA would be expected to establish conciliation arrangements, with an independent element, for resolving disputes with parents.

What are the duties placed on LEAs to provide disagreement resolution?

The SEN and Disability Act 2001 amends the 1996 Education Act by inserting the following sections:

1   A local education authority must make arrangements with a view to avoiding or resolving disagreements between authorities

(on the one hand) and parents of children in their area (on the other) about the exercise by authorities of functions under this Part.

2   A local education authority must also make arrangements with a view to avoiding or resolving, in each relevant school, disagreements between the parents of a relevant child and the proprietor of the school about the special educational arrangements for that child.

3   The arrangements must provide for the appointment of independent persons with the function of facilitating the avoidance or resolution of such disagreements.

Both the SEN Code of Practice and SEN Toolkit provide specific guidance on how such disagreement resolution arrangements should be put into place.

It should be noted that the duties are in respect of special educational needs – separate arrangements will apply to disagreements under the Disability Discrimination duties that take effect from September 2002. It is also significant that the duties cover disagreements that may arise between parents and schools, and not just those between parents and LEAs. This means that access to disagreement resolution must be available to parents of children who are supported through School Action or School Action Plus, as well as those whose children are undergoing statutory assessment or have a Statement of Special Educational Need.

What are the SEN Regional Partnerships?

Excellence for All Children (DfEE, 1997) highlighted the need to develop better regional planning arrangements for some aspects of SEN provision and to improve partnership between LEAs and other statutory, voluntary and private sector providers. In particular it was noted that significant variations existed between LEAs in the arrangements for support and provision for pupils with low incidence disabilities. As a result the DfEE established, by early 1999, five pilot projects in order to improve regional coordination of SEN provision for pupils with particular low incidence needs. These projects were tasked to help redress – through collaborative working – the variations across the country in the quality and way provision is made for pupils with special needs. The Programme of Action (DfEE, 1999) subsequently included a commitment to extend regional coordination to all areas of the country which took effect from September 2000.

There are now eleven SEN Regional Partnerships covering all the LEAs in England, with all of the partnerships receiving 100 per cent funding from the Department for Education and Skills. Each of the partnerships has a management or steering group with representation from local stakeholders. A facilitator or manager is employed to lead the work of the partnership and to secure the involvement of the statutory agencies, voluntary organisations and other interested parties. A national steering group, with broad based representation, provides overall coordination. Similar arrangements have since been established in Wales, though these are funded through the Welsh Office.

Although the focus of the Partnerships was originally on low incidence disabilities it became increasingly evident that there were potential benefits in looking at a wider remit for these regional arrangements. It was therefore determined that, from April 2001, the role of the eleven SEN Regional Partnerships would be expanded to encompass:

- developing more inclusive policies and practice;
- improving the efficiency and effectiveness of SEN processes and services;
- responding to, and engaging effectively with, government initiatives;
- improving inter-agency working.

Details of the composition of each of the regional partnerships, their work plans and arrangements for evaluation of the effectiveness of the partnerships can be found on the DfES website at www.dfes.gov.uk/sen.

Where does disagreement resolution fit in?

Disagreement resolution is not a new concept within education. The skills involved in mediation are at the heart of good negotiation. Nor should it be assumed that disagreement is undesirable, the result of a failure in the system or of unreasonable behaviour. Disagreement is not in itself anyone's fault – it is natural. Simply avoiding conflict may store up problems for later. What is needed is a culture that encourages constructive disagreement resolution. Parent partnership officers, head teachers and special needs coordinators, education officers, advisory teachers, educational psychologists, and representatives of voluntary bodies have regularly used such skills as active listening, providing impartial feedback, problem-solving, framing agreements, etc. in their day-to-day work. The duty placed on LEAs under the SEN and Disability

Act 2001 to *avoid* as well as resolve disagreements means that these skills should continue to underpin much of the work of LEA services. Nevertheless, however good LEA and school staff may be at seeking to avoid and resolve disagreements it is inevitable that they will arise from time to time, not least because of the need to reconcile demands on provision with the availability of resources. This has long been recognised as a particular tension for SEN provision in particular.

All local authorities and schools have arrangements to deal with complaints, but it is relatively rare for *formal* arrangements for disagreement resolution to be available to parents. Complaint procedures are normally designed to investigate, and seek to remedy, events that have already taken place. Disagreement resolution, on the other hand, looks forward. It is about resolving alternative ideas relating to what should happen in the future. It is important that disagreement resolution is divorced from apportioning responsibility or blame for things that may have gone wrong in the past.

A number of approaches to mediation have been tried by LEAs (Hall, 1999), but these have usually involved direct work by their own staff. Impartiality is central to disagreement resolution and both LEAs and parent partnership services have particular roles and responsibilities that may be seen to conflict with providing independent mediation. The introduction of independent, formal disagreement resolution arrangements will therefore offer a new opportunity to parents, in circumstances where communications may have become strained.

It is clear that disagreement resolution will not always be appropriate. If fundamental issues of policy are at stake, or when the parties are unwilling to consider the possibility of a mutually agreed outcome, the SEN and Disability Tribunal will continue to arbitrate. However, the evidence from other areas of public service, the private sector and in family and community work is that mediation can bring significant benefits and better outcomes for all parties (e.g. Liebmann *et al.*, 1998; Stewart, 1998).

Why have a regional approach to disagreement resolution?

Although some local authorities had begun to use Standards Funds to develop local arrangements for mediation or disagreement resolution, for the majority of LEAs the introduction of formal arrangements represents a new area of work. In anticipation of the new legislation a number of SEN Regional Partnerships had already provided a forum to discuss the potential for collaborative arrangements, and some had begun preparatory work. For example the London SEN Regional Partnership was well advanced with the development of training materials (Kuhn, 2001), which have since been circulated to all LEAs and Parent Partnership Services by the DfES.

The advantages of LEAs working together to secure the provision of independent disagreement resolution services include greater potential for:

- equity of access to, and delivery of, disagreement resolution services for parents;
- economies of scale (both for LEAs and potential service providers);
- simplification of the process for tendering for services;
- securing a larger pool of mediators with appropriate knowledge of the SEN framework;
- ensuring the delivery of the minimum standards required by the SEN Code of Practice for the provision of disagreement resolution, and effective arrangements for monitoring and evaluation.

Since the scope of the SEN Regional Partnerships had been broadened and there were clear advantages in adopting a regional approach to the development services for disagreement resolution the DfES took the decision to 'pump prime' this work. In 2001/2002 an additional £2 million was set aside for this purpose, with the funding being released through the eleven SEN Regional Partnerships. To secure this grant funding each partnership was invited to submit an action plan, following consultation with the LEAs within their area. These action plans had to specify how funding would be used to secure access to disagreement resolution, the timetable for implementation and the way in which the voluntary sector would be involved in order to ensure the independence of these services. Action plans were then subject to ministerial approval.

What are the plans for regional disagreement resolution services?

Analysis of the action plans submitted to the DfES in the summer term 2001 indicates that they broadly fall into two types: those where work had already started prior to the decision by the DfES to provide additional funding through the SEN Regional Partnerships, and those where this work had not previously been identified as a priority.

For example, the South Central and South East Regional Partnerships had had discussions with the LEAs from the combined regions and had begun work on the introduction of a tendering process to identify an independent regional service provider.

The London SEN Regional Partnership had embarked on a strategy to develop its own regional SEN mediation service as well as producing training materials.

In the West and East Midlands discussions had been taking place between the local forums for parent partnership officers with a view to setting up a service across the two regions.

Six of the eleven regions (North West, London, South Central, South East, West Midlands, East Midlands) were therefore in a position to tender for an independent service provider at an early stage and their action plans were therefore based on identifying and contracting with an independent service provider at the earliest opportunity.

Four of the other regions (Merseyside, North East, South West, Yorkshire and Humberside) did not expect to be in a position to tender for an independent regional service provider by the time the duties came into force. Furthermore it was evident that in some areas a minority of LEAs had set up service level agreements with local providers, which were already operative. These partnerships therefore adopted a phased approach to the introduction of regional services. In the first phase the emphasis was on securing an interim service so that all LEAs were in a position to meet their statutory duties from January 2002. This was achieved either by recruiting and training a small, temporary team of mediators or by purchasing additional capacity from existing providers. In the second phase a tendering process was used to identify suitable independent providers of either regional or, in the geographically largest areas, sub-regional services.

In the Eastern Region a number of authorities were already in discussions with local providers of disagreement resolution services. A decision was made to undertake further research and discussion before determining what aspects of a disagreement resolution service might sensibly be taken forward on a regional basis.

Who will provide regional disagreement resolution services?

As previously stated there can be no doubt that parent partnership services, education officers and others will continue to use mediation skills in their discussions with parents. However, the legal requirement that disagreement resolution should be provided by 'independent persons' means that it is likely that a new range of providers – at least within the field of education – will be identified. It is essential that the providers of such services have skills in mediation *and* a knowledge and understanding of the SEN framework.

So who might this be? The early indications from those Regional Partnerships that have advertised for a service is there may be a range of possible providers. These may include existing mediation services that extend their scope to include SEN issues, national and local SEN voluntary organisations that develop disagreement resolution work, and new organisations that emerge in response to the legislation.

As yet it is extremely difficult to predict the demand for disagreement resolution. There is evidence that its use in disputes between parents and local authorities can help to reduce the number of appeals to the SEN and Disability Tribunal. Since parents may seek disagreement resolution without prejudicing their right to go to tribunal it seems likely that some may want to use this route as a potentially quicker way of resolving disagreements; and provided that mediation is skilful and a mutually agreeable outcome can be found this must be a 'win–win' solution.

What is much less clear at this stage is the potential demand for disagreement resolution between parents and schools. Disputes between parents and schools concerning SEN provision which are not resolved by special needs coordinators, headteachers or governors have often resulted in the involvement of parent partnership services, LEA officers and support services but much of this work may not currently be recorded as disagreement resolution. In order to plan capacity for the future, close monitoring of the demand for disagreement resolution at the school level will be essential.

Whoever provides disagreement resolution it will be necessary to ensure that this meets the minimum standards described in the SEN Code of Practice and that effective arrangements are in place to assure the quality and effectiveness of services. This, therefore, forms a vital component within the process of establishing service level agreements at a regional level.

The future

The introduction of formalised arrangements for disagreement resolution presents new challenges for education services. The lead role taken by the SEN Regional Partnerships has promoted the rapid development of provision and strong collaboration between local authorities.

From 2003 to 2004 the funding for disagreement resolution will change. Rather than it coming through a combination of grants managed by the Regional Partnerships and through local authority Standing Spending Assessments it is expected that it will be entirely through LEA funding, since it is local authorities which have the statutory duty to ensure the service is available. While this does not preclude the continuation of regional arrangements, these would be entered into voluntarily with each LEA making a contribution toward the provision of a regional (or sub-regional) service.

The experience gained through the work undertaken by the SEN Regional Partnerships during the two years in which the DfES is 'pump-priming' developments will prove valuable. There is much to be learned about demand, capacity and effective delivery of high quality services. Regional arrangements will promote the sharing of information. In the longer term the continuation of a regional approach to disagreement resolution will depend on the willingness of LEAs to pool resources. Disagreement resolution may yet prove to be a powerful factor in developing improved regional coordination of a much wider range of services for all children and families with special educational needs.

References

Department for Education (1994) Code of Practice on the Identification and Assessment of Special Educational Needs. London: Department for Education.

Department for Education and Employment (1998) Meeting Special Educational Needs – A Programme of Action. London: DfEE Publications.

Department for Education and Employment (1997) Excellence for All Children – Meeting Special Educational Needs. London: DfEE Publications.

Department for Education and Employment (2000) Special Educational Needs Tribunal Annual Report 1999/2000. London: DfEE Publications.

Department for Education and Skills (2001) Special Educational Needs Code of Practice. London: DfES Publications.

Hall, J. (1999) Resolving Disputes between Parents, Schools and LEAs: Some Examples of Best Practice. London: DfEE Publications.

Her Majesty's Stationery Office (2001) Special Educational Needs and Disability Act 2001. London: The Stationery Office.

Kuhn, M. (ed.) (2001) SEN Disagreement Resolution in Action. London: London SEN Regional Partnership.

Liebmann, M. *et al.* (1998) *Community and Neighbour Mediation.* London: Cavendish Publishing.

Stewart, S. (1998) *Conflict Resolution – A Foundation Guide.* Winchester: Waterside Press.

Leimdorfer, T. (1998) 'Special Children – Special Conflicts', *Mediation*, 14(1).

Wolfendale, S. (in press) *Parent Partnership Services for Special Educational Needs.* London: David Fulton.

SEN Regional Partnerships

East of England

Member LEAs: Cambridgeshire (Lead), Bedfordshire, Hertfordshire, Essex, Luton, Norfolk, Peterborough, Southend, Suffolk, Thurrock.
Facilitator: Ms Jackie Jackson-Smith   **Tel:** 01245 436320
Email: jackie.jackson-smith@essexcc.gov.uk
Website: www.hertsdirect.org/senregionalproject

East Midlands

Member LEAs: Northamptonshire (Lead), Derby City, Derbyshire, Leicester City, Leicestershire, Lincolnshire, Nottingham City, Nottinghamshire, Rutland.
Facilitator: Pat Bullen   **Tel:** 01283 762 430
Email: pat_bullen@talk21.com
Website: http://www.emleas.org.uk

London

Member LEAs: Westminster (Lead), All 33 London boroughs.
Facilitator: Ms Mary Kuhn   **Tel:** 020 7217 3231
Email: mkuhn.gol@go-regions.gov.uk
Website: http://www.londonregionsenproject.org.uk

Merseyside

Member LEAs: Liverpool (Lead), Halton, St Helens, Knowsley, Sefton and Wirral.
Facilitator: Andy Simpkins   **Tel:** 0161 865 7169
Email: andyf.simpkins@tinyworld.co.uk
Website: www.merseysen.org.uk.

North East

Member LEAs: Redcar and Cleveland (Lead), Darlington, Durham, Gateshead, Hartlepool, Middlesborough, Newcastle-upon-Tyne, North Tyneside, Northumberland, South Tyneside, Sunderland, Stockton.

Facilitator: John Kirton   **Tel:** 0191 202 3587

Email: *jkirton.gone@go-regions.gsi.gov.uk*

Website: *http://www.inclusion-ne.org.uk*

North West

Member LEAs: Lancashire (Lead), Blackpool, Blackburn with Darwen, Bolton, Bury, Cheshire, Cumbria, Manchester, Oldham, Rochdale, Salford, Stockport, Tameside, Trafford, Warrington, Wigan.

Facilitator: Diane Whalley   **Tel:** 01457 867 019

Email: *diane.whalley@bigwig.net*

Website: *http://www.sen-northwest.org.uk*

South Central

Member LEAs: Hampshire (Lead), Bracknell Forest, Buckinghamshire, Isle of Wight, Milton Keynes, Oxfordshire, Portsmouth, Reading, Slough, Southampton, West Berkshire, Windsor and Maidenhead.

Facilitator: Hugh Clench   **Tel:** 01273 230 718

Email: *hughclench@btinternet.com*

Website: *http://www.scrip.uk.net*

South East

Member LEAs: Kent (Lead), Brighton and Hove, East Sussex, Medway, Surrey and West Sussex.

Facilitator: Lindsey Rousseau   **Tel:** 0208 541 9048

Email: *lindsey.rousseau@surreycc.gov.uk*

Website: http://sersen.uk.net

South West

Member LEAs: Devon (Lead), Bath and NE Somerset, Bournemouth, Bristol, Cornwall, Dorset, Gloucester, Isles of Scilly, North

Somerset, Plymouth, Poole, Somerset, South Gloucester, Swindon, Torbay, Wiltshire.

Facilitators: Dorothy Hadleigh and Nick Knapman
Tel: 01823 335491
Email: lucy_donnelly@swafet.org.uk
Website: http://www.sw-special.co.uk

West Midlands

Member LEAs: Coventry (Lead), Birmingham, Dudley, Herefordshire, Sandwell, Shropshire, Solihull, Staffordshire, Stoke on Trent, Telford & Wrekin, Warwickshire, Walsall, Wolverhampton, Worcestershire.

Facilitators: Annette English   **Tel:** 0121 445 0108
Bridget Jones   **Tel:** 01432 820159
Email: aenglish@discover.co.uk or bjones@discover.co.uk
Website: http://www.westmidlandsrcp.org.uk

Yorkshire and Humberside

Member LEAs: Kirklees (Lead), Barnsley, Bradford, Calderdale, Doncaster, East Ridings of Yorkshire, Hull, Leeds, North East Lincolnshire, North Lincolnshire, North Yorkshire, Rotherham, Sheffield, Wakefield, York.

Contact: Pip Wise   **Tel:** 01226 763313
Email: millwise@unison   **Website:** http://www.yhsen.org.uk

4.3 THE WEST LONDON MEDIATION PROJECT

Jeff Frank

Introduction

It is August and I am sitting here in the sunshine wondering why I have agreed to contribute a chapter to a book on conflict resolution. But I know the answer: by being involved in a pilot scheme I have become convinced of the potential of a mediation service to improve the way in which we work, collaboratively, for youngsters with special educational needs. That matters to me.

Mediation can be the key to a whole new mindset in the area of special educational needs and I am a passionate advocate for a different way of working. A change is well and truly overdue. The current dilemma facing LEAs has been summarised by the Department for Education and Skills (1997) as follows: it is very difficult for LEAs who are 'struggling to achieve strategic coherence and budgetary control against a statutory framework that accords uncontested priority to individual needs'. In the current climate it isn't just difficult, it often feels impossible. Yet this is the challenge, to satisfy both individual needs and budgetary control. Budgetary control is not an end in itself. Taken one step further, it is the means by which authorities can move away from funding individual needs, towards increased inclusion – with most youngsters having their needs appropriately met in local main-stream settings. The Green Paper proposed 'shifting resources', but there is a clear dichotomy: how can we move further along this road when the current draft Code of Practice is being rewritten, as I write, in order to ensure that provision on SEN statements remains both 'specific and quantified'? This does not suggest that we are working in an atmosphere of mutual trust between parents, voluntary organisations and Local Education Authorities. Rather, the opposite; the statement continues to be viewed as a necessary protection against an LEA deter-mined to withdraw provision. But what has this to do with mediation? A great deal, I would suggest. Mediation offers a new and challenging approach to conflict resolution and the result can potentially change authority–parent relationships for the better.

In this chapter I intend to describe the West London project on mediation, which was initiated in February 2000. During the course of the project an opportunity arose to participate in a study visit to the U.S.A., in March 2001, in order to learn about their Special Education Mediation Service. This experience proved to be influential in the direction taken by our project and is also reflected in the findings in this chapter. I hope to outline some of the challenges faced by the project and to outline some clear benefits. I make no bones about it, I am an advocate for mediation/conflict resolution services.

Setting up the West London project

A West London Regional Group of LEAs was established in 1999 and included Hammersmith and Fulham, Brent, Ealing, Hillingdon,

Kensington and Chelsea, Harrow and Hounslow. The group wanted to identify a project that would demonstrate inter-LEA cooperation. Mediation was selected as a suitable project. As early as 1997, with the publication of the Green Paper, there were clear indications that some form of dispute resolution was likely to become compulsory in the area of special educational needs. There was a clear gap in LEA provision. I was asked to establish a small working group that would feed back its recommendations on what was believed to be a fairly straightforward, discrete area of work. However, in reality the whole topic proved to be far more complex than originally thought.

In the spirit of partnership, right from the outset the intention was to actively involve parent support groups. In the very first meeting we were joined by both Philippa Stobbs, Principal Development Officer from the Council for Disabled Children, together with Philippa Russell. It was at this stage that I caught my first glimpse of the learning curve ahead of the group. I had assumed that we could establish a small pilot on 'conciliation', where an Officer or Parent Partnership Coordinator acted as conciliator for another LEA. Immediately a number of issues came to light that questioned such an approach. Before we knew it, the group was involved in a discussion about semantics – what sort of service was it that we were really trying to establish? I distributed a brief definition of arbitration, mediation and conciliation to the group. It seemed to me at that time that conciliation was the preferred option: *To reconcile two sides and to bring about an agreement.*

Pragmatically, I could live with this approach, which was of clear value to LEAs. I had misgivings about mediation, which seemed far too vague – the definition of mediation that I distributed to the working group offered: *To consider thoughtfully, to reflect upon.*

It seemed to me that the whole process could only have value for LEAs if the results were tangible – a significant reduction in the number of SEN tribunals being registered. The confusion was to some extent perpetuated in the draft Code of Practice. In its first version, under the heading 'Conciliation', there followed a clear description of what the steering group now understood to be mediation: 'The conciliator is not there to determine the dispute'.

Does it matter? I would argue that it does, as clarity and transparency are crucial, if trust is to be established. Imagine publishing a book on sport and in the chapter on 'tennis', outlining the rules of squash! Clearly this would be unhelpful at best and misleading at worst. As a basic principle, let us say what we mean and mean what we say. It's a good starting point.

In unravelling this issue, Philippa Russell shared her knowledge of the Minnesota experience and Philippa Stobbs was able to clarify what she had gained from a training workshop on mediation in Manchester, where the trainers were Zanne Findlay and Akin Thomas. As a group we explored the options available to us. Following further discussions and despite my original misgivings, we settled upon 'mediation', rather than 'conciliation'. I changed my view as a direct result of the group discussions. It felt right to aim at a system whereby parties came up with their own solution, rather than having a solution imposed upon them. This was better described as mediation. This concept of 'ownership' became one of the main tenets of the work of the group. Once we had agreed 'what' it was we wanted to do we were able to move on to 'how' to achieve our aim.

It was agreed that the involvement of Zanne Findlay would be of great value to the group and she was invited to join us at our second meeting. Our project began to take shape as we started to tackle the practicalities of the pilot. A number of decisions had to be taken and can be summarized as follows:

- For the purposes of the pilot, we initially intended to pilot two cases per authority, fourteen in total. (In reality, this proved to be too optimistic.)
- Cases selected as suitable would involve only two-way mediations, seen as more straightforward (e.g. not parent/school/LEA).
- Cases selected as suitable would be those likely to proceed to tribunal in the absence of intervention.
- For the pilots, all cases would be co-mediated.
- Venues would be neutral.
- There was to be no legal representation on either side.
- A full day was to be set aside for each mediation.
- The process was to be voluntary, on both sides.
- Permission was to be gained in advance to evaluate the cases.

There were areas that we did not resolve through the pilot: in the event of parents being dissatisfied with the process, would they have a right of legal recourse against the mediator(s)? Are parents to have access to a complaints procedure in the event of them being dissatisfied with the process? (Fortunately, with Zanne as co-mediator and all her experience in the field, the matter was not a real issue during the pilot. However, it would need to be resolved if both co-mediators were volunteers.) Should a choice of mediators be offered?

How practical is this? Perhaps the way forward would be to offer mediation, giving details of the proposed mediator(s) and only reconsider if either side raises objections. If either parent or LEA agreed in principle to mediation but did not accept the suggested mediators, the objections could be considered and, if reasonable, another mediator proposed. There is a related issue here, and that is how to ensure the quality of mediators.

Payment of mediators

Whilst agreeing to pay expenses, the pilot chose to view the pool of potential mediators as a voluntary group, similar to school governors. This might not work out in the long run. Here was a concern expressed that offering payment to mediators in this field could create a profitable area in which to work, in much the same way that Special Educational Needs tribunals have been viewed by some as legitimate and lucrative business opportunities in the legal world.

Identification of appropriate cases

Not all cases are suitable for mediation. Where views are so polarised that there is no room for negotiation, then arbitration (the role of the SEN tribunal) is more appropriate. But this is not to diminish the value of mediation. The opportunity to be grasped is to recognise the cases at an early stage that can benefit from mediation and so avoid a potentially protracted and negative confrontation. This is why mediation must be voluntary on both sides. There will be cases where LEAs have strong views. Also there will be cases where parents can see absolutely no mileage in negotiation. To avoid mediation becoming a meaningless sham, a necessary step on the way to tribunal, both sides must retain the right to refuse to participate.

Each participating authority was to identify one or two potential mediators who would be interested in participating in the project. The work was to be on a voluntary basis and would include a three-day training course to be offered by Zanne and her colleague Akin. The first day was to be of a general nature, as an awareness raising session. This was to include not only potential mediators but also other interested parties such as parent partnership coordinators, SEN officers and managers. (We didn't include parents, as the pilot was very much at an early stage of its development. On reflection, I believe that we should have done so.) This day proved to be very successful and served to illustrate the global nature of mediation. By raising the awareness of all those involved in SEN, the potential impact of a mediation service was considerably increased. The next two days represented the core of the training for the would-be mediators. It included the opportunity to develop skills, such as preparing an opening statement for a mediation and an understanding of the principles that underpin the process.

We were able to refine our approach to the pilot as we went along. A number of role-play exercises were carried out and proved to be both entertaining and instructive. In the course of the three-day training session, other issues arose. Through these role-play sessions, the potential hazards of involving youngsters in the process were brought home to the group. In the States, it is always the parents who attend mediation, on behalf of their child. Of course this flies in the face of the move in this country to increase participation of the child and could create serious difficulties in the event of the child and the parent(s) disagreeing on the best course of action. The advice here is to be sure to take account of the views of the child. This can and should be incorporated into the groundwork undertaken before the case is deemed appropriate to go forward for mediation. It was agreed that as part of the training, each potential mediator would have the opportunity of co-mediating a case with Zanne, before going it alone.

Our understanding of the approach offered to conflict resolution through mediation greatly increased over the three days. We adopted a number of principles for the pilot. Namely, that the process be:

- voluntary on both sides
- confidential
- with no lawyers
- neutral.

Following the training session, the next stage of the pilot was to carry out some mediations. However, there were some practical difficulties. It proved extremely difficult to identify suitable cases for mediation. There was a concern that by presenting a case for mediation, the tight statutory time-scales would not be met. So, if the mediation session did not resolve the issues, then the LEA would be in an even worse position. This concern was exacerbated by the fact that this was a pilot, which of course meant that clear and agreed procedures were not established. Another factor was that of conflicting priorities. A number of the participating authorities were carrying out best-value reviews and were undergoing Ofsted inspection. Both areas are extremely time-consuming. In addition, it was unclear which cases could go forward for mediation. There was a genuine concern that the process might raise parental expectations, to no avail. In the absence of clear and agreed procedures, there was uncertainty as to whether a case was appropriate or not. Given all these difficulties, it is remarkable that any cases were identified. Even more remarkable are the positive outcomes.

The actual experience

From the perspective of an LEA officer, I found the process both worthwhile and draining. I have presented many tribunal cases, but this was far more emotionally taxing. At one stage I was informed by the mediator that I had been speaking for an hour. This was in response to the initial issue raised by a parent. I was surprised, but strangely enough, it didn't seem excessive. We had a whole day to get this issue sorted. It was an incredible luxury to not have to be distracted by thoughts of the next meeting in the diary. I was able to devote time to the issue in hand. Certainly, the whole process was far more rewarding than tribunals. We were genuinely in the business of finding shared solutions and it was refreshing.

Learning points from the mediations carried out

- The venues were considered suitable and were both neutral and in pleasant, peaceful locations with three areas available.
- In order to ensure the right frame of mind of all participants it is crucial to set aside enough time – a full day is ideal. In both cases resolution was achieved in the afternoon sessions.
- A purpose written pack, including simple proformas, would be of great value (Zanne is working on such a pack).
- The presence of an experienced mediator clearly facilitated the process and gave all those involved confidence.
- Training for mediators, following the initial training sessions will be important. Ongoing refresher courses would be of great value.
- Co-mediation proved to be a useful approach in both cases. (In time it is hoped that the co-mediators would feel comfortable carrying out co-mediations without the need for a professional mediator to be present.)
- Lunch in both cases proved to be an opportunity for all involved to relax and the issues were not discussed.
- The process has to be seen to be both fair and even-handed.

Outcomes

Initially, the project had commissioned Zanne to evaluate the mediations carried out. However, given the fact that only two were completed, this was not considered to be a wide enough sample to be valid.

However, some outcomes are worth noting. In both instances, parents expressed the view that the process had been helpful and they had valued the opportunity mediation gave them to be heard. There was unanimity from those who took part in the process, whether as co-mediator, parent, parent advocate or LEA officer, that the process was of real value. Both the mediations carried out resulted in positive outcomes for both the parent and the LEA. Neither case went on to the SEN tribunal. In one instance a direct result of the mediation session was that a tribunal appeal was withdrawn and a satisfactory outcome was achieved. The mediation process gave the impetus to find a creative solution, involving another agency (social services). This not only resulted in the avoidance of a tribunal, but also gave a resolution, which satisfied both parties (such a solution would have been outside of the remit of the tribunal). It also served to strengthen joint-agency working.

In addition to the successful outcome in the individual case, there were a number of positive 'windfall outcomes' (unexpected outcomes). One of the participating authorities is arranging for whole-team training on mediation.

A visit to Pennsylvania

Shortly after the three-day training session, the opportunity arose to visit Pennsylvania, where a mediation service for SEN had been effectively established twelve years ago. This served to reinforce a lot of the principles the West London pilot had already established. When the system was set up in Pennsylvania, one of the first principles was: 'Mediation is a one-time session. Parties reserve the entire day for mediation.' (In practice most cases are brought to a conclusion within a four-hour time frame.)

Children do not take part in the process in Pennsylvania, nor is there a formal mechanism for securing their views. Mediation is usually scheduled within two weeks of being requested. It is important that the service is seen to be both responsive and prompt.

One of the consequences of setting up a service in Pennsylvania has been the impact on their 'due process' system (the American equivalent of our SEN tribunal). This is because their mediation service is funded centrally, as is their 'Due Process' service. In addition, the dispute resolution team share the same location as the 'Due Process' staff. Mediation has proved to be an effective use of resources primarily because lawyers are out of the frame. Whilst it is true to say that the number of Due Process cases has increased from 120 in 1985 to 320 in 2000, there is a unanimous belief that without the introduction of mediation, given the increasingly litigious nature of society in the USA, the increase would have been far greater.

When the dispute resolution service became established, the due process system became more hard-nosed. This had the added bonus of discouraging the legal route and making mediation all the more attractive. For mediation/conflict resolution to become a sustainable service and to achieve its potential it needs to be adequately resourced. In Pennsylvania the setting up of the service was accompanied by a major financial commitment.

Final thoughts

It is worth remembering that rules are made to be broken, within reason! Procedures can only serve as guidance and there will always be exceptions. For example, in one of our piloted mediations, a possible outcome would have been a second mediation, involving a third party (social services). This would have flown in the face of the principle of 'one-time sessions'. The salutary reminder here is that we are dealing with people and their needs. They do not always fit into convenient rules. A better description of any underlying principles would be as 'guidelines'. Taken in this light, I hope that the experience of the West London project outlined in this chapter is helpful.

It is to be hoped that the impact experienced in Pennsylvania on Due Process could be mirrored here with our tribunal system. Our system was set up in 1994 in the absence of any redress for parents against what could be arbitrary LEA decisions. At the time it was set up in conjunction with the introduction of the Code of Practice and was a welcome change. However, it is time for a full review as it has outlived its usefulness. Despite all the good will in the world, the system is something of a lottery, with consistency of decisions proving hard to achieve. SEN tribunals are essentially of a confrontational nature. Intervention is usually at such a late stage that resolution is unlikely to be accepted by both sides.

In addition, LEAs are encouraged to formulate local criteria for SEN, in the absence of any prescribed national criteria, which are often overruled by the tribunal. Unless all cases go to tribunal, this makes a mockery of equal opportunities. It is increasingly frustrating to try to balance individual needs against the efficient use of resources. In my experience tribunals often appear to be trying to find a 'win–win' solution in order to appease both sides. But in many instances the case would not be before them if such a simple solution were possible. The current quasi-legal status is unhelpful. Both sides would I believe, welcome a clearer role for the SEN tribunal as 'impartial arbitrator'. It would certainly be fairer and more honest. In the long run such a change of approach, together with the introduction of mediation services, could result in a reduction in the number of cases being presented to the tribunal.

Conflict resolution is a good example of 'working smarter'. Not only is it cost-effective, but it also represents good practice. Rather than the adversarial approach that is inevitable through tribunals and tends to require everything being documented, mediation is dependent upon trust. One sheet of paper outlining the issues from both perspectives is all that is required. This calls for a very different mindset from both sides. Just this fact is liberating in itself! The current system diverts resources and expertise towards bureaucracy and assessment. It is wasteful and undermines support for inclusion. In addition, the system encourages a confrontational relationship, so perpetuating the lack of trust between parents, schools and LEAs.

The value of mediation is the potential it offers to redress this situation. It is possible to develop trusting relationships. Through conflict resolution there is the real potential to change attitudes, to bring about a change of mindset that will genuinely facilitate increased partnership working. Such a change will only come about if authorities understand the process. Mediation is to be a statutory requirement placed upon LEAs and there is a temptation to purchase an 'off-the-shelf' service. Certainly this will meet the statutory requirements, but is inevitably of limited value. Whilst it can be seen to be independent, if the process is not 'owned' by authorities, then the real benefits will not be felt. The real value of the pilot was through the joint training, questioning current procedures and offering a valid alternative approach, through mediation.

Through increased awareness the way is open for improved communication and an increase in true partnership working. As Browning said: 'A man's reach should exceed his grasp'. What is so exciting is that this is not beyond our grasp. A real change in SEN practice is within our reach and mediation offers one of the means by which it can be achieved.

References

Department for Education and Skills (DfES) (1997) *Excellence for All Children – Meeting Special Educational Needs*, October.
Draft Code of Practice P11, 2.9.
Ofsted and Audit Commission, Local Education Authority Support for School Improvement, 2001.

4.4 THE LONDON SEN DISAGREEMENT RESOLUTION SERVICE

Mary Kuhn

The London SEN Disagreement Resolution Service is a regional mediation-based service developed by the London SEN Regional Partnership. The Partnership is one of a series established and funded by the Department for Education and Skills. One of the Regional Partnership's objectives is to reduce variations in provision of SEN processes and services regionally; another is to respond to government initiatives. The introduction of SEN disagreement resolution in the new SEN Code of Practice presented the opportunity to meet both of those objectives and at the same time serve the LEAs within the Partnership. Providing a regional service would allow LEAs to meet their statutory responsibilities and at the same time achieve consistency of response and economies of scale.

The time-scale was very short. Although the London SEN Regional Partnership had anticipated this development and had in fact financed initial pilot work in this area, the government's intention that the new code would come into effect in September 2001 meant that we would have to be quick off the mark. It was essential that the service was operational as soon as the duty on LEAs to provide independent disagreement resolution services came into force, in order to avoid the regional nature of the initiative being compromised through a patchwork of local plans. There was a period of six months in which to get a service up and running before the proposed regulations came into effect.

Initial market soundings highlighted a number of factors, which would need to be taken into account in developing the service. Although some LEA officers were enthusiastic supporters of disagreement resolution in SEN, many officers felt that they and their staff already used mediation skills in their day-to-day dealings with parents. Some had little confidence in this type of conflict resolution because, they believed, if it were possible to compromise or concede what the parent was asking, they would do it without mediation. Quite a number were concerned about the amount of time that would have to be devoted to an individual child when they had a responsibility to serve the needs of all the children in the authority. Additionally they found it difficult to see the point of mediation when parents still had the right of appeal to the SEN tribunal.

So it was clear that in addition to developing the service, careful work would need to be done to build confidence in the process. And, importantly, to respond convincingly to these concerns. In order to truncate development time it seemed sensible to look at what had been achieved elsewhere.

In the United States, amendment to the Individuals with Disabilities Education Act (IDEA) which came into force in 1997 placed a requirement on State Education Agencies (SEA) to offer independent mediation to parents and school districts in the event of a dispute over educational provision. In some states mediation services have been running for some years and are now mature. I therefore decided to arrange and lead a study visit to the United States to find out more and was fortunate in being able to negotiate grant funding for a visit to Pennsylvania.

Pennsylvania was the first state in the USA to introduce SEN mediation. In 1985 the state education department, concerned at the rising level of litigation in special educational needs cases, set up the Pennsylvania Mediation Task Force to investigate the setting up of a mediation service. In its report, the group presented findings to the Bureau of Special Education wholeheartedly recommending the setting up of a mediation service *as soon as administratively feasible to do so*. Interestingly though the group noted in the preface to the report that a reduction in the projected number of due process hearings was not anticipated; rather, the development of positive working relationships was the goal.

During the course of the study visit our delegation had the opportunity to meet with representatives of the Pennsylvania Office for Dispute Resolution, officers from school districts, headteachers and parents who had taken part in mediation and mediators employed by the service. All were very positive about both the process and their personal experience.

School district officers felt that disagreements with parents caused barriers to go up which made communication more difficult. In mediation, the issues became the focus, not the child, allowing for clearer problem-solving. They also felt that the process provoked reflection and re-evaluation, which had a positive impact on continuing practice.

Parent users of the service were equally enthusiastic. They emphasised that the structure and process allowed the parents' voice and through them the child's voice to be heard – the other side had to listen and respond. The role of the mediator ensured that listening happened.

These were encouraging findings. The challenge now was to bridge the gap between experience on one side of the Atlantic and expectation on the other.

Several factors seemed key to success:

- basing the service on mediation as opposed to other forms of disagreement resolution;
- raising awareness of and increasing knowledge about mediation – the process and the benefits;
- addressing LEA officers' concerns about the resource commitment;
- recruiting high-quality mediators.

The decision to base the service on mediation was taken after considerable debate and exploration of other forms of dispute resolution within the London SEN Regional Partnership. These are rehearsed elsewhere in detail but for education officers, the most persuasive argument in favour of mediation was that the parties to the dispute, having been part of the process of finding a solution, would be more likely to be able to support and maintain any agreement reached. This fitted well with good practice in many LEAs and with authorities' efforts to build more constructive partnerships with parents.

More challenging were some of the start-up issues that would need to be addressed to win support for the new service, while at the same time not losing ground in service development. The time-scale we were working to meant that a multi-track system had to be used (Figure 1).

The service had to be designed in consultation with LEAs – SEN officers and Parent Partnership Officers. We were also keen to involve

		Service design
Mediation Service Development		Progress Information to, and feedback from, interested groups
		Preparation of promotional and training materials
		Recruitment and training of mediators

Figure 1   Mediation service development tracks

the voluntary sector in order to create a broadly based consensus as a foundation for the initiative. Creating and maintaining a dialogue during the development phase was very important to the success of the project. It was also necessary to keep information about the progress of the scheme flowing out to the thirty-three London LEAs in order to avoid unintentional duplication of effort.

To be workable, the service concept had to address officers' concerns. It was clear from the many discussions that took place in the various meetings and from debate in the service implementation group that officers still believed there was little more they could do than they were already doing. They did not really have confidence that a third party might be able to facilitate agreement where it had not previously been possible and were not persuaded that the investment of time in one case could be justified.

We needed to communicate that even when mediation does not result in agreement on the substantive issue, participants often feel the process brought unexpected benefits. These benefits can improve communication between the parties and/or resolve some of the conflict if not the substantive issue. People we had met in the United States talked a great deal about the spin-off benefits of mediation:

- all parties had to come to terms with the reality of the child;
- a working relationship was retained with the school;
- it provides a safe but clear structure that gives confidence to all;
- the process allows for honesty;
- it gets to underlying issues that might not have been apparent before;
- small agreements can often be reached which can then be built on;

- it allows for reflection and re-evaluation;
- because someone else is 'in control' you can focus more on listening;
- it enables parties to 'still be nice to each other';
- it allows for a holistic view of a child as all parties know them differently – the process respects this;
- it allows for the voice of the pupils to be heard.

Inspired by the fact that the concept difficulties had been present in the early development of the Pennsylvania service but had been so successfully overcome there, we looked at putting together an SEN disagreement resolution package that would win hearts and minds in London.

Debate crystallised into a mediation-based service with the following characteristics:

- located in the not-for-profit sector and therefore provided at cost;
- high-quality;
- efficiently administered;
- an informal, paperless service – as unlike the SEN tribunal as possible;
- quality controlled;
- effectively managed and developed;
- supported by training.

We decided to develop training materials to work at getting the key messages across to LEAs and schools. Video presentation supported by written materials was considered the most effective medium and so a short promotional film was commissioned. The brief for the filmmaker was that the film should

- explain the process of mediation;
- illustrate how mediation might be used in the context of disagreements between parents and LEAs/schools about meeting the needs of children with special educational needs; and
- highlight the benefits of attempting to resolve disagreements in this way.

The preparation of the materials took place over a four-month period. The final product was a short film featuring parents, education officers and professional mediators speaking about the benefits as they perceived them together with extracts from a simulated mediation with actors playing the parts of parent, parental supporter, education officer and teacher. The film, on completion, won the endorsement of the Department for Education and Skills and was sent by the Department to every LEA and Parent Partnership service in England. Subsequently, due to high demand, the packs were made available to LEAs and schools through the DfES distribution system.

While the video was in preparation, service planning and recruitment and training of mediators had to be achieved.

Within the SEN context, disagreement resolution cannot be pure mediation. The parties to the dispute are not individuals in disagreement with one another. It is the system – education funding, the Code of Practice, the lack of integrated provisions, the absence of frameworks and protocols to promote interagency working – albeit managed by individuals, with which the parent is in conflict. The potential for resolution of disagreements is often not within the gift of either party – a factor which makes mediation in SEN disagreement resolution unlike mediation in other settings.

In the United States we had heard from all sides that there were benefits to mediation, many of which were unexpected and which helped not just to settle a matter in dispute but also to improve dialogue, understanding and relationships. We wanted to build into our service the cascading of benefits to as wide a range of stakeholders as possible and we wanted our mediators and service users to play as full a part in that process as possible.

We believed that one way of achieving our not-for-profit ethos at the same time as working towards this objective was to try to deliver the service in partnership with voluntary organisations. The plan was to recruit some of our mediators from these organisations and over time to transfer the management of the service to a voluntary organisation. The arrangement would be that the nominating organisation would receive the fee for the mediation in return for allowing the member of staff time to act as a mediator for an agreed number of days per year. The training of the candidate as a mediator would be provided free of charge. Mediators selected and trained through this process would however not mediate cases in their own area of specialism.

This strategy, which received support from the voluntary agencies approached, was intended to spread the benefit of training and the lessons learnt in service delivery through the organisations involved on the one hand, and to gain from the skill and knowledge spectrum represented by the voluntary sector on the other.

A meeting of interested organisations was held, as a result of which several agreed to identify candidates from their staff for possible selection for training as mediators.

In addition to voluntary sector recruitment we wanted to draw our mediators from a range of walks of life – people who had experience and skills on which we could build in training. Advertisements were placed in London-specific press and through LEAs in community newsletters and LEA recruitment lists:

> No specific qualifications are required but candidates will need to have excellent inter-personal and communication skills, the ability to stay calm under pressure and commitment to non-adversarial means of dispute resolution . . . We aim to build a service that reflects and celebrates the diversity of London. Applications are therefore welcome from all sections of the community and are particularly encouraged from under-represented groups . . .
>
> (*Big Issue*, 21 May 2001)

An excellent response to the advertisement resulted in a large number of high-quality candidates being recruited. Some of those had previous experience as mediators in workplace, community and international settings. Others had counselling experience. A wide range of occupations and professions were represented by the applicants. The gender balance was also good. Although black African/Afro-Caribbean representation was reasonably proportional, applications from other minority ethnic groups were low, thus exposing a weakness in the advertising strategy which the service is addressing.

The selection process involved three stages:

- completion of an application form supported by confidential references,
- interview,
- assessment during initial training.

The initial training course took place over three and a half days with assessed tasks taking place during that time. The focus during the training course was on the development of mediation skills. Subsequent training has looked at process and how the mediator uses the process to guide the parties towards looking at a resolution of their disagreement.

We have not attempted to train our mediators as experts in special educational needs. The emphasis has been kept on their role as a facilitator in control of the process but not the content. Having said that, they have had some briefing in aspects of SEN legislation and the tensions created by the competing factors within the system. Those selected as mediators for the London SEN Disagreement Resolution Service are also expected to take part in continuing professional development provided by the service and develop their own knowledge and expertise through self-study.

Our mediators are subject to quality control through evaluation by participants in the mediation, scrutiny of their record in facilitating the resolution of disagreement, the quality of the agreements they write and through performance monitoring (subject to the agreement of the parties to the mediation).

Design of the service itself has been influenced both by the concerns of LEA officers and the model of practice seen in the United States. The service does not require any administration by the LEA or parent – it is as paperless as possible. Initial contact is by telephone and subsequent documentation is drawn up by the service.

The time spent on a mediated session is intended to be not longer than about four hours. Sessions will be scheduled to start mid-morning and finish by mid-afternoon, thus allowing parents time to drop off and collect other children from school and enabling LEA officers to be at their desks at either end of the day. (There is of course flexibility about timing depending on the circumstances of the individual case.)

For the working of the referral process, see Figure 2.

Currently (2001/2002), the service is provided free of charge to London LEAs. This is possible because of grant aid from the DfES to support the introduction of SEN Disagreement Resolution. However, we are confident of longer-term, low-cost sustainability through the approach we have adopted of combining consultation with service users, partnership working, developing and disseminating training and modelling service delivery.

The mediators we have trained and recruited are an exceptional group of people. They are highly skilled and motivated individuals each with a strong commitment to empowering people to resolve their difficulties in this way. They are enthusiastic about having the opportunity to engage in the process of service development with the other stakeholders and they are very keen for the service to be a success. So at this time, as we start our service, we are quietly confident of making a small difference by providing improved opportunities for parents and LEAs/schools to listen to respond to each other, to understand each other's needs and constraints, to resolve conflict and, in so doing, to build positive relationships in the interests of children.

Referral made by phone by LEA/school or parent.
Other party's details taken and brief details of the disagreement.

▼

Disagreement Resolution Service telephones other party to explain that referral has been made, introduce the service and establish whether other party is willing to take part in mediation.

▼

| If yes, brief details of the disagreement from this party's perspective are taken. | If no, SEN Disagreement Resolution Service contacts the referrer to inform. |

▼

| SEN Disagreement Resolution Service prepares documentation for each party setting out what they have described as the main areas of disagreement. | ► | This is sent to each party to confirm accuracy. Each party is asked to sign copy and return in s.a.e provided. |

▼

| LEA is asked to arrange suitable venue and inform Disagreement Resolution Service of details, location and travel directions. | Once confirmation received copy of documentation is sent by SEN Disagreement Resolution Service to each party with the name of mediator and details of the venue. |

▼

Mediation takes place.
If agreement is reached, this is written up and a copy given to each of the parties. The mediator sends a further copy to the SEN Disagreement Resolution Service.
Participants in the mediation are asked to complete evaluation forms and return them in sealed envelope to the mediator who sends them in to the SEN Disagreement Resolution Service.

Figure 2 The referral process

4.5 ESTABLISHING A REGIONAL SERVICE FOR DISAGREEMENT RESOLUTION – THE EXPERIENCE OF TWO REGIONAL PARTNERSHIPS

Hugh Clench and *Lindsey Rousseau*

In 2001 the DfES channelled money through the recently established SEN Regional Partnerships, to assist LEAs in responding to the new legislative requirement of the SEN and Disability Act 2001 to make independent arrangement for the resolution of disagreements between schools and LEAs, on the one hand, and parents, on the other.

The account below describes the process of setting up a regional service across the South Central and South East Regional partnerships, covering nineteen LEAs in the south of England. At the time of writing the service had just been established, and will provide the participating LEAs with valuable evaluative data, which will inform their decision-making in 2003, when the grant money runs out. They will then have to decide how best to continue to offer the service.

The SEN and Disability Act 2001

The SEN and Disability Act 2001 modified the Education Act 1996 in a number of ways. In particular, from January 2002, section 332B was modified as follows:

> A local education authority must make arrangements, that include the appointment of independent persons, with a view to avoiding or resolving disagreements between authorities (on the one hand) and parents of children in their area (on the other) about the way LEAs and maintained schools carry out their responsibilities towards children with special educational needs.

> A local education authority must also make arrangements with a view to avoiding or resolving disagreements between parents and certain schools about the special educational provision made for their child.

> LEAs must take whatever steps they consider appropriate to make disagreement resolution services known to parents, head teachers, schools and others they consider appropriate.

It was in this context that a decision was taken by the DfES to make grant money available through the Regional Partnerships, to assist LEAs in responding to this new legislative requirement.

Both the South Central and South East Regional Partnerships had already identified parent partnership as project themes, and regional working groups were established in both areas. In the view of the similarity of the objectives of both groups, an early decision was taken in response to these developments to merge to form a single working group covering both partnerships.

LEA concerns

When the regional partnerships were first established there was a mixed response from LEAs. Whilst some readily embraced the concept, which in some areas reflected groupings which had already been formed, others were suspicious of a hidden government agenda to undermine the authority of LEAs and regionalise some educational services. Although these fears had largely been overcome by the end of the first year of the Partnerships, the decision to channel money through them to support the establishment of independent services for disagreement resolution reawoke these fears.

In addition, a small number of LEAs had already commissioned independent services from the voluntary sector, and they felt that these arrangements had not been recognised and would be put at risk.

Whilst this was largely a concern of senior LEA officers, a further issue arose among Parent Partnership officers who regarded themselves as independent of the LEA. Many of these had made great efforts to establish their independence from LEA decision-making processes in the eyes of parents, some having been recruited from advocacy backgrounds. There was therefore considerable discussion about the meaning of the term independent, which was not resolved until the DfES made it clear that this meant, 'not employed by the LEA'.

Gaining consensus

Within this context the process of gaining consensus across nineteen LEAs was not an easy one. Initial discussions took place in three regional working groups before the formation of the merged group covering the whole of the South East. Attendance at regional meetings rarely exceeds two-thirds due to the heavy commitments of LEA officers, which meant that membership of the same group would vary from one meeting to the next. Discussion leading to the resolution of issues at one meeting would often have to be repeated at the next meeting to ensure the commitment of all concerned.

Perhaps the most difficult of these in the early stages was reaching agreement concerning the term mediation. In initial discussions a variety of additional terms were used including conciliation and arbitration, resulting in a degree of confusion. In the event the definitions given by Jane Hall (1999) in her research report conducted for the DfES in 1999 were adopted.

Mediation: a process of dispute resolution involving a neutral third party who controls the process but not the outcome, and is not involved in decision-making. The overall aim is to achieve a win-win outcome.

Conciliation: a process that is more concerned with mending relationships and resolving problems. Conciliation may be needed both before and following mediation.

Arbitration: a process in which a neutral third party is brought in to resolve a dispute by deciding who is right. One party stands to win and the other to lose.

At the same time as these discussions were taking place through the regional partnerships a debate over terminology was being conducted at the DfES whilst the revised Code of Practice was being written. Confusion between the terms mediation and conciliation had led to the adoption of the term 'dispute resolution' as employed by Jane Hall in her research (1999). However, in recognition of the fact that not all lack of agreement results in a dispute, the word 'disagreement' was substituted.

Within the region, once the definitions had been clarified, it was agreed to adopt the term mediation and to use it synonymously with the term disagreement resolution preferred by the DfES. To consolidate the regional identity of the mediation service it was also agreed that wherever possible information linked to the service would be the same across all nineteen LEAs.

The level of demand

A further issue, which generated considerable discussion, was the anticipated level of demand amongst parents. On the one hand the view was expressed that parents would be unlikely to opt for independent mediation if Parent Partnership Officers had been unable to resolve the issue. Why would parents be prepared to engage in a further time consuming exercise when the SEN tribunal could arbitrate and give them a clear decision one way or the other?

On the other hand, some LEAs were concerned that demand could spiral out of control once parent groups became aware of their new rights, putting further pressure on LEA SEN budgets which were already difficult to control. Whilst the grant was available for the first two years to assist LEAs in setting up services, from March 2003 LEAs would be obliged to pick up the costs themselves.

It was impossible to predict what might happen, but an estimate had to be made of the likely level of demand before a tender document could be prepared. This was also necessary to reach a decision about how much grant money should be used to finance the mediation process, and how much to provide training to LEA and school staff to help them avoid disagreements arising in the first place. An estimate was made from tribunal statistics across the region, based on the number of cases actually being heard by the tribunal – i.e. registered and not resolved prior to tribunal. While it was recognised that it was unlikely that all such cases would go to mediation it was felt to be the best estimate that could be made in the circumstances.

One critical piece of information, which shaped discussion at this stage, was a series of caveats being prepared by the DfES to go in the SEN Toolkit accompanying the revised CoP relating to the disagreement resolution process. These recognised that mediation may be inappropriate if:

- either side does not wish to engage in the process;
- matters of policy are at stake;
- the main issue is one that would set a precedent on which the LEA is unwilling or unable to proceed;
- there is no goodwill;
- there is a substantial change in the relationship between the parents and the LEA or school, for instance the parents have moved or are moving to another LEA area, or the child is about to transfer to a different school.

(SEN Toolkit, Section 3, Resolution of Disagreements, para. 19)

LEA officers pointed out that the only cases which generally go to tribunal are those where matters of LEA policy are at stake, and where the LEA does not wish to set a precedent by going against its stated policies. This suggested that fewer cases might be appropriate for mediation than had been imagined.

The other significant caveat is the first one listed above, which indicates that both parties have to be willing. Elsewhere in both the revised Code of Practice, and the SEN Toolkit, the role of Parent Partnership Officers in avoiding and resolving disagreements is emphasised and supported. The conclusion was quickly reached that LEAs would not normally be willing to go to mediation unless these services, and other appropriate avenues, had been explored first. It was recognised there may be circumstances where this might not happen. However, such circumstances were likely to be the exception rather than the norm, and to reflect this regional criteria were drawn up for referral to mediation. These were:

- The issue should be an SEN issue and not another type of complaint.
- The parties (including schools where appropriate) should have met, discussed the issues, and explored alternatives and this discussion should include those able to make decisions.
- Where appropriate, other agencies should have been involved.
- Parent partnership services should normally have been involved to try to resolve the disagreement.
- If the disagreement is with a maintained school (including city academies and CTCs) the headteacher and governing body should have been involved.
- If the disagreement relates to any part of the statutory assessment process referral should only be made at key decision points.
- Possible solutions should normally fall within LEA policy.

The definition of what constitutes an SEN issue was felt to be a potentially difficult area. While it was anticipated that most cases would be clear-cut, it was felt likely that there would be some where the boundaries were blurred. One example might be where there is a complaint about the relationship between a learning support assistant or teacher and a pupil with special educational needs. Parents might view this as an SEN issue when it should normally be dealt with through the school's complaints procedure. It was felt that, over a period of time, it would be possible to build up a series of relevant examples across the region, which could be used to guide future decision-making.

Conditions of grant and priorities for the two partnerships

One of the conditions of grant from the DfES was that the voluntary sector should be involved, amounting to an average of 75 per cent across the country. In addition, the bulk of the money was seen as supporting training, although each region was free to reach its own decisions about how the money was used.

Given the new legislative requirement for LEAs to provide parents with access to independent arrangements for disagreement resolution by January 2002, our first priority was to establish an independent service across the region. We wished to involve the voluntary sector as far as possible and use some of the grant money to establish the service without any financial cost to the LEAs concerned. As well as assisting LEAs financially with the costs of this new service, the fact that LEAs were not paying would help to reinforce the independence of the service in the eyes of parents. The regional steering group would act as the monitoring body for the service.

Our second priority was to use the remainder of the money for training purposes within schools and LEAs, to improve the skills and processes necessary to avoid disagreements arising in the first place. A regional training group was established to plan this development.

The tendering process

To achieve this first priority a specification was drawn up describing the service required, and an advertisement was placed in a national newspaper inviting tenders. All information was also made available on the SCRIP and SERSEN websites.

A description of the tendering process accompanied the specification, and included the criteria, which would be used in drawing up a shortlist. Organisations, which were shortlisted by a regional panel, were invited to make a presentation. They had received feedback on their tender indicating the areas in which the panel would be seeking further information. The purpose of this was to give every opportunity for the organisation to put forward its best case. The selection process throughout was conducted on an equal opportunities basis.

At the end of this process a contract was offered to the selected provider and feedback was given to those who had been unsuccessful. The contract was signed on 18 December 2001 in time to meet the deadline for implementation of 1 January 2002.

The regional specification is reproduced in Section 10, together with a description of the tendering process. Finally, the overall SEN disagreement process, presented as a decision-making grid and flow-diagram, is shown in Figure 3.

References

The SEN and Disability Act (2001), London: HMSO.
The Education Act (1996), London: HMSO.
Hall, J. (1999) *Resolving Disputes between Parents, Schools and LEAs: Some Examples of Best Practice.* DFEE.
Special Educational Needs Code of Practice, DfES (2001).
SEN Toolkit, DfES (2001).

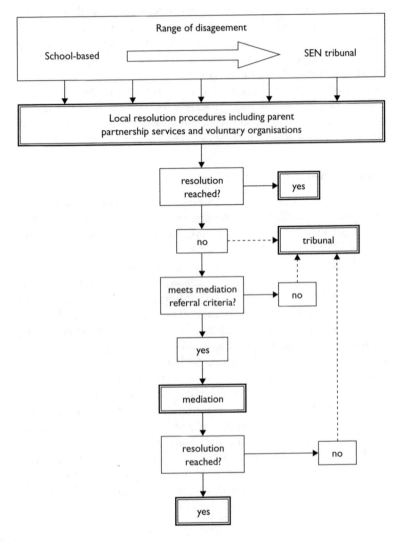

Figure 3 SEN disagreement resolution process

4.6 PEER MEDIATION: INVOLVING CHILDREN IN MEDIATION

Mari-Cruz Taboada Lopez and Moray McLaren

Introduction

Conflict in schools is currently part of the national agenda.

Social inclusion policies and the National Healthy School initiative aim to involve staff, pupils, governors, parents and the wider community in reducing conflicts both inside and outside schools.

At their heart these initiatives aim to:

- reduce problems with truancy and juvenile crime;
- encourage young people to be good citizens;
- reduce social exclusions, disadvantage and disaffection;
- encourage pupils to became healthy, mature grown-ups;
- charge them with important tasks – like graffiti control or anti-bullying strategies.[1]

For the last ten years, Southwark Mediation Centre's (SMC) peer mediation programmes have tackled many of these issues by enabling young people to develop in a positive way.

Teachers tell us that they are spending an increasing amount of time intervening in disputes between individuals. These typically are verbal insults, fights, threats and intimidation. It has been suggested that students use coercion and manipulation more than reasoning to resolve their conflicts. When conflicts escalate schools have resorted to exclusion.

Working in cooperation with teachers, our peer mediation programmes provide young people with the dispute resolution skills required to help resolve conflicts that arise between fellow students.

These programmes were introduced in order to:

- provide a forum to resolve conflicts between students in the playground;
- reduce aggressive behaviour in general; and
- improve the environment in schools.

As we shall see, peer mediation has been very successful in Southwark, in particular in the schools where it has been sustained over a period of time. The scope of the work has also expanded to include cases of serious complaints from parents about schools, as well as cases where conflicts between school students have escalated into conflicts between families.

Southwark Mediation Centre

Established in 1985, SMC was one of the first mediation centres to pioneer peer mediation in the UK. To date, we have established peer mediation in twelve schools (seven primaries and five secondary) and trained over 400 pupils as peer mediators.

One of the main messages of the centre is that conflict is a normal and natural part of our lives. Handled in the right way, conflict may lead to creative solutions to problems. In all but exceptional circumstances, we are all responsible for our own behaviour. The vast majority of people want relationships to improve and they respond positively to appeals for change.

Funding

There are a variety of ways in which we can work with schools. Typically we jointly seek external funds from bodies such as LEAs, community initiative groups and the European Union to pilot a one-year scheme. After the first year, schools often find funding from their own budget or apply themselves for funding. At this stage, we would typically develop a rolling two-year partnership agreement.

Structure

Peer mediation projects are managed by an experienced mediator in his or her role as a project coordinator. The coordinator's role includes:

- liaising with a teacher who will overview the programme;
- providing external support to teachers, saving them time by taking full responsibility for the project;
- training a team of peer mediators and visiting them once or twice a week to make sure that the mediation service is running smoothly.

Getting started

Assembly

In order to introduce the service, the coordinator makes a presentation in assembly about the mediation service and its role in developing a culture of problem-solving within the school.

Selection process

The school manages the selection of the students. Typically, students volunteer. In some cases, teachers encourage students who they feel may gain most from participating.

Teachers will short-list and select the final group. Once trained, mediators will only work with children of their own age or younger. Every year a new team is trained, with the experienced mediators providing support to the new group.

Time

Ideally the training is completed in twenty-six hours, over five school days (what we call fast-track). In secondary schools, however, a more intense curriculum means that training is divided over two to three months.

Content

The training is highly relationship-orientated, choosing methods that stress and focus on communication and the quality of personal relationships.

Training focuses on the following key skills:

* asking questions
* active listening
* understanding confidentiality as well as knowing when teachers must be informed
* the use of language and reframing negative comments into positive comments
* supporting each other in a team.

Methodology

At the start, the coordinator and students establish 'golden rules' of behaviour to follow during the training and afterwards (e.g. not arguing or interrupting each other). Students understand that participation is voluntary and requires focus and consistency.

The training is interactive, combining hard work and fun. Exercises allow the students to learn about their own emotions. They practise at school and with family at home feeding back their experiences to the group. While the coordinator guides the role play, students make up their own role play disputes.

Through acting as disputants, they better understand the emotions people feel in conflict. Teachers and support staff observe and can join in the training to have a better understanding of the concepts.

Oliver Goldsmith School has recently introduced a scheme. The deputy head, Angie Law, has suggested:

> Most of the mediators (Years 4, 5 and 6) are proud of the role and responsibility that they have, and for some young people it has been a real opportunity for them to show their strengths and skills in communication.

The mediators agreement

On completion of the training, students sign an agreement that they will obey certain rules. These include:

- to be fair and not take sides
- to listen to parties and help them to find their own solution (not tell them what to do)
- to keep everything confidential ('no gossip in the playground')
- to try to behave at all times ('not to get into arguments or put others down')
- to show respect to adults and pupils.

Certificates

After the training the group is awarded with their certificates at assembly and their roles are explained fully to the rest of the students.

Implementation

The service works normally at lunchtime but in some circumstances mediations happen after school. Schools typically have a group of twenty to twenty-four peer mediators to cover the weekly service.

The coordinator encourages students to take responsibility for organising the service. In our experience, students can coordinate the timetable and even develop systems to make the service more efficient.

Typically four mediators are on service at any time. Two circulate in the playground with a mediator badge or armband so the other children know who they are. They identify disputes and invite both parties to mediation. If the parties accept they take them to a room where the two other mediators will be ready to start the mediation process.

The mediation

All four pupils go through a careful stage-by-stage process which involves:

- Outlining the ground rules which guide the way the session will be held. The mediators typically read this from a sheet. Both parties must agree to this for the session to proceed.
- Listening to the disputants side of the story one by one.
- Identifying their feelings and needs.
- In a joint session, the parties will suggest options for progress and then agree on a course of action.
- Finally, where possible, disputants sign a short agreement outlining how they will or will not act in future. This is often accompanied by an oral apology.

Case study 1 – secondary school

One weekend, girl A received several confrontational text messages addressed to her and girl B. On Monday morning at school, girl A received another message. After discussing it with girl B they decided to speak with a peer mediator at break-time. Both felt they knew who it was and the reasons behind it. The mediator approached the alleged perpetrators (girl C, girl D and boy E) at break-time and after talking to them about the situation, they agreed to mediation.

During the session all five clients kept to the ground rules and acted with respect towards each other. The process gave parties C,

D and E a clearer understanding of the fear some text messages can bring to individuals. Forty minutes later, agreement was reached as they apologised and agreed not to send prank text messages again.

It was an intense and emotional session and the mediators considered referring the case to an adult. But they were driven by the fact that everyone concerned wanted to improve the situation. After the session, the peer mediators commented upon the new friendship between the parties.

Advantages to schools

Peer mediation schemes provide a means whereby small conflicts can be resolved before they escalate. The majority of schools report that they have become more peaceful. Students know that they have a dispute resolution system that is confidential and non-confrontational.

The reduction in fights and verbal abuse in the playground reflects on exclusion rates or cases of truancy among children intimidated by bullying or other cases of anti-social behaviour.

Teacher time and stress is reduced as some of the need for disciplining, having to judge who is telling the truth and enforcement is lessened. As a result, they have more time and energy to devote to other areas.

Headteacher Joyce Manyan at Camelot Primary School told us:

The idea of peer mediation started three years ago and is going strong with more and more youngsters deciding to take up a mediator post each year. SMC peer mediation scheme has surpassed my wildest dreams – I dreamed about all this happening. I can't believe it has come true.

Case study 2 – secondary school

This secondary school conflict – involving three pupils – had a knock-on effect that resulted in a face-to-face clash between the parents outside the school.

The conflict started with a single fight between students, then spread into a number of ongoing fights as it engulfed others. The school considered disciplinary action such as excluding the students and barring the parents from the school. This would have solved the immediate problem but not the source of conflict.

The school asked two adult SMC mediators to help resolve the conflict. After direct mediation with the pupils the original conflict was resolved, stopping the wider dispute among other pupils. SMC then engaged in indirect mediation between the parents. Finally there was a successful face-to-face mediation with the teachers and both sets of parents.

The parents felt their concerns were addressed and were happy their children could attend the school without fear of further conflict. The school felt the parents were now at a stage of working together to address issues around conflict between their children.

Advantages to peer mediators

Trusting children to solve their own problems has shown, in SMC's experience, that it can improve relationships in schools. The peer mediation scheme starts from the assumption that children can make decisions and that they will respond positively to being accepted and valued by adults and their peers.

Students develop their skills in listening, communication, negotiating and problem-solving. Children with a lack of affection, problems at home or aggressive behaviour have responded extremely positively to this experience. Their self-esteem improves and their school performance often improves too.

A ten-year-old mediator of Camelot Primary School told us:

> I now have a lot more self-control. I try not getting into arguments or put others down. It's all about staying calm and talking things over.

A fellow mediator said she enjoyed the responsibility but added that it was not about telling people what to do:

> you can't take sides and you must get those arguing to find a solution themselves.

In addition, the more experienced secondary school peer mediators have the opportunity to work alongside adult mediators in SMC's community disputes that involve children.

Case study 3 – family disputes

The case involved two families, parent A and girl B and parent C with three girls, D, E and F, who lived in the same block of flats. The children's ages ranged from six to twelve.

SMC mediators were asked by parents A and C to intervene in their conflict which started with allegations that girls D, E and F were bullying B. The parents had different theories about bringing up children. A felt C was neglecting her girls, C felt A was overprotective.

From the beginning both sides agreed that mediation was not going to establish the 'ideal' method to raise a child but it could aid communication between parties preventing future conflict.

With the permission of her parents and teachers, a SMC mediator worked with an experienced fourteen-year-old peer mediator. As they visited both families, it was clear the fear and lack of trust was a key issue amongst the children.

A joint session was prepared for the children by the peer and adult mediator and the process was adapted to take account of the age of the youngest. Through games the mediators developed a question-and-answer process. Suggestions to solve the dispute were awarded. As there was an imbalance of numbers amongst the girls, there were three short sessions with girl A (aged six) meeting the others one by one before a final joint session.

The case is being monitored and to date there have been no further incidents. Everyone has reported a great improvement in their relationship.

Serious incidents

Following on from its experience in peer mediation, SMC adult mediators have been instructed on cases where parents have become involved in conflicts related to their children. In particular, when serious problems arise amongst students, schools might find that their decision is being challenged by the parents and may therefore lead to a complaint and possible legal action. These cases are often referred to the centre by the police.

Case study 4 – primary school

The case involved two boys in conflict. One parent self-excluded their son for six months, as they felt this would pressure the school to resolve the matter. The school felt that it lacked evidence to prove allegations of violence which the alleged offender and his parents were denying.

Both sets of parents were angry, feeling that the school should resolve the issue. The school invited SMC to mediate between the boys and separately between the parents together with a school representative.

At their session, the boys explained they both had felt intimidated by the other and discussed the consequences of their behaviour on themselves, their families and the school. The session ended in agreement with both parting on good terms.

At the joint meeting with the parents, parties discussed where they felt the responsibility for the situation sat – with the boys, parents or the school. The school representative explained the procedures they followed and was asked for clarification.

The process was successful, and after the second session the self-excluded student rejoined school.

Conclusion

SMC is one of the growing number of mediation centres working with schools to provide peer mediation services.

This chapter has provided only a general overview of the subject matter and more detailed research is required on the specific advantages and disadvantages of such schemes. In particular, it would be interesting to compare exclusion numbers between schools with and without peer mediation.

Needless to say, that demand for peer mediation is growing. In an ideal world, we would provide dispute resolution training to all children, parents and teachers associated with a school. Funding is a key issue as LEAs, like schools, have limited finances.

It is perhaps inevitable that the increasing severity of disputes, especially those resulting in exclusion, lead to disputes between parents and teachers (often groups of parents and teachers). As we have seen in Southwark, it is only a small step from providing peer mediation programmes to providing dispute resolution services to a wider range of disputes in schools between teachers, parents or any members of the school community.

Acknowledgements

We are grateful to Melanie Bruce, Southwark Mediation Centre peer mediation project manager, and David Walker, Southwark Mediation Centre coordinator, for their support with this chapter.

Notes

1 Details of the National Healthy School initiative is available on the Department of Education's website.

Chapter 5

The SEN tribunal

Simon Oliver

Structure and administration

History

The Special Educational Needs Tribunal for England and Wales was established by the Education Act 1993 and started work on 1 September 1994. It was created to overcome a perceived problem of delay in the former system under which parents were first required to appeal to a local committee of the local authority and then, if dissatisfied, to appeal to the Secretary of the State. However, courts only granted the parents a remedy for a delay which was 'unreasonable' and 'reprehensible'. The intention of the new procedure was not only to make it easier for parents to appeal but also to ensure that the decision about a child's future was made as quickly as possible. The tribunal is governed by regulations which set a clear timetable for each stage of the appeal process.

The tribunal is regulated by s333 Education Act 1996 and exercises its jurisdiction pursuant to regulations. The current governing regulations are the Special Educational Needs Tribunal Regulations 2001 and the Education (Special Educational Needs) (England) (Consolidation) Regulations 2001. Trevor Aldridge QC has been President of the tribunal since it was established. In addition to the President there are two panels; the chairman's panel and the lay panel. There is a secretariat based in London and Darlington to handle appeals and service the tribunal.

Members

The President determines both the number of tribunals to be established from time to time and also the times and places they may sit. Since members of both panels reside throughout England and Wales, the tribunal is widely travelled. For example, on one day in February

2002, the tribunal was hearing cases in London, Birmingham, Bristol, Oxford, Salisbury, Carlisle, Chester, Hull and Leeds. Subject to one of the lay members being absent at or after the commencement of a hearing, the tribunal shall consist of a chairman (being either the President or a person selected from the chairman's panel) and two other members selected from the lay panel.

Clerks and the Secretary of the Tribunal

The Special Educational Needs Tribunal is based at the office of the tribunal in London (7th Floor, Windsor House, 50 Victoria Street, London SW1H 0NW). From early 1996 however, tribunals for the north of England have been dealt with from the Department for Education and Skills' office in Darlington (Mowden Hall, Staindrop Road, Darlington, DL3 9BG). The tribunal helpline is 01325 392555 and there is a website which has useful information: www.sentribunal.gov.uk.

The Secretariat staff 'clerk' all tribunal hearings, although they have no role in deciding the outcome of the appeal. The tribunal consistently received between thirty and thirty-five appeals per week in its first year but that increased to an average of sixty per week by August 2001. A clear and helpful guide to the tribunal has been produced, copies of which are available from the DfES Publications Centre (0845 60 222 60). The Secretary of the tribunal (and so the senior civil servant) is Kevin Mullany. He is senior civil servant in the tribunal. The Secretary is the person to whom, for example, all documents must be sent, who must be notified of the name and address of a party's representative and who is responsible for notifying the parties of the decision of the tribunal after a hearing.

Wales and Welsh

The tribunal has a responsibility to provide its service in Welsh to parents and local education authorities in Wales if they wish. There is a Welsh form of the Notice of Appeal. The tribunal has a chairman and lay members who are native Welsh speakers. The Education Bill 2002 contains proposals for the creation of a separate tribunal for Wales.

Council on tribunals

The Special Educational Needs Tribunal is supervised by the Council on Tribunals whose function is both to supervise the procedures and working of tribunals and inquiries and advise government departments.

Members of the Council visit tribunal hearings as observers to assess how the procedures are operating. Further information about the Council's function can be obtained from the Secretary. Both the Council on Tribunals and Sir Andrew Leggett (who conducted a review of the operations of tribunals during 2000/2001) regard the tribunal as an excellent example of how a tribunal should operate.

Northern Ireland

In 1997 the Northern Ireland Special Educational Needs Tribunal was established by the Education (Northern Ireland) Order 1996 which incorporates into Northern Ireland (with appropriate amendments) the English and Welsh parts of the Education Act. It has similar powers and functions as the English and Welsh tribunal although it is governed by different regulations (The Special Educational Needs Tribunal Regulations 1997). The tribunal has six chairmen and fourteen lay members. It is based at Alban House, 73-75 Great Victoria Street, Belfast, BT2 7AF, telephone number 028 9032 2494. The e-mail address is *enquiries.sentribunal@nics.gov.uk*.

Codes of practice

The provision of special educational needs in schools is regulated by a Code of Practice. The first code was issued in 1994 but after consultation a new code was issued in late 2001. It came into force on 1 January 2002. In addition a 'SEN Toolkit' has been produced which contains additional information. The tribunal is required to 'have regard to' the Code in considering appeals.

There is a separate Code of Practice for Wales which was published in April 2002. It is similar, but not identical, to the English Code.

Procedure for appealing

The appeal has to be lodged within two months of the date of the decision of the local education authority (LEA).

Since September 2001, the procedure has been that once an appeal by a parent has been registered, both parties have a period of time (thirty days) in which to submit a 'Case Statement'. This is done at the same time as the other party, rather than consecutively as before. The LEA's case statement must set out the views of the child about the issues raised in the appeal.

Types of appeal

The Education Act 1996 gives the Special Educational Needs Tribunal jurisdiction to hear six types of appeal:

Section 329:	against a refusal to make an assessment;
Section 325:	against a refusal to make a statement;
Section 326:	against the contents of a statement;
Section 328:	against a refusal to reassess special educational needs;
Schedule 27, para. 8:	against change of a named school, and
Schedule 27, para. 11:	against a decision to cease to maintain a statement.

Appeal against a local education authority's refusal to carry out a statutory assessment

This applies where there is no statement. The duty to assess is contained in section 323 and may be instigated by either a referral by the child's school or another agency or by a formal request for assessment by a parent. In the last case where

1 no assessment has been made within the six months before the request; and
2 it is 'necessary' for the LEA to make an assessment, there is a duty to assess.

This gives rise to the inevitable question: when is it 'necessary' to assess? The answer lies in linking section 329 with s.323. The latter states that an LEA must carry out an assessment where a child has, or probably has, special educational needs; and it is, or probably is, necessary for the LEA to determine the special educational provision which any learning difficulty the child may have calls for.

Parents may appeal against the LEA's decision not to comply with the request for an assessment whether it was made by them or the school.

It should be noted, however, that the fact that a child has special educational needs does not lead the LEA to the conclusion that a statutory assessment is 'necessary'. (R -v- Secretary of State for Educational and Science, ex parte Lashford (1988) 1 FLR 72.) In reality most cases will turn on the extent to which the child's needs are being addressed under the school-based stages of the Code of Practice. In other words, if the school is providing considerable support and the child is making progress it is unlikely that there will be an assessment. Although a statutory assessment is often seen by parents as a way of obtaining additional provision (or securing it) for their child, this is not the basis upon which the tribunal will consider the appeal.

The tribunal has the power either to dismiss the appeal or order the LEA to arrange for an assessment to be carried out. By reason of Regulation 25 of The Education (Special Educational Needs) (England) (Consolidation) Regulations 2001 and Section 4 of the Special Educational Need and Disability Act 2001, the LEA has to start the assessment within four weeks of the tribunal's order. These regulations came into force on 1 January 2002 for England and 1 April 2002 for Wales.

Appeal against the LEA's refusal to make a statement of a child's special educational needs

The appeal is found in section 325: After carrying out an assessment of a pupil's special educational needs under s.323, the LEA must decide whether it is 'necessary' for it to determine (by means of a statement) the 'special educational provision which any learning difficulty the child may have calls for'. In other words, will it issue a statement? If the LEA decides not to make a statement, parents may appeal to the tribunal. As can be seen, the meaning of 'necessary' is again an issue. It must be considered against the policy intention that only a minority of those children (usually regarded as 2 per cent) with special educational needs will have a statement. It follows that a statutory assessment does not necessarily lead to a statement.

The Code of Practice offers some guidance on what 'necessary' was intended to mean. The tribunal has power when hearing the appeal to dismiss the appeal or to order the LEA to make and maintain a statement or to remit the case to the LEA to consider whether, having regard to any observations made by the SENT, it is necessary for the LEA to determine the special educational provision which the child's learning difficulties call for.

If an LEA is ordered to make a statement, it must do so within 5 weeks of the tribunal's order or, if it is required to reconsider whether or not to make a statement, within two weeks of the tribunal's order.

Appeal against the contents of a statement

Section 324(3) of the Education Act 1996 provides that a statement must give details of the LEA's assessment of the child's needs (this is usually found in Part 2); specify the educational provision to be made to meet those needs (in Part 3); and, in Part 4, specify the type of school which is appropriate for the child and name the maintained school for which the parent has specified a preference.

Under s.326, a parent may appeal against the description in the statement of the LEA's assessment of the child's special educational needs; the special educational provision specified in the statement; or against the school named in the statement or, if no school is named in the statement, against that fact.

The right of appeal arises when the statement is first made; where the description of the child's needs in Part 2 or the provision specified in Part 3 or the school named in Part 4 is amended; or where, after reassessing the child's needs under section 323, the LEA decides not to amend the statement.

Appeals under s.326 tend to be the most complex and there is now a good deal of case law highlighting the distinction between educational provision and health, or social care provision, and on the question of 'specificity'.

Sometimes in s.326 appeals, although the parents have only appealed against the provision specified in Part 3 of the statement they are, in fact, also concerned with the LEA's description of the child's needs in Part 2. The same may happen when the appeal appears to be only against the school named in Part 4. Usually, the President will issue directions in advance, asking parents to clarify the basis of their appeal. Sometimes the matter is not raised until the hearing.

This is usually not a problem because parents may, in exceptional circumstances, with the permission of the tribunal at the hearing itself, amend the notice of appeal. In addition the tribunal may, if it is satisfied that it is just and reasonable to do so, permit a party to rely on grounds not stated in his notice of appeal.

If the notice of appeal is not amended or a parent is not permitted to rely on any new grounds, the tribunal will not be in error of law if it determines the appeal on the basis of the notice of appeal. As it is standard practice to explore the issues to be determined with the parties at the start of the hearing it should not happen very often.

Frequently, some issues will be agreed and can be incorporated into the tribunal's decision by consent. When new issues are raised by one party at the hearing, the tribunal will need to consider if an adjournment is appropriate to allow the other party to file new evidence.

It is very important to note that the tribunal does not have jurisdiction in relation to Parts 5 or 6 of a statement. These relate to non-educational provision. Nevertheless if the tribunal makes consequential amendments to a statement (section 326(3)(b)) by, for example, ordering provision for speech and language therapy to be specified in Part 3 (as educational provision) it would consequently require the reference to such therapy to be deleted from Parts 5 and/or 6.

When deciding the appeal against the contents of a statement the tribunal may dismiss the appeal or order the LEA to amend some or all of Parts 2, 3 and 4 of the statement. The jurisdiction to make orders under this heading does not seem to be limited by the scope of the parents' appeal so could include those matters which are not necessarily in dispute; or order the LEA to cease to maintain the statement.

In trying to determine an appeal against Parts 2 and 3, the issues for the tribunal are: what are the educational needs of the child and what provision is appropriate to meet those needs?

In regard to an appeal against Part 4, the legal position about naming a school is complex. Section 324(4) provides that the LEA must specify in a statement the type of school appropriate for the child; the maintained school for which the child's parent or parents has/have specified a preference.

Section 316 of the Education Act 1996 has been amended so that a child must be educated in a mainstream school unless it is incompatible with either the wishes of his parent or the provision of efficient education for other children. This does not prevent a parent expressing a wish for an independent or non-maintained special school but does not permit the LEA to require a pupil to attend a special school if it is against the wishes of his parent.

The effect of these last two paragraphs is that there is a legal presumption in favour of parental choice of school. This is displaced where a statement is first made if the school is unsuitable to the child's age, ability or aptitude to her/his special educational needs; or where the attendance of the child at the school would be incompatible with the provision of efficient education for the children with whom s/he would be educated *or* the efficient use of resources (schedule 27, para. 3).

If the LEA is not required to name the preferred school, it must name another school which would be suitable for the child. That decision may then be challenged by parents by appeal to the tribunal. The only time the LEA does not have to name a school in Part 4 is if it believes that the parent is making suitable arrangements for the education of their child (Section 9 of the 2001 Act). This means that, for example, if the LEA is satisfied that the parents are providing suitable education at their own expense at an independent school, they are freed of any obligation to pay for that education.

Any amendments the tribunal orders the LEA to make to the statement must be done within five weeks of the tribunal's order.

Appeal against the LEA's refusal to reassess the educational needs of a child with a statement

Having a statement implies constant review and reassessment from time to time. There are no regulations setting out the frequency of a reassessment but an LEA must reassess on parental request where no assessment has been made within the period of six months ending with the date of request; and it is necessary to make a further assessment. Again it will be noted that Section 328 (2)(c) links 'necessary' in this case with Section 323 and it may be assumed that the s.323 criteria apply. However, 'necessary' could have a different meaning post-statement.

When hearing the appeal, the tribunal may either dismiss the appeal or order the LEA to arrange for a reassessment, the process must start within four weeks of the tribunal's order.

Appeal against the LEA's refusal to change the name of the school specified in a statement

Under schedule 27, para. 8 of the Education Act 1996, once twelve months have elapsed since a statement was made or amended, or since an appeal against the contents of a statement was determined, parents may request the naming of an alternative maintained school. Again, parental preference determines the outcome unless the LEA can show that the chosen school is unsuitable to the child's age, ability or aptitude, or to her/his special educational needs; or that the attendance of the child at the school would be incompatible with the provision of efficient education for the children with whom s/he would be educated or the efficient use of resources.

The wording of schedule 27 means that the tribunal has no jurisdiction to name an independent school where the appeal is brought under schedule 27. Where that is the parents' objective, the appeal must be struck out. This means that an independent school can only be named by the tribunal following an appeal against the contents of a statement under s.326.

At the hearing the tribunal may either dismiss the appeal; or order the LEA to substitute the parental choice of school in the statement. However, the tribunal only has power to name either the school specified by the parent in the notice of appeal or the school put forward by the

LEA. If an amendment is ordered, the statement must be amended within two weeks of the tribunal's order.

Appeal against the LEA's decision to cease to maintain a statement

The tribunal may either dismiss the appeal; or order the LEA to maintain the statement in its existing form, or with such amendments as the tribunal may determine.

Section 6 of the 2001 Act and Regulation 17(8) of the Consolidation Regulations prohibits the LEA from ceasing to maintain a statement until the right of appeal has lapsed (two months). If there is an appeal, the statement has to continue until the tribunal has made a decision.

The issue for the tribunal is whether the needs of the child are such that it is necessary for the LEA to continue to maintain the statement. The power to amend the statement is then based upon 'appropriateness'.

In Part 4 of the Education Act 1996 'child' means any person who has not attained the age of nineteen and is a registered pupil at a school. Where a young person over sixteen attends an FE college, therefore, the LEA may cease to maintain the statement as the young person is not a 'child' and is not a registered pupil at a school. The further education sector has its own special educational needs provision arrangements and, as a statement has no jurisdiction in respect of provision in the FE sector, an appeal against cessation of a statement must be struck out.

However, in S -v- Essex CC and the SENT TLR 10 May 2000, the Divisional Court held that the tribunal does have jurisdiction where an LEA does not give notice of its intention to cease to maintain a statement until a young person has left school. 'Child', therefore, is to be taken to include a child who was the subject of a statement at the time notice was given.

Whether the tribunal orders the statement to cease or continue, the order has immediate effect unless the LEA has set a later date upon which it will cease to maintain it.

Volume of work

During the year to 31 August 2001 the tribunal received 3,035 appeals (99/00, 2,642). This is an increase of 14.8 per cent with most of the additional appeals occurring in the second half of the year. There is always a proportion of appeals received which are not registered, either because they arrive out of time or they fall outside the tribunal's jurisdiction. Nevertheless, although those cases do not proceed, they do involve work for the secretariat. Of the 3,053 appeals received, the tribunal registered 2,728 appeals last year (99/00, 2,463) an increase of 10.8 per cent over the previous year (99/00, 2.1 per cent). This is the highest percentage increase for five years. The proportionate rise is confined to England; appeals registered against Welsh authorities during the year represented 4.1 per cent of the total (99/00, 4.3 per cent).

One statistic remains constant: 75 per cent of the appeals registered related to boys and 25 per cent to girls. This has been steady for three years.

Not all appeals registered resulted in an hearing. In the year to 31 August 2001, 1,368 appeals were withdrawn. This is an increase (99/00, 1,225) of 11.7 per cent, representing 53.1 per cent of appeals registered by the tribunal. During the year the tribunal heard 1,165 cases (99/00 1,155) and struck out 41 (99/00 41). The informal research carried out by the tribunal as to the reason for the large number of withdrawals suggests that in some 51.1 per cent of cases the LEA had fully complied with the parents' requests and in 34.7 per cent of the withdrawn cases there had been a negotiated settlement.

Types of appeal

868 cases were against a refusal to assess (being 31.8 per cent of the total) (99/00 774, 31.4 per cent);

229 cases were against refusal to make a statement (8.4 per cent) (99/00 264, 10.7 per cent);

53 cases were against a refusal to reassess (1.9 per cent) (99/00 56, 2.3 per cent);

74 cases were against a refusal to change the name of a school (2.7 per cent) (99/00 38, 1.5 per cent);

50 cases were against a decision to cease to maintain a statement (1.8 per cent) (99/00 61, 2.5 per cent);

10 cases were against a failure to name a school (0.4 per cent) (99/00 7, 0.3 per cent);

387 cases were against the contents of Parts 2 and 3 of the statement (14.2 per cent) (99/00 375, 15.2 per cent);

652 cases were against the contents of Parts 2, 3 and 4 of the statement (23.9 per cent) (99/00 604, 24.5 per cent);

405 were against the contents of Part 4 of the statement (14.8 per cent) (99/00 284, 11.5 per cent).

Nature of special educational needs in cases heard 00/01

Nature of SEN	Cases	%	99/00	%
Autism	402	14.7%	319	13.0%
Emotional and behavioural difficulties	384	14.1%	315	12.8%
Epilepsy	24	0.9%	31	1.3%
Hearing impairment	82	3.0%	75	3.0%
Literacy (including SpLD)	919	33.7%	932	37.8%
Moderate learning difficulties	139	5.1%	142	5.8%
Multi-sensory impairment	7	0.3%	4	0.2%
Physical difficulties	178	6.5%	124	5.0%
Severe learning difficulties	101	3.7%	75	3.0%
Speech and language difficulties	291	10.7%	274	11.1%
Visual impairment	36	1.3%	31	1.3%
Other/unknown	165	6.0%	141	5.7%

Outcome of appeals

Of the 1,206 decisions issued in the year to 31 August 2001, 79 per cent were upheld and 21 per cent dismissed (99/00 78 per cent upheld and 22 per cent dismissed). These figures should be treated with caution because, as 2/3 of the decisions concern the contents of a statement, they have to be recorded as successful even if there has been only a minor change to the statement.

Mediation

The tribunal does not undertake mediation itself. However, at a hearing it is some times possible to help the parties reach an agreement on proposed amendments to Parts 2 and 3 of the Statement (if the appeal is against the contents of a statement). Hitherto many LEAs have established a quasi-independent Parent Partnership Service. From January 2002, however, the Special Educational Needs and Disability Act 2001 has placed a statutory requirement on LEAs to inform the parents of the availability of conciliation services when informing them of the decision. The availability of conciliation does not affect the right to appeal, which must be brought within two months of the decision by the LEA. Unusually, because the Welsh Assembly has not yet passed similar amending regulations, these provisions do not apply to Welsh authorities.

Disability discrimination

The biggest change since the creation of the tribunal occurs in September 2002 when its remit is extended to cover claims of discrimination on the grounds of disability. Until September 2002 education was excluded from the provisions of the Disability Discrimination Act 1995 (DDA), albeit that it did apply to employment within schools. Part 2 of the Special Educational Needs and Disability Act 2001 has inserted into the DDA a new Part 4. From 1 September 2002 the Special Educational Needs Tribunal will be renamed The Special Educational Needs and Disability Tribunal (known as SENDIST).

There is a Code of Practice due to come into force on 1 September setting out the framework for avoiding discrimination on the grounds of disability which has been prepared by the Disability Rights Commission. In addition to the Code of Practice for Schools, there is one for post-16 education as well. It is intended that both Codes of Practice will be published in May 2002.

A claim of discrimination on the grounds of disability can be brought on the basis of 'less favourable treatment' or 'failure to make reasonable adjustments' except in the provision of auxiliary aids and services and physical adaptations. There is considerable (but not total) similarity with special educational needs as not all children who are defined as being disabled (by Section 1 DDA) have special educational needs and vice versa.

The provisions of Part 4 of the DDA extend to every school and cover every aspect of school life. That is admissions, exclusions and education and associated services, which means the teaching and learning, break times, bullying and special educational needs. For the first time the actions of an independent school are to be regulated.

Any claim of disability discrimination is to be made to SENDIST within six months of the discrimination complained of. The time limit is extended to eight months if the dispute is referred to the conciliation service. If the complaint is about discrimination in the admission or permanent exclusion of any pupil from a maintained school, that appeal is to the Independent Appeal Panels established by the School Standards and Framework Act 1998. Complaints about temporary exclusions from maintained schools and about admissions and exclusions from Independent schools have to be made to the tribunal.

In hearing a claim, the tribunal cannot order financial compensation but may, for example, require disability training for staff, the preparation of guidance for staff on combating disability discrimination, a review or alteration of school or LEA policies or a formal written apology to a child.

It is possible that there will be a claim made to the tribunal on both special educational needs and disability discrimination grounds. In those circumstances it is important to note that there is no extension to the two-month time limit in bringing a SEN appeal just because there is a disability claim as well.

The Disability Rights Commission is going to establish an independent conciliation service but whether this is going to run as a precursor to making a claim to the tribunal or to run in parallel with it is still unclear. The purpose of conciliation is to promote the settlement of claims without going to the tribunal. Further information about the conciliation service and the DRC can be obtained from the DRC helpline (Telephone 08457 622 633, Textphone 08457 633 644) or the website: *www.drc-gb.org*.

The extension of the tribunal's remit will require fresh regulations which will set out the procedure to be followed. Whilst there has been consultation as to what these should include, the draft regulations have not yet been published. It is expected that they will be finalised by June 2002.

A fuller discussion of the Code of Practice, the Special Educational Needs Tribunal's powers and interpretation of the legislation by case law as well as the extension of the tribunal's jurisdiction can be found in Special Educational Needs and the Law (2nd edition) by Simon Oliver, published by Jordans (0117-918-1490).

Chapter 6

Mediation skills and techniques

Adam Gersch

6.1 TYPES OF MEDIATION

Mediation is most effective when the parties understand the differences between the mediation process and other processes, such as litigation or tribunal hearings. In litigation, or a case conducted before a tribunal, the emphasis is on putting the best case forward in an adversarial approach.

Mediation however is flexible, non-confrontational, and allows the parties to be involved and exercise control over the outcome. The emphasis is on interests and concerns rather than legal issues, and all parties work together to formulate creative solutions.

Other disagreement resolution processes are outlined in Chapter 1 on ADR concepts. Whilst mediation is useful for resolving disagreement at any stage, it is best placed as a process when a solution could not be reached by negotiation, but before any more formal process. Since mediation has the status of a 'without prejudice' discussion and matters raised are confidential, the process can continue despite ongoing litigation.

Effective mediators encourage active participation of all parties, listen carefully to the respective interests and feelings of the parties, and generate an atmosphere of openness.

Education disputes lend themselves to resolution through mediation as they involve non-legal as well as legal issues; often emotional factors prevail, and the mediation session provides the time and space to allow feelings to be expressed and differing perspectives to be understood.

This section examines skills and techniques useful to both participants and mediators. We first look at the different types of mediation, explore the process and then review some general pointers for participants, case managers and then mediators. At the end of this chapter is a checklist of skills recommended for effective mediators.

The SEN Toolkit (Chapter 10) sets out the main principles of disagreement resolution at Section 3. The full section is reproduced in Chapter 10, and provides at paragraph 11:

- any agreement has to be to the satisfaction of all the parties concerned
- all parties agree that a resolution is needed
- the process is voluntary and confidential
- the facilitator is, and is seen to be, independent and neutral
- the parties have all agreed the choice of the facilitator
- the process does not prejudice any rights to take issues further, for example to the SEN tribunal
- those involved have the authority to be able to settle the disagreement.

It is suggested that 'where a joint meeting is held, the discussions can often be concluded in less than one day' (Section 3, paragraph 13).

Mediation procedure and practice can vary, but there are three main models for mediation – commercial mediation, community mediation and family mediation. Family mediation is mostly concerned with divorce settlements and care proceedings, and we concentrate here on commercial mediation and community mediation, and review the differences in approach.

Commercial mediation

This outline describes the model favoured by CEDR (Centre for Effective Dispute Resolution) and several other commercial ADR training organisations. There are five phases to the mediation, and the mediator should ensure that ample time is dedicated to each phase as may be appropriate in any particular case. The phases are: (1) Preparation Phase; (2) Opening Phase; (3) Exploration Phase; (4) Negotiation Phase; (5) Concluding Phase.

During the Preparation Phase the purpose is to explain the process and engage the parties and persuade reluctant parties to be involved. It is during this phase that the agreement to mediate is obtained from all parties, any relevant papers are exchanged, the ground rules are agreed including confidentiality, authority to settle, people expected to attend, timing of any meeting, selection of the mediator, arrangement of the venue and, where appropriate, fees to be paid. The venue should be neutral ground for all parties, and refreshments are usually arranged to ensure the comfort of all participants.

The Opening Phase is the actual start of the mediation session. Parties are met at a neutral venue, usually comprising one large meeting room with private meeting rooms (one for each party) to allow a private and secure environment for each party to consider matters in confidence. The mediator checks seating at the venue with thought given to appropriate seating arrangements. It is usual to use a round or oval conference table with parties sitting opposite each other and the mediator at one end. Introductions are made and the mediator gives an address setting the ground rules – emphasising confidentiality, voluntary and non-binding nature of the process, and checking that all parties have appropriate authority to settle the disagreement. During this phase, the mediator invites each side to make an opening presentation and encourages the parties to allow each other to do this without interruption. The mediator will usually summarise the points made by each party, often using a visual aid. The mediator will also check with the parties about any previous attempts at settlement, and review offers made.

Next comes the Exploration Phase, which involves building the groundwork for settlement negotiations. After a joint session with all parties, the mediator will often ask them to retire to their private meeting rooms so that the background to the disagreement can be explored in confidence with each side. The mediator uses this time to clarify the needs, key issues and interests of the parties and looks to uncover the hidden agendas. Strategies for settlement are also identified, and the mediator will normally ask a lot of 'open questions' and avoid assumptions. This phase also concerns the rebuilding of relationships and trust between the mediator and each party, and also between the parties. During the Exploration Phase, the mediator may shuttle between the parties or may choose to bring parties together as the mediator feels is appropriate. Experience has shown that looking behind the current disagreement is vital to understand the different perceptions of parties, and critical to finding a solution acceptable to everyone.

The Negotiation Phase follows with a mixture of indirect negotiations, using the mediator as a shuttle diplomat, and direct negotiations between the parties in joint session. This is where the mediator's role is critical, helping to break deadlock, reality-checking and facilitating movement. The mediator works creatively with the parties to help them discover possible areas of resolution.

Finally, in the Concluding Phase, the mediator explores any proposed settlement to check for potential problems or loopholes. The mediator will often write up the agreement, and explain back to all the parties in joint session what has been agreed. If agreement is not reached, the mediator may wish to summarise the progress made and discuss possible alternatives. It is usual for the mediator where appropriate to thank participants for their efforts and at this stage evaluation forms, if available, can be completed by the parties. Some post-mediation contact may be appropriate after a suitable period to see if the parties wish to reconvene, or where a settlement has been reached, to check that it has worked.

Community mediation

This outline is based on the model at Section 3, Annex A of the SEN Toolkit based on the seven stages developed by Mediation UK: (1) first contact with the first party; (2) first contact with the second party; (3) preparing to work on the dispute; (4) hearing the issues; (5) exploring the issues; (6) building agreements; (7) closure and follow-up.

At the first stage, the first party is seen and the mediator introduces him- or herself and the process. The mediator finds out about the background, acknowledges feelings and builds rapport. Agreement is sought to continue the mediation and confidentiality is explained. Next steps are decided between the mediator and the first party.

Stage 2 is the first contact with the second party who now has an opportunity to explain things from their perspective. Once again, the mediator builds trust and establishes their impartiality. Confidentiality is explained, and maintained by the mediator.

Stage 3 involves preparing to work on the dispute. The mediator usually identifies the best way to continue the mediation, prepares the conflicting parties, establishes commitment from each to the mediation process and arranges a suitable venue.

The issues are heard at Stage 4 in a joint meeting with the mediator. The parties are introduced by the mediator together with the main issues. Ground rules of confidentiality etc. are established and the mediator explains the process and gains the agreement of both parties. Each side has uninterrupted time, and the mediator manages any early conflict or hostility. A safe environment is provided for constructive dialogue, and the mediator establishes a climate of honesty, trust and openness. Key issues are summarised and the parties, through the mediator set the agenda and time limits.

Stage 5 involves exploring the issues, which are then established and presented. Good communication is encouraged, and the mediator checks understanding, clarifies assumptions, identifies fears, concerns and reservations. Any differences are acknowledged to allow the discussion to move on. Again, a safe environment is maintained and the mediator seeks to change the focus from the past to the future. Areas of agreement and remaining areas of disagreement are summarised.

During Stage 6, agreements are built. The mediator brainstorms with the parties for alternative and creative solutions. Options are evaluated and problem-solving is encouraged with a view to constructing agreements. Fallback agreements are established, and where there is no agreement, next steps are identified.

Stage 7 is the closure and follow-up. The joint session is closed and the mediator arranges any necessary follow-up.

Section 3, Annex B of the SEN Toolkit provides an adaptation of this model for use in the resolution of disagreements about SEN.

Commercial versus community mediation

Commercial mediators come from a variety of professional backgrounds and are usually paid for mediation work. Community mediators tend to be unpaid volunteers from all walks of life, and usually work in pairs rather than alone.

Training for commercial mediators is usually intensive and expensive. Commercial mediators often invest thousands of pounds in intensive training courses and are members of dispute resolution organisations such as CEDR that insist on continual professional development and further expensive training courses. Community mediators are usually trained in-house or through a variety of short courses run by Mediation UK.

Unlike commercial mediators who are used to providing a detailed CV, community mediators are not usually asked to provide a CV and there is usually limited choice of community mediator. Most community mediation is provided free to parties.

Commercial mediators are used to preparing documents and reading about the issues in advance. Community mediators tend to avoid documents. In SEN mediation, the use of a child's Statement may be essential reading by a commercial mediator but a community mediator may prefer to learn about the concerns of the parties without the distraction of any paperwork.

In commercial mediation, the focus is on the mediation session, where all parties meet on neutral ground. In community mediation, much pre-meeting work is conducted between the mediator and each party. It is usual for community mediators (working in pairs) to visit each party in their home and discuss the case, building trust and understanding. Commercial mediators would hardly ever meet a party at their home, and outside the context of a joint mediation session as this would be seen to compromise their neutrality and independence. In a commercial mediation, all parties agree who is to be seen first by the mediator during the Opening Phase.

In SEN mediation, there are different approaches to the model used in different regions. It remains to be seen whether the commercial mediation or community mediation model will be preferred or whether, in fact, a hybrid model will be developed over time.

In the SCRIP/SERSEN scheme for the South East and South Central Regions, Global Mediation Ltd has set up a panel of twenty-five mediators whose backgrounds are in either commercial or community mediation. The framework used for SEN Mediation is a mixture of commercial and community mediation. The mediator makes contact with the parties in advance of the mediation, usually by telephone, to build trust and establish a rapport. A face-to-face mediation session is arranged, which is usually a four-hour meeting with all parties present, and mediators determining procedure as they see fit. The child's statement or tribunal case summaries are provided to the mediator in advance, but little else, and there are no exchanges of lists of issues or summaries provided in advance of the mediation session, other than that which the mediator may glean from the parties in the initial contact.

Whatever model is used, it is essential that the mediator remains impartial, does not accept contact by the parties outside the mediation process (Global Mediation does not give out individual mediator's contact details), and that confidentiality is maintained throughout. Proper control of documents and destruction or return of sensitive material is important for the integrity of the process.

It is a reassuring development that the Regional Coordinators of the various mediation providers working in the field of SEN disagreement resolution have agreed to maintain contact and contribute to the debate and the development of SEN mediation.

In any model, it can be helpful for a mediator to explain to all parties how to prepare for mediation as part of the mediator's role in managing expectations and managing the process. Rather than sending in great swathes of papers or correspondence, parties can be invited to bring a list of issues with them to the mediation session.

6.2 PREPARATION FOR MEDIATION

Many parties attending a mediation session for the first time are unsure what to expect or how to conduct themselves. In a negotiation, we normally know the ground rules, know what to expect and can anticipate how matters will proceed. Attending a tribunal or court can be daunting, but, again, most parties realise that proceedings will be quite formal and have some preconceived ideas about what is expected. In a mediation session, parties are often unsure whether they should be prepared for an informal negotiation or more formal proceedings.

In one mediation session arising from a legal dispute, all the lawyers attended in suits apart from one who wore a very colourful Hawaiian short-sleeved shirt and casual trousers. Clearly it is important that participants feel comfortable about their role as well as understanding what will take place.

Part of the skill of the mediator is to create the right atmosphere and manage the expectations of the parties. There is always a tension between allowing everyone the time and space to resolve issues, and the fact that time is usually limited. Parties can ensure that time in the mediation session is used effectively by preparation before the day.

Mediation is designed to be quick and easy. The process is flexible and designed to be user-friendly. Below, are some time-saving tips for parties getting ready to prepare and present their case at a mediation:

1 Select a good mediator or mediation agency. Most mediation organisations will suggest a mediator or provide a list of suitable individuals. In SEN mediation, there are likely to be arrangements with one or more providers funded by the LEA. There may still, however, be some choice as to the actual mediator. Check the mediator's experience, qualifications and insurance. Review the mediation procedure. What arrangements are in place for ensuring confidentiality? Will the organisation set up the mediation session for you, contact other parties and provide a suitable neutral venue? Before instructing a mediator, check the cost and level of service – who is funding it; are preparation, travel and other disbursements all included?

2 Know your case. Effective preparation need not take a long time. Remember that the session involves a discussion of the case rather than presentation of the evidence as would be expected at a trial. Identify key facts, witnesses and documents and list the main arguments. Be clear about your objectives.

3   Prepare a short case summary to give to all parties prior to the mediation. Give consideration to a confidential settlement statement for the mediator's use only. Identify the main documents essential to explain the case. Bear in mind that the focus is on what will happen in the future rather than on the history of a case. Some mediators do not use any papers at all – check the position before putting pen to paper! Even if papers will not be distributed, you may find it helpful to make notes of point for your own use.

4   Make a list of the strengths and weaknesses of your case and that of your opponent. Consider your potential settlement range. What could you learn at the mediation that would alter your view concerning settlement? Give thought to your negotiating strategy and be prepared to assist the mediator in determining the best way to persuade the other side of your position.

5   Determine who should attend the mediation, and how they will participate. In SEN mediation, could the child or young person make a contribution, and would it be helpful for them to attend? Statements from a child or young person can be very effective, but attending a mediation could also be daunting. Which officers from the LEA should attend, and will they have sufficient authority to settle the case. All parties should understand who will be attending before the mediation session. If you have any doubts, ask the mediator.

6   Prepare and practise a short opening statement for the first joint session. Introduce yourself, go over the main facts and explain your view of the case. Keep the presentation concise. Be prepared to acknowledge weaknesses and try to appear objective and reasonable. If your presentation is after others, indicate any agreement or disagreement with their statement. Describe previous attempts to settle, and reiterate your willingness to resolve the dispute. In SEN mediation, everyone will be looking to what is in the best interests of the child, even though there may be disagreement; it may be helpful to acknowledge this.

7   During the mediation, examine the points of agreement and disagreement. Consider the best likely outcome if the case is not settled. Then discuss the worst likely outcome, assess the risks and explore areas of potential movement. Rank demands in order of priority – you may be surprised! Be prepared to discuss creative settlement options at the mediation and remember that nothing is binding until an agreement is signed.

Finally, keep in mind that the large majority of mediation sessions do result in a settlement. Even where no settlement is reached, the number of disputed issues is usually reduced. Invariably you will have gained an understanding of some of the difficulties, learnt more about your opponent's case and perhaps observed new aspects of your own.

6.3 CASE MANAGEMENT

Different mediation services work in different ways. The key principles are that the service should be completely independent and neutral and have proper systems for ensuring confidentiality, privacy and data protection. Most services have case managers or intake workers who are the first point of contact. Whatever the status of support staff, any disagreement resolution service should ensure that the whole service, as well as the neutral mediator involved, is covered by adequate professional indemnity insurance.

Some smaller services are simply a collection of mediators who manage cases, deal with all administration and take telephone calls themselves. Other larger services use case managers to set up the logistical arrangements, help with the selection of a neutral mediator, send out any necessary paperwork and explain the process before passing the case to the mediator. Case managers may or may not be mediators, but should be well versed in mediation procedure and covered by a proper code of practice.

The advantage of a mediator doing this background work is that they have an understanding of the process, and can take the opportunity of establishing rapport with the parties. The disadvantage is that there can be attempts to influence the mediator, and the mediator may not appear to come to the case from a position of neutrality. For this reason, the SCRIP/SERSEN scheme run by Global Mediation uses mediators to contact parties once the initial details and referral procedure is complete. In SEN mediation, it is helpful for the mediator to be involved in pre-mediation negotiations about who should be present.

Aside from the challenge of administration and privacy and confidentiality safeguards, case managers have a considerable challenge in getting the right people to the table at the same time. This can be a pre-mediation mediation itself, and requires some thought by whoever undertakes this role. There are often issues about the balance of numbers of people attending to be weighed against having all the key decision makers together. Parents may feel that having too many LEA/school staff appears unfair as more people present can be perceived as suggestive of more power. This must be balanced against the fact that the mediation would be of little value if the right people are not present. There is some value in the mediator assisting with these process decisions, and guiding the parties prior to the mediation session.

There is no one secret to getting people to participate in the process – some will be only too keen to be involved, and others will need some encouragement. The section on 'Common Myths' in Chapter 1 can be useful in dispelling any fears of participants or concerns about the process.

In SEN mediation, there may be ground rules set by LEA policy, such as referral criteria. (See SCRIP/SERSEN referral criteria in Chapter 10.) For example, there may be a requirement that parents should have tried other methods of resolution, attending meetings, liaising with Parent Partnership Officers etc. prior to referring the case to mediation. At the time of writing, regional referral criteria are being developed by other regions.

The South East and South Central Region has also arranged that each LEA has an induction meeting with the local mediators provided by Global Mediation to discuss variations in local procedure, learn about local issues and answer questions about the process and discuss the service. Each of the nineteen LEAs involved has established a named contact who will ensure that cases proposed are suitable for referral to mediation. The named contact has responsibility to ensure that referral criteria are applied, and it is hoped that a regional picture will gradually emerge from these case-by-case decisions.

Soon there may be less demand for formal mediation as a culture develops techniques for early intervention of disagreement. Cases suitable for mediation may then be identified at an early stage. In the meantime, a case manager may provide a useful filter to ensure that a case is suitable for mediation for those services where parents have made direct contact with the mediation service.

At present, referrals may come (a) from parents directly to the provider; (b) from parents via the LEA/school or (c) from the LEA/school. All parties must consent to participation in the process, and the case manager establishes that there is agreement to mediate.

How far should the LEA/school go to explain mediation and encourage participation? It is suggested that details of the independent mediation service be provided to parents and that they then be asked to contact the service direct. The pattern of referrals to date indicates that there is a high take-up of the service where the LEA has simply provided a leaflet or phone number and asked the parents to contact the provider directly.

Where the parent must express their wish to the LEA/school or even where the LEA/school explains too much about how the service works, there is often a perception from parents that this suggestion has been made to suit the LEA/school, 'to waste more time' or a suspicion that the service is not in fact neutral. SEN mediation cases typically involve a serious breakdown in trust between the parent and LEA or school. The evidence seems to suggest that LEAs should do little more than highlight the existence of the service and suggest that parents make direct contact if they wish to find out more.

Where this model is used, the role of the service case manager can be critical to the success of the service. Where the LEA handles the referral process, the officer responsible may be acting as case manager albeit from a perceived non-neutral position. Given the context of SEN disagreement, it is essential for the service provider to demonstrate outstanding efficiency, reliability and quality of communications with parents and carers who are very often emotionally charged and completely disillusioned and distrustful of others involved in the process.

The following suggestions may be useful to a mediation service case manager or other individual fulfilling that role:

1   Listen and be sensitive to the position of the parties – there is a fine line between empathising with a position and agreeing with it. Anyone involved as an impartial neutral must be careful not to give advice or express judgement. LEA officers should establish and be clear in advance of discussions whether their role is to explain the process or discuss the merits of the case or both. Summarising a position to check understanding can be a useful technique.

2   Explain the role of the mediation service. It is a good idea, especially when dealing with people unfamiliar with mediation to establish the ground rules at an early stage. Rules on confidentiality should be explained as early as possible, together with the procedure used by the service to facilitate mediation.

3   Ensure that the concept of mediation is understood. Part of managing the expectations of the parties may well be to clarify the way that mediation works. It is best to make clear that there will be no binding judgement and that the process is voluntary. In SEN mediation it is important to explain that the mediation will not interfere with other statutory rights, such as referral to the SEN tribunal.

4   Be prepared to answer questions and concerns about the mediation process.

5   If appropriate, complete a mediation referral sheet and take full details. Any records kept are subject to the Data Protection Acts and the service must be registered for the handling of data to comply with the law. Be clear about what happens to any information taken from a party, and what will be done with it at the end of the process. Clarify to whom communications may be made – i.e. can a partner or other family member take a message, and is it appropriate for the mediation service to leave a message on an answer-machine. These finer details are important.

6   Make and confirm arrangements for a mediation session, taking into account the need for a neutral venue, transport, dates and times when all parties can be available and any statutory time-scales, i.e. for lodging a tribunal case if not done already.

There should be confirmation that the parties due to attend have 'authority to settle'; i.e. the right parties will be attending who have an ability to make the decisions required to settle the case. This does not mean that every person attending has complete authority to consider all options – by definition everyone has a limit to their authority. What is important, however, is that parties who attend have a reasonable range of authority to enable a solution to be agreed without delay. In difficult cases, a fund-holder or higher authority may be available by telephone, but if this is the arrangement that person must be actually available.

The involvement of children at the mediation is another area worthy of discussion. The SEN Toolkit and other guidance recognises the right for children to be heard, together with the right of parents to involve a supporter or advocate (but not a lawyer). If children are involved, care should be taken to ensure that they can understand what is going on, they are told the options and all parties understand in advance that the child or young person will attend, that they can make a valid contribution, that their involvement would not cause them upset, trauma or distress. It should also be borne in mind that children as well as people who speak for children can make mistakes about what is in the child's best interest.

7   Follow up the mediation session with a quality survey evaluating client satisfaction, providing an opportunity to develop best practice and gathering statistical data for any reports.

6.4   THE ROLE OF THE MEDIATOR

Mediation is an emerging profession. Accordingly, there are a number of different styles and philosophies of mediation. For the purposes of this text, mediation is purely facilitative as distinct from 'conciliation' which implies a more evaluative and expert role or the use of a facilitator who is not entirely neutral. (See Chapter 1 for ADR concepts.)

The mediator must possess a number of skills. To facilitate effectively, the mediator should be a convenor, educator, communicator, counsellor, translator, questioner and clarifier, confidante, diplomat, manager of the process, reality-checker, creative genius, wordsmith and draftsperson. In summary, the mediator's ultimate role is to do anything and everything within their power to assist the parties to reach a settlement.

A mediator should not, however, feel personally obligated to ensure the parties reach a settlement, as trying too hard, or taking ownership or a personal interest in the resolution of the disagreement would be counter-productive. The parties bring their disagreement, and it must always be for the parties to arrive at their own solution with the assistance and facilitation of the mediator.

We now examine some of the skills of an effective mediator assisting parties in mediation. First, the various roles of the mediator are examined before reviewing some useful techniques and completing a checklist of key skills.

Broker/case manager

The mediator or case manager should encourage the parties into the process, manage the interaction between the parties and arrange the mediation session, setting appropriate ground rules.

Information source

Parties need to be educated about the process of mediation. This will include information on other alternatives, how issues can be addressed in mediation, what types of resolution can be expected and how these can be enforced.

Communicator

The essence of mediation is communication. A mediator must therefore be an outstanding communicator, able to interpret verbal and non-verbal communications and to ensure that each party is fully heard in the mediation process.

Counsellor

Listening and empathy skills are essential in mediation. Parties must feel that their concerns are being taken seriously. Effective mediators often use visual aids, such as flipcharts to note the main points made by parties so that their contributions are explicitly acknowledged. In facilitative mediation, care must be taken to acknowledge concerns but not to side with one party or appear judgemental, which could compromise impartiality.

Investigator

The mediator must look behind the problem to unlock the real obstacles to agreement. This may involve asking open questions and keeping an open mind. Parties' statements need to be probed and important leads followed.

Translator

The mediator should reframe, rephrase or explain communications where necessary to ensure that statements are better understood. Reframing is an important skill, especially useful in cases of strong communications, such as a demand for an apology.

Clarifier

Every significant statement made in mediation should be summarised by the mediator who should check their own understanding. Assumptions can be damaging, and the process of clarifying and checking understanding also serves to build confidence and establish rapport. An effective mediator is an active listener who summarises points made and ensures absolute clarity of communications.

Confidante

Keeping confidentiality and managing sensitive information is key to the effectiveness of the mediation process. A mediator should ensure that they present as a person in whom the parties may confide. By explaining the confidentiality of the process and refusing to compromise on this, and by checking what may be revealed at the end of each private session, the mediator demonstrates his/her commitment to confidentiality of communications and builds trust in the process.

Diplomat

An effective mediator must be able to deal with tensions and emotions in a sensitive and impartial manner and without negative comment. Managing tensions is an integral part of the process, turning hostility or resentment into constructive thinking. An effective mediator is able to recognise when tensions may be useful in a shared environment, and when it would be better to split the parties and deal with them in private session. The mediation process allows such feelings to be aired. Once parties have had this opportunity, and observed the strength of emotions, the consensus-building approach can be started.

Manager of the process

The mediator must build confidence in his/her own ability to manage the process and the interaction between the parties. For this, it is important to be clear, organised, decisive and confident, consulting all parties and developing a clear agenda. Parties will often challenge the decisions of the mediator, but after time an effective mediator comes to be trusted to suggest procedures for making progress, deciding the order of meetings, etc. Persuasion and presentation skills are important with the mediator appearing relaxed and engaged and presenting information positively. Maintaining authority must be balanced with a flexible approach.

Reality-checker

An effective mediator challenges assumptions, plays devil's advocate and questions the practicality of suggested solutions. This is generally known as 'reality-checking' and an effective mediator is able to do so in a non-judgemental way, helping the parties to explore their own solutions and ensure that all perspectives are considered.

Creative genius

The parties have to come up with their own solutions, but an effective mediator may offer options for consideration by asking creative questions.

Avenues of collaboration should be explored and problem-solving skills are essential to help the parties reach agreement. An effective mediator avoids premature commitment to solutions but helps to generate the right atmosphere for creative problem-solving. Brainstorming and 'thinking outside the box' are useful skills for promoting creative solutions. An effective mediator provides the right prompts for creative thinking, and asks questions that cause parties to think in a wider way.

Wordsmith and draftsperson

In the same way that apologies may need reframing, an effective mediator is able to come up with language acceptable to all parties in writing a memorandum of settlement. Good use of written communications and ability to draft a written agreement that sticks are essential skills of an effective mediator.

6.5 SOME USEFUL TECHNIQUES

Challenging assumptions

One of the biggest single causes of conflict is false assumptions. Mediators are taught not to make assumptions, but, more realistically, to be aware of assumptions made. How often do we know all the facts?

Some years ago vast amounts of time and money were spent building a computer that could beat any Grand Master at chess. The machine succeeded for a few games, until one challenger spotted the assumption. He moved a pawn forward. The computer moved. Then he moved the pawn forward another square on his next turn. Such moves made no sense. Lights flashed on the computer but no response came. The computer had only been programmed to deal with logical moves, and could not play against a seemingly irrational opponent.

Human behaviour can be unpredictable and therefore assumptions can be dangerous. By challenging the assumptions made by parties, a mediator can often facilitate a framework for settlement that has not been previously considered, or reconsider suggestions that have been discounted on the basis of incorrect assumptions.

Sometimes both sides simply say of their opposite numbers, 'They would never agree to that'. When both sides feel able to agree on a course of action, but are sceptical that the other would consent, the mediator knows the parties have a clear way forward. In a recent SEN mediation, neither party truly believed that the other would turn up to the mediation – when each did, both parties were surprised and felt duty-bound to continue.

When acting as case manager, I often hear parties say, 'We would agree to mediation but the other side are so unreasonable they would never consent to this'. This sentiment is usually repeated when I have contacted the 'other side'. Challenging assumptions and keeping all options open are therefore important skills.

Reality-checking

As described above, an effective mediator challenges assumptions, plays devil's advocate and questions the practicality of suggested solutions. Whilst a mediator should not disagree with a party, as the mediator should not express a view, it is perfectly valid to challenge the assumptions of a party or to ask them about the consequences of the statements. 'Reality-checking' can be conducted in a non-judgemental way, and can be very effective in getting parties to rethink their decisions from different perspectives. A classic reality check in a £50,000 commercial dispute is as follows:

Mediator:	The other side are prepared to offer almost all of your demand, but there is now £5,000 difference between what you are prepared to accept and what they are offering.
Party:	I am simply not prepared to consider this settlement.
Mediator:	What is the consequence of you rejecting this offer.
Party:	We sort it out in court.
Mediator:	How long would it then take to get a decision?
Party:	A trial could be listed for later in the year.
Mediator:	And a final decision?
Party:	Next year perhaps, assuming there are no appeals.
Mediator:	How much would it cost you to litigate this dispute?
Party:	I don't care – probably £20,000.
Mediator:	What are the chances of losing your case?
Party:	We have a strong case – an 80 per cent chance of success.
Mediator:	If you win, will you recover all your costs?
Party:	Costs is a different issue, but probably not . . .

> *Mediator:* What would be your exposure to costs if you win?
> *Party:* Maybe £8,000–10,000.
> *Mediatior:* Let me just summarise. You would rather engage in costly litigation that would take over a year, involve an outlay of £20,000, have a 20 per cent chance of losing and may result, even if you win, with losses of up to £10,000 – you'd rather that than accept an offer £5,000 less than you wished?
> *Party:* Put like that, I suppose we should make a counter-offer . . .

Risk is the mediator's most helpful tool, and this simple technique is very valuable in helping parties re-evaluate their positions. In SEN cases, parents/carers risk foregoing the most appropriate provision available for their child; LEAs/schools risk an unfavourable tribunal or court ruling that could set a precedent, and both sides risk wasting time, and possible further breakdown in trust and goodwill if issues remain unresolved.

Using non-verbal communications

It is now commonly accepted that a large percentage of communication is non-verbal. To make use of this, good communicators use techniques such as 'matching' to build rapport and gain the confidence of parties. Matching is a technique whereby the mediator mirrors the posture of the party. For example, if the party has an open posture – hands outstretched, legs uncrossed, facing the mediator, the mediator should mirror this posture (within reason!). In cases of mismatching – i.e. where the mediator has folded arms, clasped hands and crossed legs – it is interesting to note that the party tends to feel less of an affinity and rapport with the mediator. As an exercise on matching and mismatching, you may find it helpful to listen to a friend for three minutes and try to mirror their gestures subtly. Repeat the exercise doing the opposite, and ask them how comfortable they felt after each exercise. The results are hilarious, but quite an eye-opener. As an exercise in persuasion, watch the non-verbal gestures and posture of a good salesperson at work. Salespeople have learned about the power of matching and its value in gaining a rapport with an audience, and thus improving their powers of persuasion.

Active listening and summarising

Listening and active listening are two entirely different skills. During a training exercise, pairs were encouraged to talk for three minutes with the other person simply nodding and offering non-verbal encouragement. It is quite astounding to have the rare experience of being listened to absolutely, even for such a short time. This does demonstrate that most dialogue and conversation is lost with distractions, interruptions, background noise, etc. Observe how often it appears that a participant in a conversation is thinking of something to say, whilst we speak. How often do you have 100 per cent of someone's attention with no interruption or distraction? An active listener uses a range of techniques including prompting, summarising, paraphrasing and acknowledging points using visual aids. Good eye contact is essential and use of non-verbal cues such as matching – see above.

When listening to a person, it is useful to summarise your understanding of what they have said at the end, before any further conversation. This is an extremely useful technique for ordering the points made, and to gain an idea of the key issues. Noting the main areas of information on a flipchart can help emphasise the fact that these points have been acknowledged and understood. Note how hard it is to summarise everything said by another person when you are not working very hard to actively listen to them! Active listening requires a lot of energy, concentration and sometimes restraint.

Silence and prompts

Use of silence can be very effective. Anyone who watches a good stand-up comedy routine will appreciate the value of good timing. This is simply good use of silence. The same joke told with different timing, and different use of silence is not as funny. Equally, the mediator should appreciate the powerful tool of silence in discussions and also in negotiation.

Once a proposition or reality-checking question has been floated, the mediator should not say anything until the party has had time to reflect and answer. Co-mediators have been reprimanded in the past for answering a mediator's question, when the mediator was making deliberate use of silence! Silence can also be used to promote effective listening. We are all familiar with how annoying it is when somebody finishes your sentence for you. Equally, it can be empowering to be given the time and space to explain something in your own way and with your own choice of words. For persuasion and listening skills, effective use of silence can be extremely powerful.

Questioning

Language used in questioning can be significant. Lawyers are taught about the different types of questions. Open questions are questions where the answer is not suggested in the question, such as 'What happened next?'. Closed questions, sometime called 'leading questions', suggest the answer – for example, 'Were you upset?'. Closed questions can often be answered by a simple 'yes' or 'no'. Open questions require more explanation. Mediators make use of open and closed questioning in communicating with parties. In the Exploration Phase, open questions can be useful. Where clarification or confirmation is needed, closed questions should be used, i.e. 'Is that correct?'. A worthwhile exercise is for a friend to make up a fictional scenario. The mediator should than practice asking them about the experience using closed questions only, and then open questions. It is interesting to see how many assumptions we make when we ask too many closed questions, and how many of these assumptions prove to be false.

Another factor is that the language used in questions can influence the answer. In a famous experiment,[1] subjects were asked to watch a video of a car accident. Some were asked 'about how fast were the cars going when they *hit* each other?'; others were asked the same question with the words 'smashed', 'collided', 'bumped' and 'contacted' in place of the word 'hit'. Results indicated that the form of the question (even changes to a single word) produced markedly different responses. We all look at a situation through different goggles, and it is important that a mediator understands the power of language and form of words when dealing with the parties.

Generally speaking, open questions give the parties maximum opportunity for expression, closed questions close down the creative possibilities. Conversely, where a party rambles on and moves away from areas of possible relevance, closed questions can help shift a discussion back to the points of interest. By practising on friends, we can become more aware of open and closed questions and use them at will as part of our mediation practice.

Breaking down issues

Some issues can be ones of general principle and some can be quite specific. By tackling the higher-order principles first, or by breaking down the larger issues into smaller ones, mediators can often facilitate agreement where the parties are in deadlock. In any mediation, it may be that the process is able to assist agreement on a number of issues and the remainder can be listed as agreed areas of disagreement.

Creative problem-solving

There are a number of techniques for generating creativity. One only has to watch young children at play to observe that we lose our creative ability as we get older. As we learn about life, we come to accept the constraints, and comply with rules imposed on us. Young children are blissfully unaware of rules and conventions and therefore able to be more creative. In the United States, the expression for creative thinking is to 'think outside the box'. The general principle for creative thinking is to think in an uninhibited way, like a child.

Brainstorming

This is a well-known technique but often misapplied. Suggestions should be called out to a scribe and noted without comment. They may be abstract, bizarre, unrealistic, outrageous or absurd, but this does not matter. The golden rule is that they should be noted down without comment on a flipchart or visual aid. Only after a minimum period of three to five minutes should the items noted be discussed. The mistake most people make is to start commenting on suggestions as they are made. Real brainstorming can lead to very creative results and prompt new ideas.

Visual representations

Putting suggestions on a chart or even representing the problem as a visual picture can be very useful and lead to creative results that inspire solutions. I once observed a group of people who had been stuck for words to describe their current situation contribute to a fantastic stormy picture with the issues represented as clouds and the possible solution under a rainbow. The use of a visual representation generated ideas and suggestions and promoted creative problem-solving.

Mind-pictures

Using words to create mind-pictures can also be effective. For example, 'Pretend the disagreement was a car journey – how would you describe it?'. Answers may include, 'We are on the motorway, travelling too fast and unable to stop', or 'The car keeps breaking down and there is nobody able to fix it'. Such mind-pictures can be extremely useful in getting parties to understand each other's point of view and generate creative thinking. They also provide a helpful technique for helping parties articulate their feelings. By replacing the subject matter of the disagreement with a common everyday situation, our brain is somehow able to think of the problem from new angles, and describe feelings and concerns more vividly.

Use of apology

As in any type of conflict or disagreement, apology can be a powerful aspect of mediation where one party feels aggrieved. In SEN mediation, a parent may feel that they can only rebuild trust with an LEA if apologies are made for past mistakes or incompetence. An LEA may be concerned about apologising for fear this imparts some admission of liability, but this need not be the case. Equally, there may be scenarios where a parent has behaved unreasonably towards staff, and an apology can help to restore faith on all sides – LEA staff are human too!

Most of us have witnessed situations where opportunities have been lost because of the failure of one party to apologise. Whilst an apology is not part of the problem-solving or negotiating process, it is a process that can assist the process of mediation and assist in reaching a successful agreement.

Apology can be difficult and obstacles such as fear and shame make the process of apology more difficult. A mediator can play an important role by preparing parties for apology where appropriate, and helping them formulate a form of words that would be acceptable.

Where an apology is demanded by one party, there are essentially two approaches. Firstly, the mediator can 'park the issue' – i.e. focus on present issues and come back to the apology later; if a good agreement is reached, parties may be less concerned about apologies. Secondly, the mediator can act as diplomat and wordsmith in helping the parties with a form of words that allows the process to move on. Even where one side is not prepared to accept any wrongdoing, they can often be encouraged to make an expression of regret about how the other party perceives their treatment. Such a gesture can be an important part of rebuilding the trust needed to work together to move towards agreement.

'Parking' an issue

Sometimes positions become entrenched and parties 'dig their heels in', for instance over an apology or a particular wording. Noting the disagreement and moving to another topic can help, as an issue is sometimes easier to resolve once some ground has been made in another area. Mediators sometimes refer to this as 'parking' an issue, or 'agreeing to disagree' so that other issues can be explored.

During one commercial mediation, neither side was able to move towards settlement discussions until the other had apologised. The mediator was able to get parties to agree to discuss the issues, 'park' the apology obstacle and revisit the issue of apologies later on. Once a mutually agreeable settlement proposal had been agreed, neither side was troubled by the earlier request for an apology, and in fact neither side raised it again. Once the resolution was near, the priorities of the parties had changed and the apology ceased to be a live issue.

Differing values

In addition, the principle of differing values can be used. Where parties have both made a list of priorities, there are often some areas which one party considers important that is less important to the other party. In one such example, I was asked about a commercial landlord who wanted to sue its tenant for disrepair of the property. Litigation would have proved expensive, stressful and time-consuming. On exploring further, the tenant happened to be a retail supplier and the landlord owned a retail business. It was easy to see a line of questions that would enable one party to give something away for little detriment that would be of great benefit to the other. The tenant was pleased to propose a non-financial settlement involving the supply of cheap retail goods, and the landlord felt that the saving was equivalent if not more than the value of the lawsuit.

By getting the parties to rank the issues in priority or importance, the mediator can gain a bird's-eye view of all the issues and it may be immediately clear that one side is able to concede something of little importance to them that represents a high priority to the other party. In SEN cases the LEA/school may be concerned about how something is to be financed, whereas parents may value trust and certainty of an agreed outcome that does not in itself attract any cost.

Enlarge the cake

Rather than negotiating each issue on the basis of concessions from both sides, the mediator can help the parties formulate approaches that increase the range of options and thus 'enlarge the cake'. Timing of implementation, a phased approach, new suggestions, involving new people, examining the amount of any resource and whether it can be substituted with other alternatives are all ways of enlarging the range of settlement options. In an SEN case, where the parties are in total deadlock over the suitability of a proposal, they may be able to agree to abide by the recommendation of a neutral expert agreed by all parties.

Mediator's ownership

In breaking deadlock, the mediator can be invaluable. Often a settlement option is discussed in private session with the mediator but as a matter of principle, or to save face, the party cannot or will not propose that settlement. However, if the mediator makes the suggestion and all parties agree, nobody has to show their perceived weakness by making the very same suggestion. Equally, if the other party rejects the idea, it is the mediator's crazy suggestion and not that of the party who really wanted to try out this settlement option.

Timing of disclosure

It is worth remembering that the mediator is not simply a shuttle diplomat, and need not communicate every offer or suggestion made immediately. If the mediator feels it is more appropriate, she or he can hold on to a suggestion or idea until the time is reached when the proposal would be most effective. Some offers may be made that are conditional – they are only mentioned when certain conditions arise, but the mediator is told the proposal at the outset. Mediators may also be able to solicit two offers – one of which is disclosed, and the other to be used as a hypothetical and only becomes a firm offer if it will unequivocally resolve the case.

Private sessions

Breaking up parties in various combinations can be a useful way of resolving deadlock and exploring the issues and agendas privately. These provide a good opportunity to 'task' the parties – see below.

The mediator should also bear in mind that the mediation process can be stressful, and breaks are useful to relieve the strain.

Tasking

A good mediator will use all the time available, even when one party has been left alone in a private session. If the mediator is talking to one party, the other should be left with a task to complete. Such tasks may include listing out objectives or issues and putting these in order of priority or looking at the problem from the other party's perspective. By getting one party to argue the case from the other point of view, some understanding of the limits on an agreement may be better appreciated. Also, hidden agendas or assumptions may be revealed that would not otherwise have been noticed. Brainstorming possible solutions also can be useful for private sessions, as can use of visual representations and examining each parties BATNA (Best Alternative to a Negotiated Agreement) and WATNA (Worst Alternative to a Negotiated Agreement),[2] or creating decision trees.

Co-mediation

Where there are co-mediators, they should take time out to discuss their respective assessment of the process and their views on the progress of the mediation outside the presence of the parties. As different people see different aspects and may pick up on different issues, a discussion by the mediators may prove useful to brainstorm ideas for moving the process along.

Notes

1 E. Loftus and J. Palmer (1974) 'Reconstruction of Automobile Destruction: An Example of the Interactions between Language and Memory', *Journal of Verbal Learning and Verbal Behaviour*, 13, 585–9.
2 These acronyms are derived from Roger Fisher and William L. Ury, *Getting to Yes* (New York: Houghton Mifflin, 1981).

6.6 AN EFFECTIVE MEDIATOR

The following descriptions are designed to illustrate the positive and negative aspects of mediator styles. They are not intended to represent any individual, and are all entirely fictional, although some characters may be familiar. You may wish to list out the different characteristics of the characters and see how many positive or negative characteristics you can find.

All ears

Sandy Sun is always smiling, calm and positive. She appears to be even-handed and understanding, and always has time to listen. Sandy is very good at empathy but avoids bias and is never judgemental. She generates good working relationships based on trust and understanding and encourages others to make their own decisions. Her communications are clear and precise.

Ingrid Ice appears to be in a muddle and is always running late. She can never find the right piece of paper or note. She never quite gets the right point, and asks multiple questions that can be confusing or misleading. She regards herself as an excellent negotiator but seems to threaten rather than persuade. Once she has made up her mind, it is difficult to get her on your side and she appears to quickly choose her favourite version of events. Ingrid often interrupts parties and challenges their views. She does not 'suffer fools gladly' and is quick to explain what is relevant and what is not. Ingrid considers that she is the best judge of the important issues and if people listened to her analysis, the mediation would go a lot smoother and quicker.

List of characteristics

   Sandy Sun   **Ingrid Ice**

Give us a clue

Carl Cluedo always sees behind the problem. He subtlely analyses state-ments made by the parties, and looks for underlying positions and hidden agendas. He asks insightful and relevant questions that demon-strate his grasp of the situation under discussion. Carl often asks prob-ing questions in order to clarify positions and seems to be able to keep track and manage all the information, which is always at his fingertips. Even when the parties change positions, he appears to be in total control of the current state of play.

Lucas Clueless asks questions that are often irrelevant. He appears distracted and his list of pre-written questions seems disorganised.

Lucas fails to follow the lines of inquiry one would expect and often returns from a private session having forgotten to ask the most impor-tant question. He appears to be overwhelmed by all the information. When he comes into a room, it is usually just to say that he has forgotten something and will return again in a moment. Parties make suggestions for settlement, but these somehow get forgotten and Lucas simply says 'yes – great, I think I understand' and wanders off when settlement options are discussed.

List of characteristics

Carl Cluedo	Lucas Clueless

People politics

Jemma Jem quickly earns the confidence of the parties in a mediation. She is fair but firm and collects everyone's views before deciding on the order of presentations by the parties. Jemma manages client relationships extremely well and is never fazed by emotional outbursts or tensions.

Andy Arbitrary is confused by complex explanations. He asks the parties to present their views in a strange order that appears illogical. When challenged, Andy allows a dominant party to take over the proceedings and this seems to impede progress. Then, when he wishes to regain control he undermines the dominant party causing them to lose confidence and alienating them in front of everyone present. Andy does not appear to have a firm grip on the proceedings, which appear to take their own course despite his interventions.

List of characteristics

Jemma Jem   **Andy Arbitrary**

Persuasion and presentation

Trudy Trainer is a pleasure to listen to. She appears relaxed, alert, enthusiastic and engaged in the process. Trudy is confident and appears a dab-hand. Her explanations are clear and her analysis positive. She is extremely articulate and maintains good eye contact with all participants. Trudy's non-verbal communications and gestures are open and her use of a flipchart and neat handwriting ensures that everything is clearly understood and logically organised.

Tim Timewaster appears flustered and looks uncomfortable when engaged in public speaking. He is difficult to hear and seems to repeat the same points in a long-winded fashion. When asked questions, he is evasive and non-committal. Tim has a way of halting and never finishing his sentences. He never looks at the parties and when challenged always corrects himself and apologises.

List of characteristics

Trudy Trainer   *Tim Timewaster*

Managing tensions

Millie Manager is acutely aware of rising tensions in a mediation. She always has a good anecdote to tell, or humorous story that deflects tension and parties seem to get back on track in no time, as you can't help but like her. She encourages people to 'take a step back' and consider things from a broader perspective. Millie always brings out the best in people and parties work hard to get to a solution.

Simon Serious never cracks a smile. He frowns upon humour as a waste of time and wants to 'get down to business'. Simon sees things in black and white and does not feel it is possible or realistic to expect anyone to change their view. Simon does not agree with public displays of emotion, and suppresses any such expressions when he is in the chair. Problems appear large and difficult and everything seems so much more serious and complex when he explains it.

List of characteristics

Millie Manager   **Simon Serious**

6.7 A CHECKLIST OF SKILLS FOR MEDIATORS: SELF-ASSESSMENT ACTIVITY

The following is a checklist of skills for mediators. Training to be a mediator can be a revealing exercise, as it is first necessary to know your own strengths and weaknesses before you can improve. You may wish to rate yourself using the following checklist of skills of mediators. Complete the score boxes as appropriate.

Assess your skill beside each quality using a sliding scale from 1 to 5 where 1 = poor, 3 = average and 5 = excellent.

How well are you able to:

1 Act independently, be seen as absolutely impartial and fair-minded, and resist the desire to give advice to parties.
2 Inspire the trust and confidence of parties, maintain confidentiality and command authority and respect when managing the process.
3 Express yourself articulately and persuasively, and summarise others' views succinctly and sensitively.
4 Set an atmosphere of civility and cooperation, using humour and energy to inspire the parties to want to succeed.
5 Apply experience as a mediator in selecting techniques for progressing discussions and breaking deadlock.

6 Listen well and patiently without interruption and be an 'active listener', keeping an open mind and avoiding assumptions.
7 Understand and consider parties' different motivations and relate easily to them without making assumptions.
8 Cut through the baggage, analyse complex problems and get to what the parties agree are the core issues, without simply producing your own solution.
9 Be a good problem-solver inspiring creative and imaginative proposals with a good sense of timing.
10 Show a thorough understanding of the negotiating process.
11 Act in a flexible, patient, persistent way and be upbeat in the face of difficulties, turning negative views into opportunities for resolution.
12 Be reflective – know your own prejudices, examine your contribution to the process, your underlying needs and feelings, future training needs and need for support.

Score 45+
Excellent. Either you are scoring yourself generously or you are an extremely effective mediator. Would others who know you give you the same score? If so, you have all the right skills of an effective mediator.

Score 35–44
Well done. You have many of the skills of an effective mediator, and you have identified those areas that need fine-tuning. With a keen eye on your weaknesses, you could make an effective mediator.

Score 25–34
Good. Whilst you have many positive skills, some further training may be worthwhile to push up your score. It is a good thing to be aware of shortcomings, provided that you can work on the areas that require improvement.

Score 24 and below
Next . . . either you have underestimated yourself, or you have plenty of work to do before you should be mediating cases.

Reflective practice

When you have completed your first mediation, you may find this form helpful for self-evaluation.

Self-evaluation – plan of action

1   Which techniques did you employ during the mediation and what went well?

2   What are the possible areas of improvement for future practice?

3   Training needs – what skills or techniques areas could be strengthened?

4   Further action – personal action plan

References

Fisher, R. and Ury, W.L. (1981) *Getting to Yes*. New York: Houghton Mifflin.

Moore, C.W. (1996) *The Mediation Process: Practical Strategies for Resolving Conflict*, second edition. San Francisco: Jossey-Bass.

Nierenberg, G.I. (1986) *The Complete Negotiator*. London: Barnes and Noble.

Scanlon, K.M. (1999) *Mediators Deskbook*, CPR Institute of Dispute Resolution Inc.

Chapter 7

Ethical issues and dilemmas

Adam Gersch

Ethical issues arise in any problem-solving process. In this chapter, we examine some of the common ethical dilemmas by providing case examples and comments. All scenarios are fictional, but where examples are based on the real experiences of mediators, names and circumstances have been changed.

> **'A local scandal'**
>
> Mr and Mrs Brown have a son, James, who has dyslexia. They are in dispute with the local education authority over special needs provision. The Browns feel that James should attend a special school outside of the local authority. The LEA suggests that James can be educated quite adequately within a mainstream school. Mr Brown has invited his neighbour Edward Adair to attend the mediation to assist them. Edward has no special knowledge of mediation or education, but he did launch a successful campaign against the local authority some years ago to have yellow lines painted around the school.
>
> In a joint session, Edward proceeds to assert that there is no money to send James to a special school because the local councillors have stolen it all. He threatens to expose the local authority to the press, and places a tape-recorder on the table, saying he wishes to record the mediation session on tape, so he can prove the LEA is lying. Mr and Mrs Brown appear to be embarrassed and uncomfortable with these accusations.

Fortunately, this is not typical of SEN mediation! This is an extreme example and the mediator has a number of challenges here.

Confidentiality

Confidentiality of the mediation process is fundamental to the progress of the mediation session, and works in two ways (with limited exceptions). Firstly, nothing mentioned in the mediation may be disclosed outside of the mediation without the consent of all parties. Secondly, everything disclosed to the mediator by a party remains confidential between that party and the mediator unless consent is given for the information to be disclosed. The only limited exceptions to these rules are where some serious criminal conduct is disclosed which requires the intervention of others (i.e. child protection issues) or where there is an order of court or tribunal that matters be disclosed. These limited exceptions rarely arise.

It is generally accepted that there is a distinction to be drawn between a parent discussing offers made by the LEA amongst the child's close family and friends who would normally make such decisions, and disclosing an LEAs offer or position to a wider audience.

By ensuring confidentiality, a foundation of trust and confidence may be built between the parties and the mediator. On the basis of such trust, the mediator is better placed to understand the respective positions and priorities of the parties, and generate the right atmosphere for a settlement.

In the example given, Edward immediately challenges the mediator and the ground rules of the meeting by trying to use a tape-recorder to record what is said. The use of the tape-recorder as a non-verbal threat is probably more important to Edward than its intrinsic use. Whilst the mediator must ensure that the ground rules are not broken, this issue must be handled carefully to ensure that Edward does not lose face when the mediator challenges him.

Neutrality

Face-saving is an important factor here. If the mediator challenges Edward too strongly in front of the other parties, she or he risks the possibility that Edward will feel that the mediator is one-sided and judgemental. Edward may also feel embarrassed or undermined if challenged, and the mediator risks creating further confrontation.

In a training exercise where a similar situation arose, the individual was asked to turn off the tape-recorder. He then refused, stating that he wished to use it. The situation was diffused when the mediator asked him to turn it off temporarily, and they would then discuss the issue in a private session. The individual was thus given a face-saving way to appear to continue his argument in private. In the event, the tape was put away, and the issue was never raised again.

Status of the parties

At an early stage, it is apparent that there may not be a unified approach from the side of the family. Mr and Mrs Brown may be more willing to talk about the central issues than their representative. Such dynamics are frequently encountered in commercial mediations where a lawyer may wish to silence the client for fear that she or he will say the wrong thing. Mediators should observe carefully for signs of these intra-party issues, and seek to clarify the positions of each party in a private session. Mediators are trained to look for such hidden agendas. If Mr and Mrs Brown and Mr Adair all agree, it may be worthwhile for a mediator to speak to each privately. The mediator does just that in this case.

Mr Brown says that he regrets asking Mr Adair to the mediation, as he only has one argument and appears to be taking over, but does not want to offend him. Mrs Brown is very angry with Mr Brown for inviting Mr Adair in the first place, without asking her opinion. She insists that Mr Brown ask him to leave, which Mr Brown is not prepared to do himself; he suggests that Mrs Brown speak to Mr Adair, but she is not happy with this. Edward Adair says that he feels that he 'really has the government on the run now'. In the end, with the Browns' agreement, the mediator approaches Mr Adair, thanks him for his input and explains that there are now some sensitive matters that need to be discussed and the parties would all feel happier if he were to come back again if required. Reluctantly, Mr Adair leaves his phone number and bids the Browns farewell.

It is rare for a difficult party to leave the mediation meeting altogether, however, and the reality is that other parties will have to try to bring themselves or the other party round to a conciliatory approach, or adapt to the situation as it presents itself. It is worth noting that many opening sessions start off in a confrontational way, with accusations and high emotions frequently displayed. Patience, tolerance and understanding in the mediation can allow the parties to vent such feelings, as a precursor to the discussions that lead to settlement.

When concerns that appear to be invalid are dismissed out of hand, their importance magnifies. It is only when all views have been heard that more constructive work can begin. Once all perspectives have been acknowledged, the mediator can assist the parties by steering them towards a consensus-building approach. Parties often have a need for their contributions to be acknowledged. Mediators achieve this by summarising points made, and using visual aids, such as flipcharts to note down issues as they arise. Such techniques help reassure parties that their input is valuable, and that they are retaining control of the settlement process.

In this case, there appeared to be problems with the representation of the Browns. By exploring this in a non-judgemental way, the mediator was able to iron out some more fundamental problems within the team. Although it happens rarely, if a party (especially a representative) leaves the meeting, the mediator has to be particularly sensitive to the appearance that this may give to the other side. With this in mind, the mediator agreed with Mr and Mrs Brown that the LEA would be told that, 'Unfortunately, Mr Adair was unable to stay for the rest of the session, but has left his telephone number'.

Allegations of criminal conduct

Serious accusations within the mediation can cause potential problems. In SEN mediation, the duty of confidentiality does not extend to child protection issues. Thus, if suggestions of child abuse became apparent, the mediator would be entitled to disclose any such information to the relevant authorities.

It is important to distinguish between that which is simply levelled as an emotive insult, and that which is seriously asserted as a criminal offence. The mediator would be quick to explain that allegations of criminal conduct are unlikely to be resolved within the mediation, and would be unhelpful for a party to raise within that context. Such complaints must be made elsewhere and dealt with in an appropriate way.

The underlying 'hidden agenda' for the mediator is that of distrust between the parties. The parties would be encouraged to work towards a settlement that meets the best interests of James. Edward would be asked questions to help him appreciate that accusations of theft against LEA employees may not be the best mechanism for achieving a helpful outcome. Using a process of 'reality-checking' the mediator challenges the positions of the parties to help them look at issues from different perspectives, rather than simply giving a view or judgement.

The mediator will assist the parties to foster an atmosphere of trust within the mediation, but the parties themselves must be content to proceed. If a party feels that they are being threatened or unfairly accused, this issue can be discussed to see whether ground rules can be reached for the mediation to continue.

It is likely that the mediator will spend some time with each party in private before bringing all parties together to decide how to continue. The fact that Edward left the mediation after making accusations of criminal conduct does not necessarily mean that this issue will go away.

Focus on settlement

The Browns are keen to reach a solution that meets the best needs of their child. The LEA will also be looking to provide the correct level of provision for James. By focusing on the shared interests of the parties, negotiations can be advanced. Participants are often greatly relieved, and reassured to see that the other party has the same interests. Disagreements are usually about the manner and type of the appropriate provision, and thus it is useful for the mediator to emphasise this at the start, and at relevant points during the mediation.

'Bubbles Away'

Margaret Muddle attends a mediation session with Sanjit Singh from the LEA. They quickly reach agreement about special travel arrangements to and from school for Miss Muddle's daughter Sarah who is severely disabled. Mr Singh and the LEA are pleased because Sarah's transport can be combined with proposed arrangements for another child in the borough. Just before signing the agreement, Miss Muddle discloses for the first time that Brian Bubble is the appropriate parent to be dealing with any agreement. Mr Bubble is in fact Sarah's father and has recently been awarded care of his daughter. Margaret says that she only wanted to attend so that she would not have to make any arrangements for Sarah herself. Mr Bubble cannot be contacted as he is away on holiday.

One of the ground rules of the mediation is that both parties come to the table with authority to settle. Whilst it must be appreciated that an LEA representative may have authority to settle within defined limits rather than arriving with a 'blank cheque', the mediator must establish from the outset that all parties are the right parties to be involved and that an agreement can be achieved amongst those present. Clearly one of the ground rules has been broken here.

If a mediator has not checked the participants' authority to settle, they have overlooked an important ground rule. One of the key skills of the mediator is to ensure that all parties understand the same point. What is obvious to one party may need explanation to another. As the expression goes, we are all people divided by a common language!

Many at this point will be thinking, What next? An important principle in mediation is that parties bring their problems to the table and the solution also lies with the parties. The mediator will assist the parties in finding the solution to any problem, by way of helping the parties to help themselves. As soon as the mediator goes further than adopting a facilitative role, they become an expert or adviser and lose their impartiality.

In this case, applying these principles, the mediator gets all parties together to discuss what is to be done. The parties (not the mediator) agree that Margaret will contact Brian on his return from holiday, with a view to carrying forward the agreement. The LEA agrees to keep the offer of transport on hold for a further two weeks.

'A Legal Challenge'

Julie Bolt has engaged the services of Cheatham, Beatham & Runne, a firm of solicitors who specialise in commercial litigation. They propose to attend the mediation with their full legal team – a leading and junior barrister and Mr Cheatham, Senior Partner of the solicitor's firm. Mrs Bolt and her team claim that her son Bobby, aged fourteen, has been unfairly excluded from school and they wish to claim substantial damages for the potential damage to his future career. They refuse to accept the LEA's assessment that Bobby has learning difficulties and that he requires extra input from the school's psychological service. On the Friday, Mr Cheatham threatens that, if Bobby is not allowed back to school on the Monday, he will immediately issue legal proceedings in the High Court. The LEA is concerned about the costs involved in going to court; the file has been sent to the borough solicitor who is away on a cruise in the Bahamas for another three weeks.

Often parties come to mediation from an entrenched position. The mediator's task is to help break deadlock; the fact that there has been a breakdown in trust or communication is nothing new for the mediator.

When arranging mediations, we have found that Party A often claims that they would be pleased to attend a mediation but their opposite number, Party B, is unreasonable and would never agree. When speaking to Party B, they often claim, in turn, that they are happy to attend but cannot see that Party A will agree to their offer to mediate. By framing an offer of mediation in the right way, communicating it in a manner acceptable to both parties, it is often possible to bring people around a table who would otherwise refuse to negotiate further with each other.

Interestingly, in SEN mediation lawyers are specifically excluded from the process. How this can be reconciled with human rights jurisprudence remains to be seen. It appears that there is nothing to stop lawyers attending a mediation providing they state, 'I am not here in my capacity as a lawyer, merely to provide support . . .'

The issue here is one of imbalance of the parties. The parent appears to have adopted a legalistic approach, but the LEA does not have the same legal resources to hand.

An important part of the agreement to mediation is the agreement as to who should be present on the day. In order that there are no surprises, all parties should be informed in advance the names and roles of the people who will attend.

In this case, a case manager would encourage some balance between the parties by trying to limit the number of people attending, and thus allow the time used in the mediation to be more effectively spent. The mediator may also wish to speak to Mrs Bolt to explore whether it is really appropriate to have all those representatives present; the mediator may be able to reassure her of the purpose of the mediation and explain that nothing discussed in the mediation will be capable of hindering any legal proceedings. No settlement will be binding unless all parties agree.

Mediators often have to deal with deadlines imposed by parties. The hidden agenda is usually indicative of a breakdown of trust and frustration rather than a real need to have matters resolved by a particular day. If Mrs Bolt can be given a date for the mediation session, she and her legal team may wish to extend their deadline. Similarly, they would be free to continue with any legal proceedings and the mediation or agreement to mediate does not prejudice any legal remedies they may have.

The LEA may wish to arrange a date for the mediation that coincides with the borough solicitor's return. Equally, it may be that someone else can properly represent the LEA's position in the mediation. The mediator will be keen to point out to the LEA that proceedings are voluntary and no agreement will be reached without the consent of all parties.

Rather than hide behind their respective legal teams, seeing each other around a table working together to generate the best outcome for Bobby may actually assist the parties to reach a settlement. The mediator's main challenge is to re-establish the purpose of the mediation and to try to rebuild the lines of communication to facilitate some constructive dialogue. When the framework for the mediation is set, and the other legal matters put to one side, a resolution may be achieved despite the unfortunate history of the case.

It should also be noted that the mediator's role is to facilitate an agreement where possible, not to protect the rights or give advice to the respective parties. In circumstances where one side may be disadvantaged in negotiations, the mediator would normally explore these issues with the parties.

Since the best interest of the child is the foundation for any SEN mediation, it is debateable how much legal advice would assist a settlement. This may be the rationale for the exclusion of lawyers in the SEN mediation process.

'A small confession'

During a mediation session, Kim Li who has attended the mediation as a representative of both parents, approaches Linda Libra, a specialist education mediator. Kim explains to Linda in confidence that she wishes the session to end in a settlement at any cost, as she has missed the deadline for submitting her client's case to the tribunal and is worried about being sued for professional negligence.

There are two issues here for the mediator: first, confidentiality, second, hidden agendas between Kim and the parents she represents.

Confidentiality

Whilst matters disclosed by one party in confidence remain confidential, it is not clear-cut whether confidentiality extends as between individual members of a team. Whatever the agreement on the terms of confidentiality, the most important thing is that all parties understand the nature and ambit of the agreement, and that there are no surprises.

Even if the terms of the confidentiality agreement are that nothing is disclosed, Linda is clearly put in a difficult position by the matters raised by Kim. Linda may decide that Kim should be persuaded to reveal this information to the parents she represents. If Kim persists, Linda may find that she has to withdraw from the mediation.

Mediators should be bound by a written Code of Conduct, which may vary between different organisations. Usually, a Code of Conduct would allow the mediator to withdraw in certain circumstances such as where their neutrality is compromised. Linda may be faced with such a situation here. If the parents remain ignorant of Kim's omission, and this has a significant effect on the mediation process, Linda would be placed in a compromising position and is unlikely to be able to continue.

Hidden agendas

There are often situations where there is internal conflict between parties on one side. These may be unresolved issues between parents; disagreements between parents and representatives or disagreements between members of the same LEA. Mediators are trained to look for such 'hidden agendas' even where these are not expressed. Sometimes, talking separately to individuals within one time can help to gain an understanding of the differing perspectives.

Even if Kim had not expressed her fears, Linda may well have sensed that there were different hidden agendas and that the discussions should be handled with care.

'Time for tea'

Charlie Chancer has been asked to mediate an education dispute. Mr and Mrs Gupta are concerned when Charlie arrives in the same car as Terry Teflon the named officer from the LEA. When Mr and Mrs Gupta are asked into the joint meeting room, Charlie and Terry both have their jackets off, have cups of tea in front of them, and appear to have started to make some notes.

In any case of conflict, it is essential that independence and neutrality are maintained. Parents often feel they are not part of the system and appearances and perceptions can be extremely powerful. The non-verbal message from Charlie and Terry was unfortunate here, and Mr and Mrs Gupta would have been right to express concern.

As it happens, Charlie had made his own way to the session by public transport but recognised Terry from a previous session when his car stopped at a red light. Since it was about to rain, Charlie took up Terry's offer of ride for the remaining two blocks. When they arrived the meeting room had just been used, and left in a mess. Charlie and Terry took their jackets off to shift some chairs and tidy up. The notes and tea had been left from a previous meeting. All these factors, however, did not assist the appearance of neutrality and started the mediation session off on a negative footing.

An effective mediator should be aware of such non-verbal messages and the impact they may have. Consideration should be given to the arrangement of chairs, provision of pens and paper, order of seating and the way parties are greeted. Ideally, parties should be brought into a room together, and, where they are used, private meeting rooms for each party should have equal facilities.

Where refreshments are offered, they should be offered to all. Even drinking coffee from a mug, when parents are given coffee in a plastic cup can give the appearance of favouritism, particularly where the mediator and LEA representative have mugs! Often, if a LEA representative has been involved in a number of mediations, they will know the mediator. Care must be taken to restrict any social pleasantries and chitchat to a private session to avoid the appearance of impartiality. If parents perceive that there is some affinity between the mediator and the LEA at the start of the mediation session, it may not assist them to place their trust and confidence in the mediator, and this will impede a settlement.

Whilst the mediation is informal, it is important not to underestimate first impressions by parties who are unfamiliar with such a process. Traditionally, barristers do not shake hands, which may seem strange given the relatively small size of the profession. The practice arose centuries ago, from a desire not to appear to lay clients to be making deals behind their backs. Impartiality and the lack of any appearance of impartiality remain as important as in those first days long ago when barristers decided to stop shaking hands. It goes without saying that the same rules apply to hugs and kisses!

There can never be a prescriptive list of all the possible issues that could possible arise, but by giving thought to the underlying principles of mediation, sound decisions can be made to deal with unexpected situations. In order to keep alert to possible ethical problems, mediators need to be aware of five 'eyes': Integrity, Independence, Imbalance, Illegality and Insurance.

Integrity

The mediator should be regarded as having the highest standards of integrity and parties must have faith that the mediator will deal honestly with them throughout the process. Whilst preserving confidentiality, the mediator must never knowingly mislead parties and should develop a stock response for questions that cannot be answered fully.

Independence

Mediators should ensure from the outset that there are no potential conflicts of interests and that they are perceived as fair, neutral, impartial and independent. Where a mediator has had any connection with a party previously (e.g. a previous mediation), this should be explained to all parties so that it does not emerge later and undermine independence. Where a previous relationship could be regarded as a potential conflict of interest (real or perceived) the mediator should decline to act.

Imbalance

A mediator should be sensitive to any possible manipulation of the mediation process or imbalance in the number or status of the parties attending. It is not the mediator's role to intervene if a party appears to have been badly advised as this would compromise the independence of the mediator who can be very easily sucked into giving advice. Where a decision has to be made and parties appear to be under too much pressure, a 'cooling off' period could be suggested as part of the process.

Illegality

Whilst uncommon, the mediator should be prepared with a response should any illegal or criminal conduct be proposed during discussions. The mediator should challenge the wisdom of such ideas, consult with his or her professional body if necessary and, ultimately, may refuse to act. It is of great assistance for the mediator to be bound by a formal Code of Conduct which sets out the procedure in such circumstances.

A similar discretion may form part of the Code of Conduct in cases of racist, sexist or discriminatory or abusive conduct by parties.

Insurance

The mediator should be aware of the boundaries of their own professional conduct and act in accordance with their professional indemnity insurance cover. Broadly speaking, two main areas may give rise to a claim against the mediator – breach of confidence and negligent advice. The latter should be extremely rare, as mediators should not be perceived as giving advice, but the former is a danger. If an error occurs, the mediator should withdraw and take professional advice and a written Code of Conduct should provide procedures for this. Claims against mediators are almost unknown in this country but a number have emerged in the United States and mediators should ensure that they are adequately covered by a policy of professional indemnity insurance.

This section has explored some of the ethical issues that may arise in SEN mediation, as food for thought.

Mediators often report that time taken to stop and think in the absence of either party during a mediation can be extremely useful. Similarly, a co-mediator can be useful to bounce ideas off; some organisations provide a 'buddy system' for mediators so that a mediator can discuss a situation with another mediator over the telephone as it arises. The process can be extremely draining on a mediator, and those who mediate have found all of the above techniques helpful.

Chapter 8

Training to be a mediator

8.1 INTRODUCTION

Mediation is a new and unregulated industry, and there is no single, universally accepted qualification of 'mediator'. In fact, anyone can set up shop and call himself or herself a mediator although happily, most practising mediators have suitable training and experience.

Some courses are more extensive than others, and some organisations have developed CPD, or Continuing Professional Development regimes to ensure that skills are kept up to date. Most organisations provide what is called 'accreditation' or 'certification', e.g. a school may offer an 'accredited' course but the accreditation or certification is usually by the training organisation itself.

Mediator regulation is still a topic of debate, with many organisations currently looking for ways of ensuring quality and consistency. It has taken over two decades for regulation in the United States with the introduction of the Uniform Mediation Act, and it is likely to be a long time before mediation is formally regulated in the United Kingdom.

In SEN mediation, some mediators now have some forty hours training on a recognised mediation skills course or courses, together with at least two days' training in the background, legislation and sensitivities of SEN work. Additionally, mediators should be selected for their experience in mediation and their personal skills and ability to deal with the unique challenges of mediating SEN cases.

Some contact addresses for training courses appear in Chapter 10, although this list is not exhaustive and new training courses are being developed all the time. Potential mediators should consider factors including reputation and experience of the training provider, course content, opportunities for mediation and cost of a course and compare the areas covered by different courses. Other countries such as the United States where mediation has been around longer offer a wider range of opportunities for mediation training.

In the next section, Zanne Findlay writes from the perspective of a mediator trainer.

8.2   THE ESSENCE OF MEDIATION – A TRAINER'S PERSPECTIVE
Zanne Findlay

I am a very lucky person – I get to train mediators. Most of my working week is spent suggesting to people who already have highly developed 'people skills' that if they package them a little differently they can empower those in dispute to solve things for themselves. The most difficult part of my day is asking those same delegates to stop fixing other people's problems and to allow creativity to emerge from chaos.

I am not sure which creates the most challenges: chaos or creativity. Chaos brings with it those uncomfortable seconds of silence, the rawness of deep emotion, the dawning realisation that no one solution is perfect and that each choice brings with it its own particular brand of compromise and disappointment. Creativity suggests new precedents, a different way of doing things which might elicit reactions and resistance once the resolution is unveiled outside of the confidentiality of the mediation room.

Mediation is a powerful and transformative tool. It unlocks creativity and creates an ownership of resolutions, which our normal bureaucratic processes tend to stifle. This can be liberating for local government officers and parents but it needs careful implementation and clear thinking.

In its essence mediation is compact, creative and person-centred. Therefore mediation sessions need to concentrate on the key issues, as identified by the parties and incur the minimum amount of paperwork. It helps if the main session is restricted to the parties involved with the central concerns. If necessary part of the session can be used to agree how any remaining issues will be dealt with later. If the mediation, or alternative dispute resolution (ADR), process ever grows to replicate the tribunal then the uniqueness of the process will be undermined.

In complex cases try visualising ADR as a number of concentric circles and work through the complexity of agencies and professional involvement one by one. Visualise a target, see yourself starting at the bull's eye and working out. Start with the key agencies and issues that will rebuild communication and trust. In this way you create an early sense of shared ownership and understanding between the LEA and the parents. As they then move out from the bull's eye to deal with the other agencies or issues, their dependence on the facilitator is likely to decrease, because they will have developed the confidence, and shared language, to deal with the issues themselves.

Mediation is a complex and dynamic activity. It is one, which deals with relationships, power imbalances and human nature and can frequently highlight political issues and tensions. It is an empowering process because it gives people the space, and the tools, to take responsibility for shaping their own future. I was struck by the comments of one mother who had been through a SEN mediation. I would sum up her sentiments as follows:

> I have to know that I have fought for my son. It is not that I have to win, but I have to know that I tried my best. He is so dependent on me. I know him better than anyone and until today no one has really asked me about my fears and concerns. Just having the space to share them, in the presence of a third party, so that I know that the LEA has to listen, is a release and a relief. I now feel I can engage in making the real practical choices about his future.

In order to support the introduction of ADR there is a whole raft of training, planning and discussion which needs to take place to ensure five things: first that the process reflects the fact that the child's needs are central; second, that parents are given the support, advice and advocacy that they need; third, that individual officers are supported and enabled to partake fully and confidently in the process; fourth, that the officers who attend have the managerial status, and support, to be able to make decisions there and then on behalf of their Authority; finally, that any learning outcomes, which naturally emerge from individual cases, are used to inform and improve LEA procedures and processes for the benefit of others.

Setting the context

One of the ways in which training has been used during 2001–2002 has been to establish the context in which the mediation, or ADR, service will be operating. What is challenging about mediation is that although it might be viewed as an idealistic model which concentrates valuable resources on one child, it can also highlight how a more holistic and reflective approach can promote change, not just for the individual, but within the system as a whole.

I am aware that during two different mediations with the West London Project that some of the outcomes were diverse and wide reaching. For example, in one instance the LEA officer arranged for the whole team to have training, to raise their awareness of mediation and to spread the skills and approach amongst those working directly with parents.

In another case a creative solution was found which involved a second agency. Interestingly this solution could not have been achieved if the process of mediation had not been offered. The mediation session enabled the participants to be creative, once they had rebuilt communication, understanding and trust. This particular outcome could not have been achieved through the Tribunal system because they would not have had the necessary jurisdiction.

This mediation enabled a holistic response because it moved beyond the educational needs to the social environment. But it did so in a way which did not compromise the responsibility of the LEA, because the education officer was in control of shaping the resolutions and carrying them through. From the parent's point of view the problem was always holistic, as the division between education and social care seems arbitrary and irrelevant when you are a full-time carer. It means having a range of professionals to reason with, all of whom require exhaustive and repetitive story-telling in order to try and gain even the most basic level of support.

LEAs and voluntary agencies tend to adopt one of two approaches when asking for training. One approach is to involve all the stakeholders in one meeting: the decision-makers, referring agencies and staff, education professionals and potential mediators. This forum enables a basic understanding to be developed about the scale of the task and the principles and processes which need to be put in place. It allows all those involved to work together to look at the local implementation and adaptation of those procedures. It builds joint ownership and lays a firm foundation either for the writing of tender documents for an external provider, or for training in-house mediators.

A second approach invites us to work with those who will be asked to mediate, or attend mediations. It provides them with the skills and the knowledge they will need and presents the issues that they will need to consider with their managers or clients. This has given people on the ground, usually those who already resolve a great deal of conflict, time to consider the potential opportunities and limitations of mediation and then engage the more senior staff and wider parents' group in that debate.

Both approaches are designed to equip delegates with some conflict resolution skills which we hope they will apply in their day-to-day activities irrespective of whether they progress to use the skills more formally. It is not the launching of an elaborate mediation service that heralds success but incremental change. What we hope to engender is a culture of conflict resolution, which inspires people to look afresh at all their interactions from answering the phone, to writing reports.

Training in mediation

There are times when I wonder why any training in mediation is needed at all. Are the basic concepts not so simple that we all do them naturally? Am I not just peddling the professionalism of good human interaction, based on respect and understanding?

Well, to some extent that may be true. The skills of mediation are not new, either within society today or ancient societies; moreover, it is not new to SEN. There are a number of individuals and professionals in the many fields which surround SEN who currently mediate, negotiate, conciliate and arbitrate creatively, quietly and very successfully. Often when these people join us in the training sessions the most valuable thing we offer is to differentiate between the roles, and suggest (gently) that even super-heroes cannot be both a mediator and negotiator within the same dispute, or with the same family.

In my opinion the different roles do imply different approaches; negotiation implies talking to others to achieve an agreement. Negotiators tend to have their own preferred outcome and direct involvement in the issues under debate. Conciliation often uses an expert from the field to broker an agreement. Arbitration requires the arbitrator to take an expert view on the different merits of the arguments and make a decision. Mediation, however, is about managing a process, whereby the parties in dispute can resolve matters to their satisfaction. The mediator has to be neutral and impartial and does not give advice or offer solutions.

None of the processes are exclusive and there is a time and place for all of them. Many of the skills and the personal attributes required are very similar. Therefore what is it that differentiates mediation from all the others?

How people perceive the role of the mediator

At the start of our training seminars we ask people what mediation means to them. It is an easy question because everyone has a view: standing in the middle; seeking compromise; problem-solving; negotiation; listening; holding the space; and so the list goes on. The list usually includes some 'being' words; being impartial; being non-judgemental, for example, and for me it is in the being that the essence of mediation lies. Certainly mediators need a range of specific and technical skills, but I would describe the primary skill of mediation as creating a reflective space.

I see mediation as a simple and a complex activity at one and the same time. It is as easy as placing stones in a flowing river. Its complexity lies in making sure that the water is a stream and not a torrent, that the chosen stones can bear the weight of the people, match the length of their stride and carry them to the destination of their choosing.

It is both a passive and an active role. It is active in that as a mediator you have to do a lot of things in preparation. I see one of the tasks as easing the focus of the mediation on to the most central issues and away from the peripheral. Therefore, I think mediators should take an active role in relation to the paperwork, attendees, venue and the rules of engagement. One of my mantras is 'no surprises on the day' for the very simple reason that everything that has to be sorted out within the mediation session has the potential to become a point, which can be won or lost. Therefore, it is better to deal with as much of the administrative and procedural matters as possible outside of the session. This helps to ensure that if these matters do then dominate the proceedings it is because that is how the parties wish to explore their differences, not because the service has been inefficient or unintentionally partisan.

There is also a more passive, or reflective, side to mediating. In psychotherapy training they might call it 'managing the energy'; some psychoanalysts describe it as 'the observing ego'. Freud advised his therapists to develop an 'evenly hovering attention' which takes in whatever passes through that awareness with impartiality, as an interested yet unreactive witness.[1] It is this awareness, which is unique to mediation because it is not about making judgements, using expertise or assessing the relative merits of different positions.

It is this awareness that can allow the unstructured periods to occur, the chaos mentioned earlier, without engendering much of the fear associated with so many roles where you feel you have to find a way through the chaos towards agreement. It is this feeling that prompts people to fill any unstructured space, to suggest solutions, or offer their own particular insights into the situation. If a mediator can maintain this point of awareness it enables him or her either to let the space linger to see what might emerge, or, if the parties are looking uncomfortable, to reflect back what is taking place in front of them, without assigning motive or reason to the observation.

By freeing the mediator from the task of seeking a solution, you also free him or her to work at the pace of the parties concerned. For example, there are some people who can work through difficulty, express their feelings, have them validated and then move on from there to forge new relationships. But others take longer perhaps to express their feelings, or to move beyond those feelings to a position where they feel they can trust the other party enough to move forward. A mediator can observe these different needs and, as his/her responsibility is to build ownership and satisfaction on both sides, he or she can concentrate on assisting the parties to agree on a process which will allow them to move at their own pace. The mediator's success is measured by the satisfaction of the parties, not by the creation of a binding agreement within a specific time-scale.

Creating an inner reflective space

When we train we are often asked, 'But how do you deal with angry outbursts, unreasonable people or explosive situations?' Our answers tend to be technique-based: 'You match their behaviour and lead them into new behaviour; you take a break; you manage the flow of information and concessions to create a sense of equality and progression . . .'

However, I suspect that what is behind that question is how will I manage a potential explosion of emotion between the parties within myself? At the root of that question is fear, the fear mediators have of losing control or of showing bias. I think the main way a mediator can create some emotional distance and achieve the 'evenly hovering attention' is to move to a point of equilibrium within themselves – a reflective space – and adapt their techniques from there.

The task of a mediator is to steer a steady course through the issues, emotions and resolutions, which the parties bring to the table. The emotions in any particular interchange may be difficult for the parties, but they should be part of the mediators palette of expectations. Some emotions may be unacceptable when expressed clumsily or angrily during a mediation session, but the mediator needs to concentrate on the need which is being expressed, not on the manner of expression, unless there are issues of personal safety. I have found the work of Marshall Rosenberg, *Nonviolent Communication*,[2] to be inspiring on the issue of needs and the use of language.

One of the challenges mediators face is to remain visibly unmoved, or unshaken, while taking appropriate steps to deal with angry outbursts. I believe that most parties subconsciously watch the mediator to check out if there is any visible sign of the mediator judging them to be 'mad' or 'bad'. If they see an expression of disapproval, no matter how fleeting, they may have been given just the excuse they need to react against that judgement and often the process as a whole.

Each mediator will develop their own manner of creating a reflective space within themselves. Some might use meditation, relaxation, or other forms of therapeutic or self-reflective techniques. The manner of preparation is immaterial. The important thing is that it is done effectively, and that any mediation service builds in, and expects, a mediator to take time to prepare him- or herself (and to debrief and self-reflect afterwards).

Some people might associate this reflective space with the place within themselves where they experience their spirituality, their religion and their most deeply held beliefs. But this place is beyond belief or religion. In this place it is impossible to judge, but easy to feel compassion. It is easy to stand firm in the face of buffeting emotions because you are connected to a still point of energy that is within you and connected to a greater whole at one and the same time.

Movers and fixers

One of the things which most people bring to our training sessions is their great ability as movers and fixers. As a society we should all be heady with success and fulfilment, because the skills and the commitment to fixing things is palpable in most of our training sessions. I have no doubt that these skills are invaluable and much appreciated but, if people are asking for mediation, then somewhere along the line they have not worked this time. Or, more possibly, the potential resolutions have all been explored and discussed but the work has not been done to build ownership, or to draw a line in the sand and allow a new dawn to emerge.

Unfortunately being a mover and a fixer is not in the job description of a mediator, and that drive, or automatic response, can be one of the barriers to finding, or remaining in, that inner reflective space.

I acknowledge that I am fortunate in that I am either mediating or training mediators and therefore I do not have to change hats too close to the start of a resolution meeting. There will be mediators who are switching between professional roles and that presents a challenge. So often the work of local government officers is like panhandling for gold in a fast-flowing river, and the task of working through complex and very personal issues is shoehorned into tight bureaucratic forms which are designed to administrate the work of the system efficiently and effectively. I believe that if we allow mediation to be shoehorned into the same structures then the same limited resolutions will emerge.

What we need to create in mediation is a different form, a more expansive and reflective form which has the space within it to consider this one individual child, separate for a moment from the other demands on resources and time. In my experience, the outcomes may not differ that much, but what does differ is the quality of the experience. Parents and LEA officers who have experienced mediation, appreciate the quality of the interaction and the increased levels of communication and understanding without necessarily having had to commit additional resources.

What does that mean in practice? It means looking closely at the venues, the more comfortable and informal the better. It means planning the timing of sessions to give the maximum flexibility to both parents and officers. It is important to keep the sessions focused and realistic in terms of time commitment, but it can be very frustrating to lose the possibility of a resolution for the sake of an optional twenty minutes. When people are pushed for time they tend to limit their choices – often between the soft option which can mean no substantial change; or leaving it to the Tribunal to decide; or agreeing to the proposals under discussion, not because they feel any sense of true ownership but so they can leave with a feeling of accomplishment.

What we suggest is that the sessions are time-limited, but that the parties are advised not to book something in the period immediately after the session. That allows two things: first, some flexibility, if needed; second, some time to relax after the session, as it can, in the words of one officer, leave you feeling 'drained'.

Mediation is an eclectic art form

The more I explore the concepts of mediation and have the privilege of being asked to mediate, the more I realise that we are dealing with a very eclectic and individual art form. Yes, there are structures and procedures, which are very important and lay the foundation for the mediator's practice. But it is what happens within the session that is important.

Mediators may well draw on counselling skills, especially brief or solution-focused counselling, management experience, professional knowledge, legislation and good practice. They certainly need a good deal of self-reflection and awareness and emotional intelligence as defined by Daniel Goleman. How much of that can be learnt through training courses, however long, I think is debatable.

I prefer to think that as trainers we awaken what is already there. Mediators need to tap into the skills and values that often lay dormant within the technical and collective structures which tend to protect professionals who are doing a difficult task most of the time. Sometimes I feel the training offers those people who already take the creative and the humanistic approach the confidence to continue to do just that. Perhaps we provide them with a few new structures, which increase their self-confidence and give them some leverage to engender more support for the work they do.

Sometimes the training is about recognising limitations, both personal and professional. However impassioned I feel about mediation, I recognise that it has limitations and therefore it is important that neither individuals, nor services, are set up to fail.

In conclusion, a word from some SEN delegates. At the end of three days of training they were asked to find a quote, which defined mediation for them. They came up with many inspired choices, here is just one: 'We cannot control the direction of the wind but we can adjust the sails.'

Notes

1 Daniel Goleman, *Emotional Intelligence*. London: Bloomsbury, 1996, p. 46.
2 Marshall Rosenberg, *Nonviolent Communication*. Puddledancer Press, 2000.

Chapter 9

Conclusions – emerging themes and future possibilities

Irvine S. Gersch

This book has surveyed the field of disagreement resolution at this particular point in the history of SEN development in the UK. We have presented a number of projects involving negotiation, conciliation and mediation. The skills and techniques of mediation have been reviewed, and some ethical issues explored. The final section lists some key sources of further information which we hope will provide a handy resource bank for professionals working in this area and for parents.

Looking to the future, it is our view that, as experience and practice grow, there will be a greater emphasis on early disagreement resolution than on adversarial legal battles.

It is likely that we will see an even further development of a staged approach to disagreements, involving:

1 direct negotiations between the parties concerned;
2 internal help using advocates (e.g. Parent Partnership officers);
3 conciliation;
4 independent mediation;
5 and then, as a last resort, the SEN tribunal and other legal redress.

The hope would be for there to be a total ethos in special education of conciliation and mediation, such that the practice is regarded as routine and expected. This may well require widespread training and support of all professionals working in the field of SEN, and perhaps all educators.

There could be no more worthwhile area of education where such an approach is required than in dealing with children with SEN, with a view to promoting the best interests of this most vulnerable group of children in the system. There is often highly emotionally charged circumstances surrounding SEN casework. Conciliation and mediation are likely to offer a much more conducive and profitable experience and outcome for children and families, than months of unresolved conflict between LEAs, teachers and parents. We do know that children need consistency in their management by key adults responsible for their care, and that they need to feel that the adults around them can work together actively on their behalf. Indeed, as a message to children for the future, a positive disagreement resolution process may itself provide a lasting lesson of value to children. Indeed, for the future, peer mediation looks to be a most exciting and fruitful development which will serve to educate the next generation in problem-solving without continued conflict.

It must be recognised, nonetheless, that there will be some cases in which processes other than conciliation and mediation are required, and indeed which require arbitration and legal resolution, through, for example, the SEN tribunal. Fischer and Ury (1981) have invented a useful term which reminds us of this possibility called 'BATNA' which stands for 'Best Alternative to a Negotiated Agreement' which can clearly be applied to disagreement resolution.

John Wright (1999) writing in an article for the Independent Panel for Special Education, (but in a personal capacity) has argued that conciliation can be unhelpful as simply 'placating peasants' when those who are doing wrong should simply be corrected and forced to comply with their legal duties. Whilst disagreeing with the extent of his negative view of conciliation, his article does act as reminder that one should not lose sight of justice, and that conciliation should not be used simply to continue wrong practices. His idea that such services should be linked to the SEN tribunal warrants serious consideration.

The concept of a staged approach is helpful in reply to Wright's critique; it would be hoped that the development of conciliation and mediation services would have the effect of keeping SEN tribunal hearings and other court actions to an absolute minimum, reserved for their cases when absolutely necessary.

For the future, we would envisage:

- a greater use of direct negotiation, conciliation and mediation;
- professional regulation of neutral mediators and facilitators in SEN;
- universal codes of conduct;
- emerging and universal operational formats, which are based upon successful track records; recognised training for SEN mediators and conciliators, plus continuing professional development programmes leading to agreed standards and qualifications to practise;

- teachers and special education professionals being specifically trained in negotiation and disagreement resolution techniques;
- children and young people being encouraged and trained in negotiation, conciliation and mediation and thus able to undertake peer mediation;
- a focus upon equal opportunity issues and issues of diversity, enabling a greater understanding of cultural, religious and other background circumstances;
- research in mediation, examining the factors that contribute to effective resolutions, which cases might be amenable, what are the characteristics of effective mediations, what factors contribute to successful versus unsuccessful outcomes, selection procedures, evaluation of services and the development of new initiatives, particularly those involving children and peer mediation. The field is ripe for rigorous empirical evaluative and comparative research, and perhaps detailed studies of mediation in action, using video and up-to-date computer methods to identify key processes and skills.

We are at the start of the development of potentially one of the most important processes in the SEN context, and there is considerable professional goodwill and excitement about the possibilities.

Effective, early and positive disagreement resolution promises to contribute greater harmony in this area. Bearing in mind the many challenges facing children and young people with SEN in their lives, there can be no more deserving group of people who might qualify for a chance to reduce conflict, dissension and argument in favour of a speedy and effective resolution of disagreements.

We hope that this book will raise issues for debate and change, that it will be of help as a training resource, and mostly that it will make a contribution to the development of disagreement resolution services.

References

Wright, J. (1999) IPSEA on Conciliation: Placating Peasants. Independent Panel for Special Education Advice (IPSEA Files). Website:www.ipsea.org.uk/placatingpeasants.htm.

Fisher, R. and Ury, W.L. (1981) *Getting to Yes*. New York: Houghton Mifflin Co.

Chapter 10

Sources of further information

In this chapter you will find:

10.1   EXTRACTS FROM THE DfES SEN TOOLKIT

Section 3: Resolution of disagreements

This section is intended primarily for Local Education Authorities (LEAs) in England, parent partnership services, and organisations working in the field of disagreement resolution. It will also be relevant and of interest to parents and schools. It provides information on good practice on making arrangements for resolution of disagreements between parents and schools or LEAs about matters relating to special educational needs.

It should be read in conjunction with Chapter Two of the SEN Code of Practice.

Resolution of disagreements

- LEAs must make arrangements for avoiding or resolving disagreements that parents have either with them or with schools about SEN matters
- Independent persons must be appointed to facilitate these arrangements

Preventing disagreements:

- Good communications between parents, schools and LEAs is the key to good relationships
- Parents, schools, LEAs and others should start talking as soon as difficulties become apparent. This can prevent problems from developing into disagreements
- Feedback from users of the new arrangements can help schools and LEAs prevent similar disagreements in the future

Resolving disagreements:

- In delivering effective disagreement resolution services, LEAs should meet the minimum standards set out in the SEN Code of Practice

- SEN disagreement resolution is designed to achieve early and informal resolution of differences of opinion
- The informal arrangements bring different parties together in the presence of an independent/neutral facilitator to seek an agreement
- The people in disagreement, not the facilitator, decide the terms of the agreement

Introduction

1. This section explains the legal requirements as set out in the Education Act 1996, and the provisions in the Education (Special Educational Needs) (England) (Consolidation) Regulations 2001. It offers additional detailed guidance to that set out in the SEN Code of Practice. It draws on research looking at what LEAs were doing voluntarily in resolving disagreements, identifying different models that have been adopted, and looking at previous good practice.[1]

2. Although the framework for disagreement resolution is statutory, and must therefore be complied with, this Toolkit is not intended to be prescriptive. This section sets out considerations that LEAs should take into account when establishing or modifying their disagreement resolution arrangements. It aims to strike a balance between what is expected of an effective disagreement resolution service and allowing LEAs the flexibility they need to deliver services that meet local requirements. An approach that meets the needs of parents in one LEA will not necessarily meet the needs of those in another.

Preventing disagreements

A local education authority must make arrangements, that include the appointment of independent persons, with a view to avoiding or resolving disagreements between authorities (on the one hand) and parents of children in their area (on the other) about the way LEAs and maintained schools carry out their responsibilities towards children with special educational needs.

A local education authority must also make arrangements with a view to avoiding or resolving disagreements between parents and certain schools about the special educational provision made for their child.

LEAs must take whatever steps they consider appropriate to make disagreement resolution services known to parents, head teachers, schools and others they consider appropriate.

See Sections 332B, Education Act 1996

3. Parents,[2] schools,[3] LEAs and others should start talking as soon as difficulties become apparent. Talking about concerns as soon as they arise may help prevent potential problems from developing into major disagreements. Dialogue should be built on a foundation of trust, respect, clarity and openness. Schools and LEAs should be flexible in the way in which they encourage early dialogue and ensure that they are able to respond to parents' needs in the most appropriate way. The views of parents should be actively sought and valued.

4. Good communications and the sharing of information between parents and schools, and between parents and LEAs is the key to good relationships. By talking early on there is greater chance of resolving potential problems. The longer things are left, the harder they become to resolve. Parent partnership services can play an important role in preventing disagreements by encouraging dialogue between the parents and the school or LEA, as soon as difficulties arise, to explore different options at an early stage.

5. Under the Education (Special Educational Needs) (Information) (England) Regulations 1999, every maintained school is required to publish information about any arrangements

made by the governing body relating to the treatment of complaints from parents of pupils with special educational needs concerning the provision made at the school. Many schools and LEAs already have successful informal processes for resolving disputes. As soon as a difficulty becomes apparent therefore, parents and schools, and parents and LEAs should, in the first instance, have informal discussions with the aim of resolving their differences locally. Where these discussions or the normal complaints procedure have been exhausted and matters cannot be resolved, any of the parties may then wish to consider recourse to the statutory SEN disagreement resolution process.

6. Parent partnership services can encourage the parties to come together and help to keep lines of communication open by:
   - assisting the parties to assess their relevant positions
   - negotiating between them, or on behalf of them
   - identifying areas of compromise
   - making suggestions or recommendations about possible ways forward.

   In exercising this function, parent partnership services should be neutral and should not be an advocate for any one party.

7. As part of the arrangements for disagreement resolution, LEAs should actively seek feedback from parent partnership services and independent facilitators on completion of disagreement resolution cases. The feedback should include information on the reasons that gave rise to the disagreement so that LEAs and schools can identify ways of improving their policies and practices to avoid similar disagreements arising in the future.

Disagreement resolution

8. SEN disagreement resolution is an entirely voluntary process. It brings people who are in disagreement together with an independent neutral party (or facilitator), who then helps them to reach an agreement. Ideally, disagreement resolution

should take place well within the two month statutory time limit for appeal to the SEN tribunal, but can also take place once an appeal is lodged. A fundamental principle should be that the child's welfare and needs are key considerations.

9. The people in disagreement, not the facilitator, decide the terms of the agreement. The facilitator does not offer advice or solutions. An example model of the disagreement resolution process is at Annex A. Annex B shows how this model could be used in resolution of disagreements about SEN.

10. SEN disagreement resolution is designed to achieve early resolution of differences of opinion between parents and schools or LEAs about the provision being made for their child's special educational needs. It should ensure that practical educational solutions, acceptable to all the parties, are reached as quickly as possible with minimal disruption to the child's education. Disagreement resolution should aim to prevent the long term breakdown of relationships between parents and schools or LEAs, and in time reduce the need for recourse to the SEN tribunal.

11. The principles of disagreement resolution are:
    • any agreement has to be to the satisfaction of all the parties concerned
    • all parties agree that a resolution is needed
    • the process is voluntary and confidential
    • the facilitator is, and is seen to be, independent and neutral
    • the parties have all agreed the choice of the facilitator
    • the process does not prejudice any rights to take issues further, for example to the SEN tribunal
    • those involved have the authority to be able to settle the disagreement.

12. Independence and neutrality are key principles. All the parties concerned therefore need to be satisfied that the facilitator is truly independent and neutral.

13. Where a joint meeting is held, the discussions can often be concluded in less than one day.

Minimum standards for LEAs

14. LEAs *must* make arrangements for avoiding and resolving disagreements parents have either with them or with schools about matters relating to the SEN provision for their child. The arrangements *must* provide for the appointment of independent persons to facilitate the avoidance or resolution of disagreements.

15. In delivering an effective disagreement resolution service, LEAs:

- should take responsibility for the overall standard of the service and ensure it is subject to Best Value principles
- should have clear funding and budgeting plans for the service
- should ensure that the service is neutral and **must** involve an independent element
- should ensure that the service, whether outsourced or provided in-house, has a development plan that sets out clear targets and is regularly reviewed. Such plans should specify arrangements for evaluation and quality assurance
- *must* make the arrangements for disagreement resolution, and how they will work, known to parents, schools and others they consider appropriate (section 332B(5) of the Education Act 1996)
- *must* inform parents about the arrangements for disagreement resolution at the time a proposed statement or amended statement is issued, and that entering disagreement resolution does not affect their right of appeal to the SEN tribunal (Education) (Special Educational Needs) (England) Regulations 2001
- should ensure that the independent persons appointed as facilitators have the appropriate skills, knowledge and expertise in disagreement resolution;

an understanding of SEN processes, procedures and legislation; have no role in the decisions taken about a particular case, nor any vested interest in the terms of the settlement; are unbiased; maintain confidentiality; carry out the process quickly and to the timetable decided by the parties

- should establish protocols and mechanisms for referring parents to disagreement resolution
- should ensure that those providing the service receive appropriate initial and ongoing training and development to enable them to carry out their role effectively
- should establish a service level agreement for delivering the service which ensures sufficient levels of resources and training, and sets out the appropriate standards expected of, and the responsibilities delegated to, the provider
- should have appropriate arrangements for overseeing, regularly monitoring and reviewing the service, taking account of local and national best practice, whether the service is provided in-house or bought-in
- should actively seek feedback from the service to inform and influence decisions on SEN policies, procedures and practices
- should monitor and evaluate the performance of the service.

From 2:25 SEN Code of Practice

The disagreement resolution process

16. The Education Act 1996 requires SEN related disagreement avoidance and resolution arrangements to be available to *all* parents whose child has SEN if their child is a registered pupil at:

- a maintained school, maintained nursery school, pupil referral unit, City Technology College, City College for the Technology of the Arts, City Academy
- a non-maintained special school
- an independent school named in the child's statement of special educational needs (where the disagreement is between the parent and the school).

However, LEAs may use their discretion and make SEN disagreement resolution available to other parents if they wish. Representatives of LEAs and of the types of educational establishments listed above can request and participate in disagreement resolution. Parents, of course, can also initiate the use of the service – though participation by either party is voluntary.

17. Depending on the nature of the disagreement, the parties involved may be the parents and the school, the parents and the LEA, or the parents, LEA and a maintained school.

The benefits of a structured disagreement resolution process

18. It is essential that parents, schools and LEAs recognise the need to deal with, and move on from what has happened in the past. It is also essential that all parties involved recognise the need to allocate sufficient time for the process of disagreement resolution. Disagreement resolution may have implications for schools' and LEAs' resources, but a structured process can bring benefits:
    - *in exploring outcomes* – the solutions reached tend to be more creative than through other processes
    - *to build trust and ownership* – which in turn might elicit outcomes that are more likely to be followed through. Because the resolutions are identified by the parties who have to carry them out they are more frequently complied with than those imposed

- *to facilitate communication* – because the parties have solved the problem together, they will have needed to communicate positively and build greater understanding. This creates a new pattern of communication for the future
- *in using a tiered process* – enabling the parties, at separate sessions, to work through their differences e.g. the school or LEA, and then parents separately.

Limitations

19. Offering a structured session may be inappropriate if:
    - either side does not wish to engage in the process
    - matters of policy are at stake
    - the main issue is one that would set a precedent on which the LEA is unwilling or unable to concede
    - there is no goodwill
    - there is a substantial change in the relationship between the parents and the LEA or school, for instance the parents have moved or are moving to another LEA area, or the child has or is about to transfer to a different school.
20. There will always be cases where it is not possible to reach agreement through the disagreement resolution process, for instance where there are legal restrictions on the action schools or LEAs may take. In such cases, it may be more appropriate for the parents to seek recourse to the SEN tribunal.
21. Disagreement resolution arrangements are not the appropriate vehicle for parents who have disagreements with the school about issues other than special educational needs, for instance the general conduct of the school. In such situations, parents should direct their complaint in the first instance to the head teacher or the governing body. All LEAs must have separate procedures for handling complaints about the actions of governing bodies and LEAs. In these cases the person with the complaint should first take the matter up with the governing body, or if after having done so they are still not satisfied, with the LEA.

SEN disagreement resolution

22. There are a number of models that LEAs might adopt to include an independent element in their disagreement resolution arrangements, for instance:

    • using a panel of trained facilitators, affiliated to a recognised body in the field of disagreement resolution. LEAs could then buy in the services as they were required

    • expanding existing disagreement resolution services that cover a wide range of areas across the work of the authority to include SEN expertise

    • using regional panels funded by a number of neighbouring LEAs, perhaps using the SEN Regional Partnerships. The LEAs within the region would then have access to a pool of facilitators.

    Whichever model is adopted it is essential that the facilitator is acceptable to the parties involved. LEAs *must*, however, appoint independent persons to help facilitate their SEN disagreement resolution arrangements. These independent persons cannot be LEA officers.

23. Many organisations have expertise in disagreement resolution and are able to provide trained and experienced independent facilitators. LEAs should therefore consider working in partnership with other organisations in making their arrangements for disagreement resolution services – but see paragraph 40 on *Advocates*. LEAs should ensure such organisations are reputable bodies with expertise in the field of disagreement resolution.

24. The role of the independent facilitator[4] includes:

    • taking responsibility for the process of resolution, not the content

    • enabling all the parties concerned to articulate their view of the problems, either through separate or joint meetings, and their preferred solutions

    • managing the process so that people, on all sides, are given an equal opportunity to tell their story, have their perceptions validated or challenged, and to work through the possible outcomes

- exploring and testing any agreements, including reaching an understanding on what happens if agreements are not complied with
- assisting, if required, in drafting those agreements that the parties involved agree to abide by
- assisting, if required, in drafting any feedback to the LEA so that the general lessons arising out of the disagreement can be fed back for wider consideration.

25. The need for confidentiality means that some boundaries have to be defined. For example, where child protection issues emerge during disagreement resolution they cannot be treated as confidential. This should be made clear to all the parties in advance. Taking part in disagreement resolution is entirely without prejudice to parents' rights to appeal to the SEN tribunal. There should therefore be an agreement about any information that may be subsequently relayed to the tribunal. As a general principle, nothing discussed during disagreement resolution should be made available to the tribunal without the consent of all relevant parties.

Following up agreements

26. In cases where an agreement has been reached about steps to be taken, school and LEA representatives should check that what has been agreed is being put into practice, at regular intervals, to be decided by the parties to the agreement.

Facilitator independence

The arrangements must provide for the appointment of independent persons with the function of facilitating the avoidance or resolution of such disagreements.

See Section 332B(3), Education Act 1996

27. The Education Act 1996 requires LEAs' arrangements to include the appointment of independent persons to help resolve disagreements. The 'independent person' (the facilitator) must be someone who:
   - has no role in the decisions taken about a particular child's case
   - has no vested interest in the terms of the settlement
   - is unbiased
   - maintains confidentiality
   - carries out the disagreement resolution quickly and according to the timetable decided by the parties involved
   - is not an LEA officer.

This is to ensure that the parties feel that their views are being properly considered and given equal weight. Perceived bias is likely to cause resentment and hinder progress towards resolving disagreements. Where all parties are seen to be equal partners the facilitator is more likely to succeed in encouraging communication, and therefore reach an outcome that is acceptable to all.

Principles and minimum standards for independent facilitators

28. LEAs should use their best endeavours to ensure that those appointed as independent facilitators:

   - unbiased and always act in good faith; have no vested interest in the outcome of the disagreement or the terms of the settlement; act fairly at all times showing no favouritism or bias; keep all concerned informed of progress and make any information available to the parties as is required; and have no personal involvement with any of the parties

- maintain confidentiality (as this encourages the parties to open up and be honest with the facilitator); should retain as private all information or materials received by them from any party unless disclosure is expressly authorised by the party concerned. There may, however, be exceptional situations where the rules of confidentiality would have to be set aside – such as in the case of disclosure of child protection issues when confidentiality would not be appropriate and legal requirements may require disclosure
- outline the procedures at the outset and ensure that all parties understand the process, and the role and neutrality of the facilitator; carry out the disagreement resolution expeditiously and according to the timetable decided by the parties involved
- ensure that all parties understand the proposed settlement and that they have had time to consider it thoroughly; where more than one resolution procedure is being considered, ensure that the parties are clear about the different procedures and the consequences of revealing information during one procedure which may later be used for decision making in another – see paragraph 48
- do not act fraudulently, deceitfully or in any way unlawfully, nor use their position to gain personal advantage for themselves, family or friends; do not accept gifts, favours or hospitality from any party that may be construed as an attempt to influence them
- have the necessary skills, expertise and knowledge to fulfil their role effectively, including an understanding of SEN processes, procedures and legislation.

The skills required of the independent facilitator

29. The independent facilitator needs to have a wide range of knowledge and skills including the ability to:
    - manage the process
    - be an active listener
    - uncover the real issues
    - remain neutral and unbiased
    - ensure equality
    - provide neutral and accurate feedback
    - assist others to problem solve
    - recognise similarities and differences
    - frame agreements.

30. It is particularly important to avoid apportioning blame or to let the past dominate the entire session. Some discussion of the past may be necessary in order to enable the parties to move forward, but the session itself should be managed in order to draw a line under the past and move towards the future. Throughout the session, or sessions, the facilitator should work to re-establish direct communication between the parties. Part of the role of the facilitator is to demonstrate good communication. Enabling and encouraging the parties to communicate effectively during the facilitated sessions provides an opportunity to lay a foundation on which to build continuing positive relationships for the future.

31. A range of experiences, knowledge and qualifications is essential for those involved in SEN disagreement resolution, for instance:
    - training and experience in disagreement resolution
    - counselling and negotiating skills
    - the ability to establish and maintain communications
    - knowledge of SEN legislation, the SEN Code of Practice and other educational issues.

32. Prospective facilitators will therefore need initial and ongoing specialist training to ensure they are kept up to date with developments. The precise nature and level of such training will depend to a great extent on the approach adopted by

the LEA but should include training on SEN legislation, the SEN framework and the SEN Code of Practice and information on local LEA SEN policies and procedures.

Implementing the process

Providing information

> The authority must take such steps as they consider appropriate for making the arrangements known to the parents of children in their area, the head teachers and proprietors of schools in their area, and such other persons as they consider appropriate.
>
> See Section 332B(5), Education Act 1996

33. LEAs *must* inform parents, schools and others they consider appropriate about their arrangements for avoiding and resolving disagreements. In addition, the Education (Special Educational Needs) (England) (Consolidation) Regulations 2001 requires that LEA *must* inform parents:
    - about the arrangements for disagreement resolution when they give notice of their decision not to carry out a statutory assessment, and at the time a proposed statement or proposed amended statement is issued; and
    - that, where parents have a right of appeal to the SEN tribunal, taking part in disagreement resolution does not affect that right (see paragraphs 46 and 47).

    It is important to ensure that parents, schools and all relevant LEA officers are fully aware of the arrangements – what is available, when they may have access to disagreement resolution, and where it might take place. One way of helping to achieve this – particularly when schemes are set up – might be to organise a series of workshops for parents, LEA SEN officers, governing bodies and school staff to raise awareness of what disagreement resolution entails, how it would operate and what the benefits are. Such sessions could be organised at a local or regional level.

34. LEAs should consider other ways of publicising the scheme, for instance through the parent partnership service as discussed in Section 2 of this Toolkit.

35. Information should be available in community languages. It should also be available in alternative formats for parents who may not be able to gain access to material through more conventional means. Schools also have a key role to play in promoting disagreement resolution and in passing on information to parents.

When and how disagreement resolution could be used

36. Disagreement resolution can be entered whenever relations between parents and the school or LEA are becoming strained, or misunderstandings are developing. Any party (i.e. parents, schools or LEAs) can request disagreement resolution, or it can be suggested by the parent partnership service as an appropriate way forward. It is essential, however, that parent partnership services, schools or LEAs do not disclose parents' details to a third party without obtaining their prior agreement. Ideally, disagreement resolution should take place well within the two month statutory time limit for appeal to the SEN tribunal, but can also take place once an appeal is lodged.

37. Independent disagreement resolution can take the form of a 'shuttle' service whereby a facilitator moves between the parties, or the parties come together at face-to-face meetings. Face-to-face meetings will usually be more fruitful. However, where relations between parents and the school or the LEA are strained, or where one party would have difficulty getting to a meeting, disagreement resolution by telephone may be appropriate. Whatever approach is adopted, it is important that all parties are aware that participation is voluntary.

Where and when meetings should take place

38. Careful consideration should be given to where and when the meetings take place. Wherever possible, disagreement resolution meetings should be held at a neutral place, and at a time convenient for and agreed by all parties. If it is not possible to hold the meetings in a neutral place, other possible locations include the LEA or other council offices or the child's school, although meetings at the LEA offices or school might not be seen as neutral, and might not be acceptable to some parents. However, there may be dvantages in that they provide quick access to important information.

39. At the first meeting, it is beneficial if the parties decide who will attend any future meetings. Each case is different, but it will usually be helpful if the same people attend each meeting. This is helpful in sustaining dialogue and ensuring that the parties feel they are equal partners in the process. It is particularly important that parents are enabled to take part in negotiations on an equal footing. Independent Parental Supporters can play a valuable role in helping parents prepare for, and in providing support at, meetings. Parents should be encouraged to bring along their Independent Parental Supporter where they would find that helpful.

Advocates

40. Advocates speak for and on the behalf of their clients, usually parents. Where a voluntary organisation has been contracted to provide parent partnership services, or are involved in supporting parents, they are in effect acting as parental advocates and cannot also be facilitators in disagreement resolution. Similarly, LEA officers act on behalf of the LEA and cannot also be facilitators.

41. It is not envisaged that the various parties would require legal representation at this stage; that would be contrary to the spirit of informal disagreement resolution. Where less formal advocates, for example Independent Parental

Supporters, are involved then they would need to be aware that disagreement resolution works best where clients are enabled to speak for themselves. The facilitator's role includes ensuring that all parties are fully supported and are given ample opportunity to confer privately.

Accessibility

42. Any disagreement resolution service needs to be credible to parents, schools and LEAs, and flexible enough to be commissioned quickly and, where appropriate, within the statutory time limit for lodging an appeal to the SEN tribunal. Taking part in disagreement resolution is entirely voluntary: parents, schools and LEAs cannot be forced to participate. Disagreement resolution will only work if the parties are willing to engage in the process. Wherever possible, both parents should be invited to take part in disagreement resolution, particularly where they may have different views.

43. Parents can feel daunted by meetings with officers of the LEA or senior school staff. LEAs and schools should therefore consider agreeing to parents bringing a friend with them. Similarly, parents may need the sort of information and advice that is available from the parent partnership service, in advance of and during the structured disagreement resolution process. Parents need to have an understanding of SEN policies and procedures, and their entitlements under SEN legislation, so that they are empowered to participate fully and effectively in disagreement resolution discussions – see Section 2 of this Toolkit. As a matter of good practice, support might include training in effective communication and assertiveness techniques. LEAs and schools may also wish to hold pre-meetings to help them identify what they want to achieve from disagreement resolution and the points they want to raise.

44. At the first meeting it is often helpful for the parents to speak first, to set the scene from their point of view. This

may help them to develop confidence in the process and feel at ease in expressing their views and concerns. Similarly, the school and LEA representatives should have the opportunity to explain the authority's position and the factors influencing it.

Role of children in disagreement resolution

45. Chapter Three of the SEN Code of Practice emphasises the importance of the rights of the child and the necessity of involving them in decisions taken about the provision made for them. In most cases, it will not be appropriate to involve children in the disagreement resolution discussions that take place between their parents and their school or LEA. However, whilst they may not be involved directly in disagreement resolution meetings, they should be consulted to determine their wishes, needs and views. Every effort should be made early on in the process to ensure that the child's own point of view is established. It should also be recognised that the views of the child and their parents may differ. Children's views might be presented in various ways, for instance video, audiotapes, drawings. Further suggestions can be found in Section 4 of this Toolkit. Discussions that do not have the child at the fore can deteriorate into a battle between the parents and the school or LEA. It is therefore essential that the child's needs and best interests remain at the fore.

Appeals to the special educational needs tribunal

46. One aim of disagreement resolution is to help resolve as many disagreements as possible without recourse to the more formal mechanism of the SEN tribunal. However, it is essential that disagreement resolution is *not* suggested as an alternative to parents registering an appeal with the tribunal. At any stage parents can exercise their rights to go to the SEN

tribunal. In certain circumstances, the SEN tribunal may be the only option (see paragraphs 19 and 20).

47. LEAs *must* inform parents in writing that their legal rights to lodge an appeal continue regardless of whether they decide to enter disagreement resolution. Disagreement resolution should not therefore be presented as an additional process that parents have to go through before being able to register an appeal. That is likely to be seen by many as a delaying tactic and will do nothing to facilitate discussion during disagreement resolution meetings. Rather, it is expected that disagreement resolution should be offered or requested as soon as disagreement is evident, and, where possible and appropriate, within the two month statutory time limit for making an appeal.

48. Disagreement resolution discussions should be seen as confidential. However, during disagreement resolution the parties can make an agreement about any information that can be relayed to any subsequent tribunal hearings. For instance, it would be appropriate to inform the tribunal of any issues agreed during the process of disagreement resolution, thus narrowing the focus for the tribunal hearing. If any other points made during disagreement resolution meetings are raised at the tribunal, they should not be held against either party.

49. Separate arrangements apply under Part III of the Disability Discrimination Act 1995 where a person believes that a service provider (or person managing the premises, for instance an LEA or school governing body) has unlawfully discriminated against them on the grounds of disability. The appropriate avenue for resolution of disputes about disability discrimination under Part III of the Act is the independent conciliation service established by the Disability Rights Commission. Information and advice about the conciliation service is available from the Disability Rights Commission's Helpline on 08457 622 633. The Helpline also provides information and advice to disabled people about their rights

under the Act, to employers and service providers about their obligations under the Act, and advice for those seeking to deploy best practice.

Monitoring and evaluation

50. LEAs should review their arrangements periodically to ensure they are delivering a high quality service that is capable of development and improvement to meet changing needs. This can be achieved by:
    - sharing information and comparing their service to others
    - collating information from users and seeking the views of non-users
    - monitoring the effectiveness of staff and volunteers
    - thorough independent evaluation.

    Users' views can then be used to improve or enhance the service.

51. There are many reasons why parents seek recourse to the SEN tribunal. Many appeals could be avoided if LEAs were aware of the reasons and took steps, where possible, to avoid the need for parents to appeal. Therefore, as part of the monitoring process, LEAs should obtain feedback from the disagreement resolution service on the factors that appear to trigger disagreement. This will identify changes that can be made to local SEN policy and practice to improve communications and practices, so minimising the potential for disagreement.

52. Benchmarking will be key to the success of monitoring and evaluation, including the benchmarking of funding, appeals to the tribunal and against minimum standards.

    Other methods of evaluation could include:
    - monitoring who the key users are
    - monitoring different aspects of the service
    - regular feedback from LEA staff and other users
    - monitoring individual casework.

53. LEAs should be aware that Ofsted, as part of the normal LEA inspection process, will carry out monitoring of the provision of disagreement resolution services.

Annex A

The disagreement resolution process – a suggested model

Note: although specific to mediation rather than conciliation, the principles and practices set out below are broadly applicable to disagreement resolution and are likely to be of practical assistance to LEAs.

This model is based on the seven stages that appear in the Mediation (UK) training manual. It outlines the stages and the key tasks associated with each stage in face-to-face disagreement resolution, the first three of which take place before the parties move into face-to-face disagreement resolution. The stages are:

1. first contact with the first party
2. first contact with the second party
3. preparing to work on the dispute
4. hearing the issues
5. exploring the issues
6. building agreements
7. closure and follow-up

STAGE I: FIRST CONTACT WITH THE FIRST PARTY

Key tasks:

- introductions
- find out about the situation
- acknowledge feelings
- build rapport
- explain what mediation is and is not
- seek agreement to continue the mediation process

- establish how confidentiality will work
- decide and agree upon next course of action.

STAGE II: FIRST CONTACT WITH THE SECOND PARTY

Key tasks:

- the second party has the opportunity to describe the situation from their perspective
- gain trust
- establish impartiality
- maintain confidentiality.

STAGE III: PREPARING TO WORK ON THE DISPUTE

Key tasks:

- identify the best way to continue the mediation
- prepare the conflicting parties
- establish commitment
- prepare the venue.

STAGE IV: HEARING THE ISSUES

Key tasks:

- introduce the parties and the issues
- establish ground rules
- explain and agree the process
- provide uninterrupted time for both parties
- manage any early conflict and hostility
- provide a safe environment
- establish a climate of honesty, trust and openness
- summarise the key issues
- agree agenda and time limits.

STAGE V: EXPLORING THE ISSUES

Key tasks:

- establish and present the issues
- encourage communication
- check understanding and clarify assumptions
- identify concerns, fears and reservations
- acknowledge the differences and agree to move on
- maintain a safe environment
- change focus from past to future
- summarise areas of agreement, and any disagreements that remain.

STAGE VI: BUILDING AGREEMENTS

Key tasks:

- brainstorm for alternative and innovative solutions
- evaluate options
- encourage problem solving
- construct agreements
- establish fallback agreements
- in absence of agreement, identify what to do next.

STAGE VII: CLOSURE AND FOLLOW-UP

Key tasks:

- close session
- arrange follow-up.

Annex B

The disagreement resolution process – an example

Note: this example is *one way* in which the model at Annex A could be adapted for use in resolution of disagreements about SEN.

STAGE I – CONTACT

- One party requests disagreement resolution from the person who co-ordinates the service for the LEA (the co-ordinator)
- The co-ordinator contacts the people requesting disagreement resolution to clarify the process and to discuss the issues they want to bring to disagreement resolution
- The co-ordinator has an initial conversation with the other party, or parties, to ensure there are no blockages from their point of view to proceeding
- Strategies for getting round potential blockages might include:
  - focusing on the issues that are central to the disagreement and those most likely to rebuild trust and communication. Smaller and more peripheral issues, which may require the involvement of additional parties, can be addressed separately following the main disagreement resolution meeting
  - taking a layered approach when a number of issues need to be resolved, for instance dealing firstly with the core issues, then agreeing a process to deal with the other issues
  - addressing any disagreement between the school and the LEA separately in a pre-meeting, before the start of the full disagreement resolution, so that there can be some agreement on how the issue will be approached and on the range of potential outcomes that both the school and LEA can live with
  - encouraging LEAs to look at the overall cost of possible outcomes, as well as the costs of a range of packages, to see if they can be creative within those parameters
- Following these discussions, written confirmation is sent out and the party who requested disagreement resolution is asked to complete and return a disagreement resolution request form – one side of A4 that sets out the issues and the resolutions they are seeking.

STAGE 2 – PREPARING TO WORK ON THE DISPUTE

- Upon receipt of the written material, or material transcribed over the phone if there are communication difficulties, the co-ordinator contacts the other party or parties
- The other parties then have a chance to complete a form giving the same details: the issues they wish to bring to the session and the resolutions they are seeking
- The co-ordinator ensures that all parties have copies of each other's request forms
- The co-ordinator checks that the people attending the session have the authority to settle, that everyone knows who will be present, and has a chance to raise any objections before the session
- The co-ordinator selects a facilitator whose role is to manage the discussions between the parties. The name and details of the facilitator are given to all the parties so that they have a chance to object
- A time, date and neutral venue is agreed
- The parties are asked if they would like one-to-one meetings, or telephone conversations, with the facilitator before the session, so that the process can be explained before it starts
- If there is a need for the facilitator to meet any party to clarify issues, or to alleviate anxiety, this can be done either immediately before the joint session, or by prior arrangement. If the facilitator meets one party it is important that they meet both (or all).

STAGE 3 – HEARING THE ISSUES, EXPLORING THE ISSUES

- A joint session is convened where the parties are able to meet together, in the presence of the facilitator, to go through the issues. Ideally this would start with everyone together, but separate meetings with the facilitator are possible at any time
- It is important that this session is kept as small as possible, so some issues that involve other agencies may be put on

hold while the main issues are sorted out. In this way communication can be re-established first and then a process agreed by which other issues will be dealt with

- The session should be designed to explore the lessons from the past, acknowledge any shortcomings and then create agreements that the parties can live with for the future.

STAGE 4 – BUILDING AGREEMENTS

- The facilitator should keep a note of any agreements that have been reached by the parties. When there is a consensus that all the agreements necessary have been made, or as much as can be achieved in one session has been achieved, the facilitator should bring the session to a close. The facilitator should then test the agreements, and make provision for what should happen if there are any difficulties identified during implementation
- After the voluntary and confidential part of the session has been closed, the facilitator can help to draft agreements that the parties agree they will abide by, and draft any feedback to the school or LEA about the more general lessons that can be learned from the disagreement. In order to maintain confidentiality, the feedback should be in a suitably anonymised form
- All parties should receive copies of the agreements and any feedback. Before anything is destroyed, the parties should confirm that the written agreement accurately represents the agreement reached. The facilitator should ensure the feedback goes to the school and/or LEA co-ordinator, but otherwise should destroy any other notes in front of the parties.

STAGE 5 – CLOSURE AND FOLLOW-UP

- The school or LEA (as appropriate) should monitor the effectiveness of the disagreement resolution process, ensure that agreements are complied with and that the more generic lessons are taken on board to prevent a re-occurrence elsewhere.

Copies of this publication can be obtained from
DfES Publications
PO Box 5050
Sherwood Park
Annesley
Nottinghamshire
NG15 ODJ
Tel 0845 60 222 60
Fax 0845 60 333 60
e-mail: dfes@prolog.uk.com
© Crown copyright 2001
Produced by the Department for Education
and Skills
www.dfes.gov.uk

Notes

1 Copies of the research report – *Resolving Disagreements between Parents, Schools and LEAs: Some Examples of Best Practice* by Jane Hall – can be requested from the DfES on 0207 925 5524.
2 Here, and throughout this section, 'parents' should be taken to include all those with parental responsibility, including corporate parents and carers.
3 Here, and throughout this section, 'schools' should be taken to include maintained schools, maintained nursery schools, pupil referral units, City Technology Colleges, City Colleges for Technology of the Arts, City Academies, Non-Maintained Special Schools and independent schools named in a child's statement of SEN.
4 The independent person required by section 332B(3) of the Education Act 1996. See also 27 to 32.

10.2 A SAMPLE MEDIATION AGREEMENT (GLOBAL MEDIATION LTD)

MEDIATION AGREEMENT

I agree to try to settle the disagreement (case no. ....) by mediation.

I agree that all communications in the mediation will be kept confidential.

PARTIES

The following people will attend the mediation:-

Parent(s)/carer(s) ....

Supporter (not a lawyer) ....

LEA / School (please state title) ....

....

....

MEDIATOR

The mediator will be ....

I agree that the mediator will decide the procedure and ground rules, but will not take sides or impose a solution.

I understand that the mediator will not retain any notes at the end of the mediation process. The mediator shall not be called as a witness and will not be involved in the disagreement other than as a mediator.

Anyone (including the mediator) has the right to withdraw from the mediation at any time. Mediation does not affect my rights.

Please sign below:-

....

....

....

....

This agreement should be signed and handed to the mediator.

10.3   A SAMPLE OF THE CODE OF CONDUCT (GLOBAL MEDIATION LTD)

Code of conduct

Introduction

1. This Code applies to any person who acts as a neutral third party ('the Mediator') under the auspices of GLOBAL MEDIATION.

Impartiality and conflict of interest

2. The Mediator will at all times act, and endeavour to be seen to act, fairly and with complete impartiality towards the Parties in the Mediation without any bias in favour of any Party or any discrimination against any Party.

3. Any matter of which the Mediator is aware which could be regarded as involving a conflict of interest (whether apparent, potential or actual) in the Mediation will be disclosed to the Parties. This disclosure will be made in writing to all the Parties as soon as the Mediator becomes aware of it, whether the matter occurs prior to, or during, the Mediation. In these circumstances the Mediator will not act (or continue to act) in the Mediation unless all the Parties specifically acknowledge the disclosure and agree in writing to the Mediator acting or continuing to act as Mediator.

4. Examples of the type of information that the Mediator should disclose include:
    (a) having acted in any capacity for any of the parties (other than as Mediator in other ADR procedures);
    (b) the Mediator's firm (if applicable) having acted in any capacity for any of the Parties;
    (c) having any financial or other interest (whether direct or indirect) in any of the Parties or in the subject matter or outcome of the Mediation;
    (d) having any confidential information about any of the Parties or the subject matter of the Mediation.

5. The Mediator (and any member of the Mediator's firm or company) will not act for any of the Parties individually in connection with the dispute which is the subject of the Mediation while acting as the Mediator or at any time thereafter, without the written consent of all the other Parties.

Commitment and availablity

6. Before accepting an appointment, the Mediator must be satisfied that s/he has appropriate time available to ensure that the Mediation can proceed in an expeditious manner.

Confidentiality

7. Subject to paragraph 9 below, the Mediator will keep confidential and not use for any collateral or ulterior purpose:
   (a) the fact that a mediation is to take place or has taken place; and
   (b) all information (whether given orally, in writing or otherwise) produced for, or arising in relation to, the Mediation including the existence and terms of the settlement agreement (if any) arising out of it.
   (c) details of all procedures, business documents and systems used in the course of running the mediation service, all of which may not be reproduced or used for any other purpose without the express written permission of GLOBAL MEDIATION.

8. Subject to paragraph 9 below, if the Mediator is given information by any Party which is implicitly confidential or is expressly stated to be confidential (and which is not already public) the Mediator shall maintain the confidentiality of that information from all other Parties, except to the extent that disclosure has been specifically authorised.

9. The duty of confidentiality in paragraphs 7 and 8 above will not apply if, and to the extent that:
   (a) all Parties consent to disclosure; or
   (b) the Mediator is required by law to make disclosure; or

(c) the Mediator reasonably considers that there is serious risk of significant harm to the life or safety of any person if the information in question is not disclosed; or

(d) the Mediator wishes to seek guidance in confidence from any senior officer or panel member of GLOBAL MEDIATION on any ethical or other serious question arising out of the Mediation.

9A. A child protection issue is always to be regarded within paragraph 9(c), above. In SEN mediations, parents should be made aware that any such issues will be disclosed to the relevant authorities.

Fees

10. The Mediator will not make any charge for fees or expenses beyond that which has been agreed with GLOBAL MEDI-ATION and collected as part of the fixed fee prior to the Mediation. GLOBAL MEDIATION will be responsible for the fees and expenses of the Mediator who will not approach any Party in relation to fees.

Mediation agreement

11. The Mediator will act in accordance with the agreement (whether written or oral) made between the Parties in relation to the Mediation ('the Mediation Agreement') (except where to do so would cause a breach of this Code) and will use his/her best endeavours to ensure that the Mediation proceeds in accordance with the terms of the Mediation Agreement.

Insurance

12. The Mediator will ensure that s/he is fully covered under a policy of Professional Indemnity insurance in an adequate amount with a responsible insurer. Insurance cover will normally be arranged through GLOBAL MEDIATION.

Withdrawal of mediator

13. The Mediator will withdraw from the Mediation if he/she:
    (a) is requested to do so by any of the Parties (unless the Parties have agreed to a procedure involving binding ADR);
    (b) is in breach of this Code; or
    (c) is required by the Parties to act in a way that is in material breach of this Code.
14. The Mediator may withdraw from the Mediation at his/her own discretion if:
    (a) any of the Parties is acting in breach of the Mediation Agreement;
    (b) any of the Parties is, in the Mediator's opinion, acting in an unconscionable or criminal manner;
    (c) the Mediator decides that continuing the mediation is unlikely to result in a settlement; or
    (d) any of the Parties alleges that the Mediator is in material breach of this code.

This Code of Conduct was last updated in February 2002.

10.4   SPECIFICATION FOR TENDERS FOR A REGIONAL SERVICE FOR DISPUTE RESOLUTION SERVICE – SOUTH EAST & SOUTH CENTRAL REGIONAL SEN PARTNERSHIPS (SCRIP/SERSEN)

Tenders are invited from interested parties to provide a service for the independent resolution of disputes between parents and local education authorities arising from the provision made to meet the special educational needs of children aged up to nineteen within the region.

The tendering process

Tenders should include a description of the proposed service, demonstrating how it will meet the attached service specification, including any guidance issued by the DfES subsequent to the publication of this document.

Tenders may be made to provide a service to cover the whole region, or a part of it. If the latter, then the area to be covered should be indicated in the bid. They may also be made by a consortium of providers from the voluntary, statutory and/or commercial sectors.

The costs of providing the service should be included, and should include an indicative costing per case, as well as a total amount for the region to be covered. It may be helpful for costs to be expressed in tranches of, say 50 cases – i.e. cost for 50 cases, 100 cases, 150 etc. This should include all costs incurred in providing the service as described in the specification. Estimates of costs per case in pilot schemes have varied significantly, but have not exceeded £1,000.

Tenders will be judged by a regional panel against a number of criteria, including:

1   The extent to which the service specification is met;
2   The level of training, experience, and independence of the proposed mediators;
3   The extent to which the service will incorporate the principles of Best Value;

4   The degree of involvement of the voluntary sector;
5   The overall cost.

Further criteria may be adopted by the panel, and the panel may attach differing weights to each criterion in reaching their decision.

A shortlist of candidates will be drawn up, and they will be invited to make a short presentation to the regional panel before a final selection is made. The successful candidate will be offered a legal contract for the period 1 October 2001–31 March 2003 in the first instance, or as soon as possible thereafter. The attached service specification will be a schedule to this contract.

The service provider will be accountable to the Regional Steering Group. Provision will be made in the contract for the Regional Steering Group to terminate the contract after a six-month notice period if it considers the service to be unsatisfactory.

The closing date for submission of tenders is Friday 31 August 2001.

Specification for a regional service for dispute resolution

Throughout the remainder of this document the term 'mediation' is used synonymously with dispute resolution or disagreement resolution as its meaning has been clearly defined elsewhere and is widely understood.

The legislative background

The process of statutory assessment of special educational needs is defined in the Education Act 1996 and the accompanying regulations, and is interpreted in the Code of Practice on the Identification and Assessment of Special Educational Needs (1994). The latter is currently undergoing revision, and a revised Code of Practice is due to be issued by January 2002. New legislation has recently been passed and has received Royal Assent (The SEN and Disability Act 2001) which places a duty on LEAs to provide independent dispute resolution procedures when parents and LEAs are unable to reach agreement on the outcomes of the assessment process.

The new legislation will be accompanied by a revised Code of Practice which will provide an interpretation of the law to which LEAs must 'have regard', together with updated SEN regulations. These require LEAs to establish dispute resolution procedures which are independent of them, thereby disqualifying LEAs from providing these services internally, although they may provide them to one another.

In addition, Good Practice Guidance relating to parent partnership services generally is in preparation by the DfES, and further non-statutory guidance relating specifically to the proposed service for dispute resolution is also likely to be issued shortly. Tenders made in response to this document should have regard to this additional guidance when it is issued.

The region

The area for which tenders are invited is the whole of the South East region, which includes the LEAs involved in the South East and South Central Regional SEN Partnerships. This is a total of nineteen LEAs as follows:

Bracknell Forest, Brighton & Hove, Buckinghamshire, East Sussex, Hampshire, Isle of Wight, Kent, Oxfordshire, Medway, Milton Keynes, Portsmouth, Reading, Slough, Southampton, Surrey, West Berkshire, West Sussex, Windsor & Maidenhead, Wokingham.

Referral to the service

Referrals to the service will be made by individual LEAs according to regionally agreed criteria. LEAs have a duty to inform parents of their right to access independent mediation when a proposed or proposed amended statement is issued. Normally a referral will be made when the LEA has exhausted its own internal procedures for mediation and dispute resolution involving LEA officers including those responsible for the administration of statutory assessment, parent partnership officers, and others such as educational psychologists who may have an internal brief for this kind of work. However, parents will be able to request independent mediation whenever there is disagreement on SEN issues, although both parties will have to agree to independent mediation.

In most cases it is likely that the parents concerned will have indicated their intention to appeal to the SEN tribunal, and in some cases they will have done so, or be in the process of doing so.

Unlike the SEN tribunal the proposed regional service for disagreement resolution will have no powers to impose a solution on either party, but will provide mediation between the two parties, with the intention of assisting them in reaching an agreed solution.

The mediation process

A recognised process of mediation should be followed, incorporating the following elements:

1   *Establish contact with both parties*, build rapport and engage the parties, gather information, provide explanation as necessary, and maintain impartiality and confidentiality.
2   *Prepare to work on the dispute*, identifying the best way to do so, making any practical arrangements, and preparing the parties as necessary.
3   *Hear the issues*, agreeing any ground rules, providing explanation of the process, managing any conflict, providing sufficient time within an agreed agenda and overall time-limit.

4 *Explore the issues*, ensuring good communication and clarity of understanding, acknowledging differences, fears, reservations, with a shift of focus from the past to the future, summarising points of agreement and disagreement.

5 *Build agreements*, generating possible solutions, evaluating alternatives, encouraging problem-solving, constructing agreements and establishing fall-back arrangements.

6 *Close and follow up*, making any necessary arrangements.

A more detailed description can be found in *Resolving Disagreements between Parents, Schools and LEAs: Some Examples of Best Practice* by Jane Hall – copies can be requested from the DfES on 0207 925 5524.

When mediation may not be appropriate

There may be circumstances where after initial contact has been made with both parties mediation is not an appropriate way forward. The service should have regard to any guidance issued by the DfES on this matter.

Administrative functions required

To provide this service effectively the following administrative functions will need to be provided:

A single point of contact for LEAs and parents incorporating a freephone (0800) number

If the service is to engage parents successfully it will need to be responsive and to provide easy to access at no cost. Parents are likely to have a high level of emotional engagement in their child's case, and are unlikely to engage with a service that is difficult to reach. Due to confidentiality issues it is likely that parents will have to make first contact with the service, and therefore all possible barriers to this first contact need to be removed.

Production of parent-friendly publicity

This will need to be specifically aimed at parents in these circumstances and is likely to be the main route into the service. It may expedite the referral process to incorporate a form for parental consent to referral to the service, and release to the service of relevant documentation. Sufficient copies should be provided to enable participating LEAs to have a stock from which they can draw according to demand.

Recruitment and training of mediators

A register of suitably qualified mediators will have to be maintained, and as well as having mediation skills, knowledge of special educational needs will also be necessary, together with sufficient local knowledge of the LEAs in which they will be providing mediation. The service provider will be expected to arrange any necessary training in mediation, and while accredited training is preferred, decisions about what is appropriate will be left to the appointed provider. However, the performance of individual mediators will be subject to ongoing evaluation.

Training in special educational needs, where it is required, and induction into LEA provision, policy and procedures in the LEAs where individual mediators intend to work, will be separately funded by the regional partnerships and costings for this training should not be included.

Mediators may be drawn from a wide variety of groups to provide parents with a choice, including those already working in the voluntary or commercial sectors in other specialist areas, and may include existing or former LEA staff, although the latter will be debarred from providing mediation within their own LEA.

Matching of mediators to parents/LEAs in each case

Although the service to be provided is regional the service is likely to be most effective where mediators have sufficient local knowledge so that time is not unduly spent on establishing the detail of LEA policy or provision. However, it is also important that parents are provided with a choice of mediators.

Arrangement of meeting venues

In the majority of cases face-to-face meetings will have to be arranged at a venue which is suitable and convenient to both parties. The arrangement of venues and all associated costs and other arrangements will be the responsibility of the service provider.

Monitoring of cases and the gathering and analysis of evaluative feedback

Evaluative feedback will need to be gathered for each case from both parents and LEAs, using questionnaires agreed with the Regional Steering Group. Participating LEAs will reserve the right to request the withdrawal of a mediator from the register on the basis of this feedback.

An annual report

An annual report, following a format to be agreed with the Regional Steering Group, will need to be provided including summative statistics. In addition a supplementary report should be provided to each participating LEA, including summative statistics for that LEA. A development plan for the forthcoming year should be included, based on evaluative feedback and incorporating clearly stated targets.

Required service standards

Same-day response to parents contacting the service 9 a.m. to 5 p.m. Monday to Friday excluding bank holidays

Ideally the freephone number should be staffed during the above times. If the number is not staffed or engaged in another call parents and LEAs should be able to leave a message and their call returned on the same day provided it is made before 4 p.m. on that day.

Time-scales

The service should be able to provide mediation without delay, and should have the capacity to identify a suitable mediator within five working days. Mediation should be conducted within a time-scale agreed by both parties, and except in exceptional circumstances should be completed well within the two-month statutory period following the issue of a proposed or amended statement.

Confidentiality

LEAs are not able to pass on any information about parents to a third party without their permission, or to release any relevant documentation. Confidentiality should be maintained at all times, and all documentation relating to individual cases, with the exception of evaluative data and any agreement reached, destroyed within a time frame to be agreed with the Regional Steering Group.

The only information which should be released to a third party is that which has been agreed by both parties for release to that party. Mediation should be conducted without prejudice to any proceedings of the SEN tribunal which may follow, and only agreed information released to the tribunal. This will need to be made clear to both parties.

The single exception to this is when issues relating to child protection emerge during the mediation process, and parents should be informed that if this arises, then there will be an obligation to inform the relevant authority.

The service should abide by the provisions of the Data Protection Act 1998.

Equal opportunities

The service should provide equal access to all parents regardless of their diversity, and this should be reflected in the publicity materials produced, as well as in the mediation procedures followed.

The likely level of demand

419 appeals to the SEN tribunal were registered throughout the region in 1999–2000. Of these approximately two-thirds were resolved through existing LEA procedures and therefore were not heard by the tribunal.

This gives a figure of 140 which are likely to go to tribunal in any year. However, not all parents are likely to take up the option of independent dispute resolution. Equally, some cases currently resolved by LEAs themselves are likely to be resolved through this route in future. Until the service is up and running it is impossible to provide an accurate figure as there are too many unknown variables. However, the figure of 140 per annum is probably the best guess, given that some will be added to this and some taken away.

10.5 SAMPLE REFERRAL CRITERIA – SOUTH EAST & SOUTH CENTRAL REGIONAL SEN PARTNERSHIPS (SCPIP/SERSEN)

Criteria for referral to the regional disagreement resolution service for special educational needs

'A local education authority must make arrangements, that include the appointment of independent persons, with a view to avoiding or resolving disagreements between authorities (on the one hand) and parents of children in their area (on the other) about the way LEAs and maintained schools carry out their responsibilities towards children with special educational needs.

A local education authority must also make arrangements with a view to avoiding or resolving disagreements between parents and certain schools about the special educational provision made for their child.

LEAs must take whatever steps they consider appropriate to make disagreement resolution services known to parents, headteachers, schools and others they consider appropriate.'

See Sections 332B, Education Act 1996 (as amended)

The engagement of the service

Whether or not a request for engagement of the service comes from a parent as result of being formally informed of the service or at an earlier stage, both parties have to be in agreement that the service should be engaged.

Proposed regional criteria are as follows:

- The issue should be an SEN issue and not another type of complaint.
- The parties (including schools where appropriate) should have met, discussed the issues, and explored alternatives and this discussion should include those able to make decisions.

- Where appropriate, other agencies should have been involved.
- Parent partnership services should normally have been involved to try to resolve the disagreement.
- If the disagreement is with a maintained school (including city academies and CTCs) the headteacher and governing body should have been involved.
- If the disagreement relates to any part of the statutory assessment process referral should only be made at key decision points.
- Possible solutions should normally fall within LEA policy.

Definition of SEN issues

Whilst in most cases these will be obvious, some will be less so. A complaint about the behaviour or competence of an additional teacher or LSA allocated to a pupil with SEN would not be an SEN issue, although if it were not resolved satisfactorily it may develop into one if the parent consequently became unhappy with the placement.

Issues concerning school transport are not SEN issues although parents may argue that they are. However, these may well be dealt with under the Disability Discrimination Act (2001).

Triggers for parents to be formally notified of the service

Although LEAs will be under a duty to publicise their independent services for disagreement resolution generally, and to give parents access to such a service at any stage, they are not required to specifically inform individual parents until an agreed point has been reached in the process of meeting their child's needs. The most appropriate triggers are those relating to the statutory assessment process, and the following have been proposed:

- Decision not to carry out a statutory assessment
- Issue of a proposed, proposed amended, or final statement

- Refusal to issue a statement
- Notice of intention to cease a statement
- Refusal to reassess or to change named school in the Statement.

In addition to reference to parent partnership services, statutory letters at each of these stages should include reference to the independent service, and the aim would be to complete any mediation within the statutory two month period during which parents can make representations and register an appeal to the SEN tribunal.

Further development of regional criteria

When there is uncertainty there needs to be consultation, and over a period of time a knowledge bank will need to be accumulated from which further criteria can be derived.

10.6 SOURCES OF INFORMATION AND FURTHER CONTACTS

1 DfES (2001): Special Educational Needs. Code of Practice. Nov. 2001.[1] DfES/581/2001. ISBN: 1 84185 5294; PP2/D16/44434/1101/35 701/15.

2 DfES (2001): SEN Toolkit:

Section 1	Principles and policies
Section 2	Parent partnership services
Section 3	Resolution of disputes
Section 4	Enabling pupil participation
Section 5	Managing individual education plans
Section 6	Strands of action
Section 7	Writing statements
Section 8	Guidelines for obtaining advice
Section 9	Annual reviews
Section 10	Transition planning
Section 11	The role of social services
Section 12	The role of health professionals

ISBN: 1 84185 5316; PP3/D16/44434/0701/15

3 DfES (2001): Special Educational Needs (SEN): A guide for parents and carers. Ref: DfES 0800/2001. PP1322/D21/44434/1101/25. ISBN: 1 84185 644 4. *This contains contacts for all the Parent Partnership Schemes in the UK and a list of addresses for the voluntary agencies.*

4 The Disability Rights Commission (2000): Draft Code of Practice (School) and Draft Code of Practice (Post-16). CONSULTATION on a new Code of Practice.

Copies:	Tel:	08457 622 633
	Fax:	08457 778 878
	Textphone:	08457 622 644
	E-mail:	*enquiry@drc_gb.org*
		www.drc_gb.org.

5 DfE (1994): Code of Practice on the Identification & Assessment of Special Educational Needs. DfE, Central Office of Information, HMSO.

6 The SEN and Disability Act (2001): Chapter 10.
7 SEN tribunal – two documents on preparing your case which are useful and relevant to preparing your case for mediation.[6]
(a) To help you prepare your case – what we need to know.
(b) Preparing the LEA's case.
Also useful: Guidance for coming to the tribunal.
8 SEN tribunal: Annual Reports 2000–2001, 1999–2000, 1998–1999, 1997–1998, 1996–1997, 1995–1996, 1994–1995. Available from DfES.
9 SEN tribunal (2001): How to Appeal. Available free from the SEN tribunal. Ref: TR1 U20. PP98/D16/44214/0601/653. ISBN: 1 84183 439 5.
10 The SEN tribunal (2000): Right to be heard: what to expect at the SEN tribunal. A video.
    Tel: 020 7925 6925
    Address: Windsor House, 50 Victoria Street, London SW1H 0NW.
11 National Children's Bureau: Highlights
• No. 186 SEN & Disability Act 2001;
• No. 187 SEN Disability Act 2001: Schools duties in the Disability Discrimination Act 1995.
    ISSN: 1365 9081.
    National Children's Bureau, 8 Wakley Street, London EC1V 7QE. Tel: 020 7843 6000
    Fax: 020 7278 9512
    E-mail: *library@ncb.org.uk*   *www.ncb.org.uk*
12 SNAP Cyrmru, Director: Roger Bishop, SNAP Cyrmu, 10 Coopers Yard, Curran Road, Cardiff CF10 5NB.
    Tel: 029 20 388776
    Fax: 029 20 371876
13 CREnet (Conflict Resolution Education Network). Director: Heather Prichard, 1527 New Hampshire Avenue, NW Washington, DC 20036.
    Tel: (202) 667 9700
    Fax: (202) 667 8629
    Website: *www.crenet.org*.

14 IPSEA (Independent Panel for Special Education Advice).
   6 Carlow Mews, Woodbridge, Suffolk, UP12 1EA.

Tel:	0800 0184016
Scotland:	0131 454 0082
Northern Ireland:	01232 705654
Tribunal Appeals:	01394 384711
General Enquiries:	01394 380518
Website:	www.ipsea.org.uk.

15 Global Mediation Ltd. 107–111 Fleet Street, London, EC4A
   2AB.

Tel:	020 7936 9090
Website:	www.globalmediation.co.uk
E-mail:	info@globalmediation.co.uk

Notes

1 Copies of DfES documents can be obtained by contacting:

Tel:	0845 60 222 60
Fax:	0845 60 333 60
Textphone:	0845 60 555 60
E-mail:	dfes@prolog.uk.com.

2 Copies of SEN tribunal documents can be obtained by contacting:

Tel:	01325 392 555
E-mail:	tribunalqueries@sent.gsi.gov.uk.

10.7 TRAINING PROVIDERS AND ORGANISATIONS

Centre for Dispute Resolution (CEDR)
Princes House, 95 Gresham Street, London EC2V 7NA
Tel: 020 7600 0500

ADR Group
Grove House, Grove Road, Redland, Bristol BS6 6UL
Tel: 020 7946 7180

Chartered Institute of Arbitrators
International Arbitration Centre, Angel Gate, City Road,
London EC1V 2RS
Tel: 020 7837 4483

Academy of Experts
2 South Square, Gray's Inn, London WC1R 5HP
Tel: 020 7637 0333

School of Psychotherapy & Counselling
Regents College, Inner Circle, Regent's Park, London NW1
Tel: 020 7583 5123 Contact: Paul Randolph

British Association of Lawyer Mediators (BALM)
The Shooting Lodge, Guildford Road, Sutton Green, Guildford,
Surrey GU4 7PZ
Tel: 01483 235000 Contact: Alastair/Pat Logan

The National Mediation Centre
The Hawthorns, 23 St James Gardens, Swansea SA1 6DY
Tel: 01792 469626

Certificate in Applied Mediation (SEN)
E. Consultancy, 17 Ardmere Road, London, SE13 6EL
Tel: 020 8858 2912
Website: www.appliedmediation.co.uk

Chapter 11

Bibliography

Acland, A.F. (1990) *A Sudden Outbreak of Common Sense: Managing Conflict through Mediation*. London: Hutchinson.

Department for Education (1993) *Guidelines for Grants for Education Support and Training*. London: DfE.

Department for Education DfE (1994) *Code of Practice on the Identification and Assessment of Special Educational Needs*. London: HMSO.

Department for Education and Employment (DfEE) (1997) *Excellence for all Children – Meeting Special Educational Needs*. London: DfEE Publications.

Department for Education and Employment (DfEE) (1998) *Meeting Special Educational Needs – A Programme of Action*. London: DfEE Publication.

Department for Education and Employment (2000) *Special Educational Needs Tribunal Annual Report 1999/2000*. London: DfEE Publications.

Department for Education and Skills (DfES) (2001) *Special Educational Needs (SEN): A Guide for Parents and Carers*. London: DfES Publications.

Department for Education and Skills (DfES) (2001) *Inclusive Schooling: Children with Special Educational Needs*. London: DfES Publications.

Department for Education and Skills (DfES) (2001) SEN Toolkit. London: DfES Publications.

Department for Education and Skills (DfES) (2001) *Special Educational Needs. Code of Practice*. London: DfES Publications.

Disability Rights Commission (2002) *Code of Practice for Schools: Disability Discrimination Act 1995, Part 4*. London: The Stationery Office.

Fisher, R. and Ury, W.L. (1981) *Getting to Yes*. New York: Houghton Mifflin.

Galloway, D. (1990) *Support for Learning in Tower Hamlets: Report of the Consultant in Special Educational Needs to the Chief Education Officer*. Lancaster: University of Lancaster.

Gersch, I., Casale, C. and Luck, C. (1998) 'The Waltham Forest SEN Conciliation Service: One Approach to Reducing Tribunal Appeals', *Educational Psychology in Practice*, 14(1), 11–21.

Hall, J. (1999) *Resolving Disputes between Parents, Schools and LEAs: Some Examples of Best Practice*, Special Educational Needs Division, DfEE.

Her Majesty's Stationery Office (2001) Special Educational Needs and Disability Act 2001, London: The Stationery Office.

Hornby, G. (1995) *Working with Parents of Children with Special Educational Needs*. London: Cassell.

Individuals with Disabilities Education Act, 20 USC chapter 33 as amended by IDEA Amendments 1997, Public Law 105–17, June 1997.

Kuhn, M. (ed.) (2001) *SEN Disagreement Resolution in Action*. London: London SEN Regional Partnership.

Landau, B. (1997) *Family Mediation Handbook*, second edition. Toronto: Butterworths.

Leimdorfer, T. (1998) 'Special Children – Special Conflicts', *Mediation*, 14(1).

Liebmann, M. *et al.* (1998) *Community and Neighbour Mediation*. London: Cavendish Publishing.

Minnesota Office of Dispute Resolution, MINSEMS (Minnesota Special Education Mediation Service) and related publications for parents, schools and education departments.

Moore, C.W. (1996) *The Mediation Process: Practical Strategies for Resolving Conflict*, second edition. San Francisco: Jossey-Bass.

National Information Center for Children and Youth with Disabilities (August 1997), The IDEA Amendments of 1997, National Information Centre, Washington DC.

National Parent Partnership Network (2000) Arrangements for Avoiding and Resolving Disagreements, Information Exchange, December 2000. Council for Disabled Children.

Nierenberg, G.I. (1986) *The Complete Negotiator*, London: Barnes & Noble.

Noble, C. (1999) *Family Mediation: A Guide for Lawyers*. Aurora: Canada Law Books Inc.

Ofsted and Audit Commission, Local Education Authority Support for School Improvement, 2001.

PACER (Parent Advocacy Coalition for Educational Rights), Parents' Summary of IDEA '97, PACER, Minneapolis, USA.

Pickell, N. (2000) *In Family Law, How Is Mediation Different from a Settlement Meeting?*, in *Mediation Services*, Mediation Books, USA.

Rowley, J. (1999) (Conciliation in Special Educational Needs: An Evaluative and Exploratory Study of One LEA Model), unpublished MSc dissertation, Institute of Education, University of London.

Rowley, J. and Gersch, I.S. (2001) Referrals for Conciliation: Is There a Pattern to Referrals? *Educational Psychology in Practice*, 17(4), 361–74.

Scanlon, K.M. (1999) Mediators Deskbook, CPR Institute of Dispute Resolution Inc.

SEN tribunal (2000) Annual Report of the SEN tribunal.

Smith, J.A. (1995) 'Semi-Structured Interviewing and Qualitative Analysis', in J.A. Smith, R. Harre and L. Van Langenhove (eds), *Rethinking Methods in Psychology*. London: Sage Publications, pp. 9–25.

Special Children (2002) Practice Makes Perfect: The Revised SEN Code of Practice Special Children, January 2002, pp. 20–5.

Stewart, S. (1998) *Conflict Resolution – A Foundation Guide*. Winchester: Waterside Press.

Stobbs, P. (2001a) The SEN and Disability Act 2001. National Children's Bureau Highlight no. 186, July, National Children's Bureau.

Stobbs, P. (2001b) The SEN and Disability Act 2001. Schools' Duties in the Disability Discrimination Act 1995. National Children's Bureau Highlight no. 187, October, National Children's Bureau.

The Disability Rights Commission (2000) Draft Code of Practice (Schools); Draft Code of Practice (Post-16). Consultation documents.

The Education Act (1996), London: The Stationery Office.

The Salamanca Statement on Inclusive Education (1994) Salamanca, Spain. United Nations Education, Scientific and Cultural Organisation (UNESCO).

The SEN and Disability Act 2001. London: HMSO.

Turnbull, R. and Rainbolt, K. (1997): Individuals with Disabilities Education Act: Digest and Significance of 1997 Amendments, Beach Center on Families and Disability, University of Kansas, USA.

Wolfendale, S. (2002) *Parent Partnership Services for Special Educational Needs: Celebrations and Challenges*. London: David Fulton.

Wolfendale, S. and Bryans, T. (2002) Evaluation of Parent Partnership in Wales: Executive Summary. Funded by the National Assembly for Wales and the National Association for Special Educational Needs. E-mail: *s.wolfendale@uel.ac.uk*.

Wright, J. (1999) IPSEA on Conciliation: Placating Peasants. Independent Panel for Special Education Advice (IPSEA Files). Website:www.ipsea.org.uk/placatingpeasants.htm.

Index